Helga

A Memoir of Privilege, War, and Family

©2013 Real Life Stories, LLP and Jane Edmonds Lang
U.S. Library of Congress Control Number: 2013906133

PUBLISHING
SERVICES

Real Life Stories, LLP
PO Box 248
Montreat, NC 28757
828 785 2828
www.ReaLifeStories.com

Memoir / Biography

ISBN: 9780979135583

Book design by Mason McCann Smith
Cover by Erin Kellington

Helga
A Memoir of Privilege, War, and Family

by Sheridan Hill

Helga. Tokyo. 1947.

Table of Contents

Stephen, Kurt, and Jessica. Christmas. 2011.

Dedication

This book is dedicated to my beloved grandchildren, Stephen, Kurt and Jessica. My fondest wish is that you continue to enjoy the privilege of emotional, physical and financial health; that you never know war; and that you always appreciate the importance of family.

My heartfelt thanks go to the following people who shaped my life and in many ways made this book possible:

• my grandparents, who instilled the first true sense of strong and loving family ties;

• my parents, who through times of plenty and sacrifice always made me know I was adored;

• my dearest Herzeltäntchen and Lückchen, who encouraged me to feel independent and self-confident;

• my beloved step-parents, who taught me that love has no genetic boundaries;

• my dear friends and family, alive and passed, who all live on in my fondest daily memories;

• Jesse, who gave me a place to belong and showed me what it was to be a proud American;

• my daughters Jane and Cindy, who, after listening to a lifetime of stories, thought to write them all down;

• Sheridan Hill, who patiently and wonderfully brought my life story back to life again.

- Helga Hofmeier Edmonds

Cindy, Helga, and Jane. Italy. 1959.

Prologue

A LIFETIME OF BIRTHDAY AND CHRISTMAS GIFTS hasn't left my sister and me much with which to surprise our parents. Over the years, we've learned that personal time with them and the memories that those personal experiences create is most important, and to that end, beginning in 2007 I began researching our family's ancestry. My hope was to find enough information about both parents' family lineage so I could compile my research into little books for each of them. Little did I know what stories and surprises I'd find: my paternal grandfather's 1917 WWI draft registration; the story of the Pelican Girls and our direct French link to old Mobile; the Evangeline Cajuns; the Germans who sailed east to farm and populate the lower Mississippi delta and the original ship manifest that reflected my mother's arrival in San Francisco (from Yokohama) on Valentine's Day 1948. That document, listing her nationality as Aryan, gave me pause to reflect on her life as a German teenager who happened to grow up in war torn Japan. As a result of my further curiosity, my sister, Cindy, and I gave Mom the wonderfully inventive gift of a personal biographer for Christmas 2011. I have been knee-deep in research for the book for most of 2012 and that research has been life changing.

Cindy and I always thought we had a typical Mom, until we were old enough to visit friends' homes without her around. It was then that we noticed that not all moms dressed like she did every day: stockings, a beautiful day dress, hair and make-up perfectly done, fashionable shoes. Not all moms cooked like she did: beef tongue laying on the kitchen counter, complete with icky papillae and all frayed muscles at the cut end, all waiting to be covered later with sickly cream sauce and paired with awful Brussels sprouts that had been boiling on top of the stove when we got home from school. Not all moms continually scraped their plate as if they had been starved during a war. Not all moms insisted on formalities at family dinner every night: linen tablecloth and napkins, milk never in the carton but always decanted into a pitcher, sterling monogram engraved napkin rings and flatware, heirloom Meissen china (although every now and then coupled with a dish or bowl out of the Fab soap powder box). Woe be it that a jar of jam be placed on the breakfast table straight from the fridge. Jams and jellies had their own two-tub crystal container, complete with sterling lids. Even honey had its own honey pot that was actually used!

It was only much later, when we were both grown and out of the house, when I met General Jimmy Doolittle and casually asked him to autograph a picture for my mother, whom he had bombed in Tokyo when she was 17, that I fully realized that all the stories we had been told as throw-away tales were actually true! And this tale of a little German girl, who came to be living in Munich and Tokyo during incredibly tumultuous times and eventually became a US citizen, turns out to be the incredible story of our very not-typical mom.

My research for her book has included reading and translating 70-year-old letters from my German grandparents. Doing that opened my eyes to a world I'd heard of, but never really understood. As I read those letters in date order, I was overwhelmed by two main themes: firstly, by the arc of personal and world history that they covered and secondly, by the personal insight they all brought to those events. No matter how much I may have learned during my own schooling, even through university, those letters truly brought the personal successes and joys and the historical horror of those times to life for me. Through Mom's memories, I was learning the details of her life during the war in Japan, and now via the letters, I was able to look through a crack in the door to what it must have been like for my family in Germany, as well. These letters have been a real joy for me to read, as they bring my German grandparents to life again for me now. More importantly, I begin to understand and appreciate what all of them must have had to sacrifice to continue any semblance of life during those difficult times. Family, friends, food, safety, normalcy: everything was at risk. Without personal letters like these, my generation, and certainly my son's generation, would never really be able to believe that their very own family experienced such horrible times.

I've also had to chance to read through the letters my mother wrote as she first sailed to America in 1948 to begin yet another new life. It fell to her, at only twenty-two, to tie up all the loose ends in Tokyo and of continue to care for, from America, her now desperate parents and family living in the rubble of Germany.

Mom lived through the beginnings of the Nazi upheaval in Germany, through the bombings and destruction of WWII Japan, through constant relocation, through learning new languages and customs – all before she was twenty-three years old. In spite of it all, she still says she considered herself lucky. I say she spent her life *surviving lucky!*

Leonore Jane Lang
January 2013

The Zopke family (l. to r.): Leonore, Hans, and Else (Omi).
Ottony (Herzeltäntchen) is seated. 1907.

Chapter One

Prussian Roots

THE GLAMOUR AND BEAUTY OF HELGA'S YOUTH still radiate from her face, defying both her eighty-eight years and the events thereof. Look closely and you will see a shield of Germanic pride: the self-control over her expression has yielded very little over the years. "I have tended to be stoic about life," she says, "believing that complaining makes things worse."

Only recently has she begun to sleep past 7:15 or allow herself the luxury of a nap. "I slept perfectly well in the night, and I have never thought it was right to lie around in the daytime."

Helga's life is inextricably linked to both World Wars, in Europe and in the Pacific. Born in 1925, only seven years after the end of World War I, she was torn from her beloved homeland and shipped to Japan at the age of nine. The month-long journey during winter, without relatives to comfort her, would have traumatized a different child. But Helga's young spirit triumphed over her sense of loss—all that she was leaving behind—and focused on the excitement of the journey. An ocean cruise to exotic Japan! And, at the journey's end, a reunion with her estranged mother.

For the next thirteen years, she navigated life in Japan. This German child who had studied Latin in school quickly picked up enough English and Japanese to chat with merchants and buy food and household goods. Several years after her arrival in Japan, Hitler came to power, and Helga, along with the rest of her friends, joined the Hitler

Youth. She survived the United States' 1945 firebombing attack on Japan—one of the worst military massacres in history. For a merciless six months, thousands of civilians were incinerated along with their homes. At first the flaming bombs looked like beautiful shooting stars, but they turned Tokyo into a living inferno. It was a fight to the bitter end. As Gen. Douglas MacArthur told the Republican National Convention the summer of 1952, "It is fatal to enter any war without the will to win it."

A half-century of living outside Germany has not erased Helga's accent and speech patterns—which are translated from German to English in her head. Nor changed are her old-school grace and formality. When the biographer calls for a follow-up telephone interview, Helga inquires with genuine warmth, "And how are you, my dear?"

She is a true German and a true American at the same time. "I defend America to anyone who criticizes it, and I defend Germany to anyone who criticizes the Germans," she says. "But I still to this day miss Germany . . . it was very hard for me to leave." The words are grievous, yet nothing in her face gives way to sadness. "I did not know when I left Tokyo in 1948 that I would lose my German citizenship forever. After that, I never got too sentimental about one place or another; we moved so much."

Helga was born March 11, 1925, in the University Hospital for Women in Frankfurt am Main. The beautifully appointed city was well populated as early as the 1500s and was crowned with both a castle and a cathedral. Frankfurt am Main had developed in a crook of the Rhine River where it met the Main River, and historically the local economy thrived. Throughout its history, the city was rich in academic and cultural assets. In the 1800s its native son Johann Wolfgang von Goethe stunned Europe with philosophical poetry, plays, novels, and mathematical innovations. Johann Philipp Reis studied at the Hassel Institute in Frankfurt am Main and in 1860 developed the first prototype of the telephone.

After World War II, a new name was added to the list of Frankfurt's most celebrated natives: Annelies "Anne" Marie Frank. The

Montessori-educated Jewish child famously documented two years of her family's life hiding from the Nazis in Amsterdam. She wrote, "I want to be useful . . . to all people. . . . I want to go on living even after my death!" Tragically, her wish came true. Although Anne Frank died of typhoid in a concentration camp, the diary she left behind changed how the world viewed the persecution of Jews during World War II.

Helga's maternal grandparents were Hans Zopke and Elisabeth "Else" Gleim Zopke. Her grandfather was a mechanical engineer and professor at the University of Hamburg, and regularly received interesting invitations to view new technologies. A November 6, 1895, *New York Times* article heralds the arrival in America of Hans Zopke, "a German State Engineer commissioned by his government" to look into America's methods of electrical propulsion and mass transit.

German inventor Werner von Siemens had already built the first electric passenger train in 1879; ever the diplomat, Zopke publicly lavished praise on American engineers. He said he was especially impressed with urban locomotives powered by overhead electrical lines. When he visited the Baltimore Beltline built by General Electric, he called it "one of the marvels of the age." Without a doubt, his words were appreciated in the raw young country, where Idaho and Wyoming had recently been admitted as the forty-third and forty-fourth states. Zopke was so excited that he applied for a six-month extension of his visa, telling the *Times*, "I believe the spring of 1896 will witness some of the greatest experiments with electricity the world has ever known."

Along with other niceties of living in privilege, Hans and Else's older daughter Leonore—Helga's mother—learned to sew. Else had insisted that her daughter learn the finer points of needlework and set her up as an apprentice to a well-known dressmaker. Leonore was a quick study and soon was sewing simple dresses. Sadly, Hans did not live to see his daughter blossom to womanhood: he died in 1918 at the age of fifty-two. From that day forward, Else kept his cremated remains in a jar by her bed.

Leonore Antoine Margaret Elisabeth Zopke was a mere teenager when she met Kurt Hofmeier, the debonair medical student who would become her husband. Despite the cultural gridlock against educating girls past the age of fourteen or so, Leonore had become an avid reader and a self-educated freethinker. She had grown up in the university city of Marburg with a wide exposure to books and ideas. She enjoyed the Austrian poet Rainer Maria Rilke, who was alive and writing during her youth, and often read from her autographed copies of his books. "Who, if I cried out, would hear me among the angels' hierarchies?" he wrote, in *Duino Elegies.* "And even if one of them pressed me suddenly against his heart, I would be consumed in that overwhelming existence."

Kurt Hofmeier was born in Königsberg, a magnificent city on the Baltic Sea that was the Prussian capital for more than two hundred years. (Helga's elder daughter, Jane, has traced the maternal line as far back as 1585 in Bebra, Germany. The paternal ancestry dates to 1663 in Gaildorf, Germany, under the spelling "Hoffmayer.") Modern-day maps now show Königsberg known as Kaliningrad, Russia. For centuries, Königsberg was an international trading center and a place where learned men of every European nationality traded goods and discussed politics. (Because it was separated from the rest of Germany by a narrow strip of Polish territory, Königsberg was the point of invasion chosen by Hitler in 1939, sparking World War II. The beautiful city with art galleries, museums, opera houses, libraries and a population of more than 300,000 ceased to exist.)

The stereotypical Prussian man was loyal to the prince, showed unusual valor in battle, and was typically rigid in personality—it was said that from their mother's milk, they assimilated frugality, studiousness, and productiveness. Girls were groomed to be proper wives, learning to manage family finances and run all aspects of home life. As the son of a Prussian general, Kurt was expected to join his father in service to the country. Instead, he became a physician. It was a daring move for a young man whose father must have cast a long shadow upon him.

In photographs, the younger Hofmeier is a strikingly handsome man who turns his left cheek to the camera, displaying a deep dueling scar. It was the visible sign of the upper class and of a proper but hard-won university education. At Philipps University of Marburg, one of the oldest and most respected universities in the world, Kurt joined Corps Hasso-Nassovia, a Protestant fraternity. Through the fraternity, he was introduced to Mensurfechten: fencing in a small, confined space. The blades they wielded against each other were true sabers: unlike today's flimsy, needlelike swords, these were both heavy and deadly. Protective clothing covered arms and torso only; not the head nor the sides of the face. To prove his mettle, a man wouldn't duck or step to the side to avoid his opponent's sword but rather slashed back. When blood was drawn, the duel was over. The resulting facial scar proved he could stand and take a blow.

Kurt Hofmeier's marriage proposal came soon into his courtship with Leonore. When Kurt graduated from medical school in Marburg in the spring of 1923, he and Leonore married there. They settled in Frankfurt, where Kurt worked as an assistant physician in a hospital. His salary was minimal, especially for the hours he put in, but the job included a small penthouse apartment on the roof of the building. From the beginning, Kurt was a slave to his career. He was gone from home most of the time, seeing patients each morning at the hospital and in the afternoons making house calls across the city. Leonore found herself alone more and more frequently. Soon, she also found herself pregnant.

When their baby was born, they named her Helga Else Irmgard Ottony Friederike Hofmeier. Else, short for Elisabeth, was Helga's grandmother; Irmgard was Kurt's sister; Ottony was Leonore's younger sister; Friederike was the feminine form of Friedrich, the name of all three of her godfathers.

Apparently, Leonore and Kurt each wanted a different kind of marriage from the one they had. After five years, Leonore packed her belongings and her daughter and moved to Munich, where her mother and sister lived. Everyone said the wistful-eyed Leonore was never the same afterward. In such a provincial day and time, she must have felt painfully ashamed to be a twenty-nine-year-old single mother. A list of unwritten rules and customs ran through Leonore's blue blood, pressing her toward an aristocratic lifestyle. Now, some of these would be harder, or impossible, to maintain: a proper lady possesses full silver place settings for twenty-four; servants maintain the crystal, silver, and china and open and close the front door; ladies do not work outside the home; and ladies don't divorce their husbands.

Leonore and Helga lived in a small apartment at Schraudolfstraße 11, across from an Italian restaurant and not far from the train and bus station. Whenever they walked up the flight of stairs to their apartment, Helga relished the feel of the polished wooden banister in her hands. Though the apartment was small, it had everything they needed. There was an entryway where coats and umbrellas could be stashed. Helga slept in her mother's bedroom in a child's bed with rails that could be removed when she grew larger. In one corner of the bedroom, Helga carefully stored her doll collection: her pride and joy. The tiny kitchen was furnished with a small table, a bench, and two chairs, where mother and daughter ate their meals, complete with sterling silver and white-linen tablecloths. The living room, with its light-filled bay window, included built-in shelves where Leonore arranged her beloved books.

(Sometimes when they looked out their big window, they spotted Adolf Hitler sipping his morning coffee at Osteria Italiana, the Italian restaurant across the street. Members of Hitler's National Socialist German Workers' Party often met at the restaurant, which was on the corner of Schraudolfstraße and Schellingstraße. In his first seven years of leadership, Hitler appeared to many Germans as a patriotic leader passionate about rebuilding the nation.)

From infancy, Helga had been affectionately called *Herzel*, "little heart." The sweetheart of a baby had become a perfect German girl: silky golden hair, large blue eyes, and a quick mind. Helga was a school-girl when she earned a new nickname. Her mother had taken her along to visit a friend in Saxony. The woman opened the door, took one look at Helga and offered in her native Polish, *Puppe!* The affectionate expression for "little doll" haloed Helga until she started grade school.

In German, *chen* is a diminutive term of endearment that is added to a name or nickname. In the family, Leonore was often called

Lorchen. Since the family often called Helga *Herzel*, Helga affectionately named her Aunt Ottony *Herzeltäntchen*—"aunt of my heart." She called Ottony's husband, Albert, "Lucky," or *Lückchen*.

Albert, now a dentist, set up his practice in one room of the apartment he shared with his wife. Albert had served as a medical doctor during World War I, but had lost an eye due to injury. Now fitted with a glass eye, he had to change his practice from medical to dental. Each morning, he pressed the glass eye in place and positioned a monocle over it to hold his eyelids open, giving the semblance of two good eyes.

Helga's *Omi* (grandmother) Else, lived just a few blocks away. Else, ever the patrician dowager, insisted that Helga have lessons in ice-skating and piano as well as exposure to theater. She taught the child piano herself, sometimes playing duets with her. Omi also paid for Helga's skating lessons and walked with her each week to a nearby park that had a little lake that froze in winter. Together they dressed up and walked to stores, to the puppet theater, to children's plays, and occasionally to a silent movie with a live piano player. On Saturdays, Helga placed her special doll in its doll carriage. Then, despite being only five years old, she walked alone for twenty minutes through the city to her best friend's house to play in her garden with their dolls. Life was grand.

A few months later they all moved into a larger, luxurious apartment. The new flat was two flights up, with a front and back staircase. Helga liked to use the back door, where delivery boys came and went, because it opened onto a courtyard. The arrangement benefited everyone: Omi no longer wanted to live alone, and she received a professor's pension each month. When Omi moved in, her piano came along with her.

All their familiar aristocratic customs and accoutrements continued as part of daily life. The table was set for breakfast, lunch, and dinner with a linen tablecloth, linen napkins, heirloom Meissen china, monogrammed silver napkin rings, and sterling silverware. Only crystal, china, and silver were placed on the table. Jam, butter, honey, and other food items were presented in small crystal bowls with sterling lids. For each meal, Helga arrived at the table with clean hands and face, clean clothes, and her hair freshly combed. A civilized European would not dream of coming to the breakfast table in a nightgown.

If someone came to the door, the live-in maid would open it and invite the person into the foyer. After a polite greeting, the maid would take up the little silver tray that stood on a table by the door and offer the tray to the guest, who would place his or her calling card upon it. Then the maid would bring the card on the tray to the lady or gentleman of the house.

Girls were expected to curtsey and kiss the hand of a lady guest; boys were to stand tall, click their heels and lower their heads in a small bow. Children were not to speak unless spoken to and always addressed an adult with the proper salutation of *Herr* or *Frau* (Mr. or Mrs.).

Although the Hofmeiers and Zopkes fared well, most of the country suffered from the devastation of World War I and the Great Depression of 1929. Streams of support for the Reichstag gurgled to the surface. The walls of Berlin's buildings were plastered with photographs of Hitler with the words: *Unsere letze Hoffnung* ("Our Last Hope"). Hitler was firmly associated with job creation and pro-family values. At public political events, he was a master at working crowds into patriotic fevers. Hitler lavishly praised German mothers and encouraged them to have as many children as possible. At that point, the general public—indeed, the world—did not perceive that Hitler's ethnocentricity had, at the heart of it, a very narrow nationalism. He had crafted a "final solution": a plan to exterminate individuals and groups he deemed inferior, including Jews, homosexuals, and people with below-average IQs.

Darmstädter und Nationalbank, the German national bank, collapsed in 1931. It was the second largest bank in the country. Day by day, the chances of clawing out of economic depression dwindled. Sentiment began to swell in support of any party that promised to put people to work. Chancellor Brüning created a national volunteer workforce that recruited men for civic and agricultural construction projects. Under *Freiwillige Arbeitend* ("volunteer workers"), craftsmen and construction workers were given a day's rations to clear forests, build roads, reclaim fallow or marshlands for farming, and build dams and dikes.

Meanwhile, Leonore had been secretly formulating plans that Helga was soon to discover. One evening in March, 1932, Leonore kissed her daughter good night as always—but this time she whispered different words. "I am leaving for Japan to marry Uncle Fritz. I will send for you. But first we must get settled and I must find a proper school for you." Uncle Fritz was Helga's godfather, Friedrich Kiderlen, who had moved to Tokyo in the early 1920s to work for his uncle, Rudolf Ratjen, an importer.

In the morning, Leonore was gone. Little Helga asked her aunt and uncle, Albert and Ottony Witzel, "Is my mother on the ship?"

"Not yet," they said, explaining that Leonore would travel through Germany saying her good-byes before boarding the ship. They created a niche for Helga in their bedroom, sectioned off with a beautiful folding screen. With love in their eyes, they told the suddenly motherless child: "Here is your own little room we made especially for you." They did not tell Helga that it would be three years before she would see her mother again.

Within a few months, the Witzel family moved to a larger, second-floor apartment on Prinzregentenstraße, a street built by Bavarian royalty in the center of Munich. Along with Helga, the household included Helga's Herzeltäntchen and her Uncle Lückchen, Grandmother Zopke, "Omi," and their German maid. They walked everywhere: to shop, to visit, to see theater and live music. More than seventy years later, Helga would look back on this time as the best time of her life. Helga's devoted elders placed themselves in a tight family unit around her. Herzeltäntchen and Lückchen immediately became much more than a devoted aunt and uncle: they were Helga's surrogate parents. With no children of their own, they loved and nurtured Helga as their own child. It would be several years before their own son, Max Dieter, would be born.

After the Easter holiday of 1932, Helga was enrolled in a public school near the Hofbrauhaus, a famous beer hall. A few months later, Omi was brushing the child's hair and detected tiny white specks clinging to her long hair. Else Zopke was more than disgusted at the appearance of lice in the family. "Here we have a doctor's house, and a dentist's house, and a child with lice!"

She stormed through the street to buy a lice comb and shampoo, dressed the way she always did in winter: in a fur stole and a pearl necklace. She scraped the child's hair clean and washed it thoroughly with the foul-smelling lice shampoo. Then she sat down and wrote her former son-in-law to inform him that, in addition to the child support he was already paying, he now needed to finance Helga's education at private schools.

Else could have used the telephone in Albert's office, but the telephone was still considered an impersonal invention for business use. Albert rarely touched it, but the maid answered the thing and wrote down the resulting messages and appointments and placed the notes on his desk. Else Zopke felt the telephone was for business and for people too lazy to write a proper letter.

For Helga, the humiliation of lice bugs in her hair was completely offset by the attention lavished over her. One or more family members would pour the special shampoo on her head, wrap her head in a white towel and let it sit all day. Strolling through the flat wearing her white turban, Helga felt like a movie star. She felt like Elizabeth Arden. The fact that her head was soaking in pesticide was a secondary issue.

The private school was a longer walk for Helga but one she enjoyed. On the way she passed a Jewish synagogue and elementary school, where children in uniforms sang strange songs and called out in Hebrew and Yiddish. Catholic churches dominated the landscape of Munich, and entire states were identified as one denomination or another. Hamburg was a protestant state; Bavaria was a Catholic state. Raised Lutheran, Helga remembers eating fish on Friday as the Catholics did because more fresh fish was available then. She always gave a friendly greeting to her Jewish neighbors, but Jewish children attended their own school. Helga was vaguely aware of a growing sentiment that Jews were not as German as people like the Hofmeiers and Zopkes.

Hitler had established Nazi headquarters in Munich and condemned modern art as unpatriotic. Helga often walked past construction of a new art museum across from their apartment. When finished, the *Haus der Kunst* would house what the Third Reich deemed as Germany's finest art. A patriotic parade commemorated the ground-breaking. Nazi flags bearing the swastika waved beside the German flag in gold, black, and red stripes as uniformed officers marched in precision down the street. Helga was so impressed with the spectacle that she drew a picture of it and mailed it to her mother in Japan.

The larger apartment was needed for another reason that soon became apparent as her aunt's waistband began to expand. The precious little son was born in the fall of 1933 and named Max Dieter, an abbreviation of the old German name Dietrich. Helga called him Peti and pampered him the same way she doted on her dollies. She would dress the baby like a girl, put on his booties, and try to comb the curling tuft of blonde hair on the top of his head.

Kurt Hofmeier was now a prominent pediatrician as well as director of a Berlin hospital. Over the course of fifty years, he would write a number of books on pediatric medicine, beginning in 1921 with *Schwere Falle von krupposer Pneumonie im Kindesalter (Serious Pneumonia in Children)* and ending in 1979 with *Alles uber dein Kind: Auskunfts u. Nachschlagewerk nach Altersstufen uber d. körperliche u. Seelische Entwicklung (All About Your Child: An Information and Research Guide about the Physical and Emotional Development during All Stages of a Child's Life).*

When modern thinking dictated that newborns be put in a separate unit from their mothers, Kurt worked to change the law. "The child should stay in the mother's room so they can bond and they can get used to breastfeeding," he said. "It is not right to have all of those screaming babies in the same room."

Helga enjoyed visiting her father and his new wife, the former Edith Breitschuh, in Berlin. (Kurt had remarried in 1929.) As a pediatrician, Kurt felt strongly that house calls to sick children helped prevent the spread of disease and he often took the visiting Helga with him on his rounds. Since he did not want his child exposed to illness, he left her sitting in his car (Leonore was furious when she found out). It was only for a half hour or so at a time, and Helga did not mind: she spent the time taking in the amazing sights and sounds of Berlin. It was one of the world's greatest cities, with more than four million people, modern trains, industrial plants, public beaches and amusement parks, and beautiful opera houses. There were nearly 150 daily and weekly newspapers; television had been introduced to the public for the first time at the fifth *Grosse Deutsche Funkausstellung,* and Albert Einstein addressed the public at a recent radio exhibition. As they drove through the city, Helga saw children playing, people riding bicycles, shopkeepers, shoppers, and the inevitable argument in the street.

Some of the shopkeepers were Jewish—doctors, furriers, jewelers—and that's how Helga had come to think of them, as people who worked in commerce, in the arts, in law. She knew that in movies, books, magazines and newspapers, Jewish people were increasingly referred to as "the bad Jews." Helga's parents patronized Jewish shops, but they would never have considered going to a Jewish doctor.

Helga had learned that higher levels of courtesy were due the aristocracy, and none of the aristocracy was Jewish. When certain ladies came to visit, Helga had been instructed by her mother to take the lady's hand and kiss it respectfully. When a Jewish storekeeper arrived to deliver groceries to the house, little Helgchen extended the same courtliness. But when the woman had gone, Leonore admonished her daughter and laughed, "You don't kiss the hand of the woman who owns the grocery!"

Meanwhile, Helga's father was called to treat the child of Nazi propaganda minister Joseph Goebbels. The child recovered so quickly that Kurt became a trusted family physician for Goebbels and other high-ranking Nazis. He also became a member of the Nazi party, but he did not consider himself an anti-Semite.

In his autobiography, Kurt offered the following picture of Jews in

Germany in the 1920s and early 1930s: "They were never looked upon as a different race. They were Prussian citizens and they enjoyed the same rights as everyone else. But I must say that somehow they were looked down upon. They could not become officers and yet they had to serve in the army as everyone else did. You may say the Jews were not loved, that one did not seek contact with them, but there was no talk in my youth of hatred of Jews or of racism. I only became aware much later of a rabid anti-Semitism. My parents had nothing in common with those circles."

One day Kurt parked his convertible on the street and went into a nearby home to check on a child with a sore throat. Since the child was already healing, he left his leather physician's bag in the locked car and was shocked to return to find the upholstered top slashed open. His medical bag with all of its instruments was gone. Although Helga was not with him that weekend, he took heed and never took her on house calls again. He continued to drive her to the city's landscaped parks and into the beautiful countryside and when Kurt and Edith's little girl, Röschen, born in 1930, was old enough, she began to join Kurt and Helga on the pleasure drives.

In the summer of 1932—about the time that Leonore boarded a freighter to meet Fritz Kiderlen in Japan—Helga was put on a train to Berlin to visit her father. She was happy for the chance to play with her little sister, Röschen, again, and to greet her new baby brother for the very first time. Hans Melchior had just been born in early June. Allowing Edith and the nanny time with the newborn, Vati drove Hans Melchoir's two older sisters to a resort on the Baltic Sea where they went swimming, enjoyed boat rides, and made sand castles every day. After several weeks, Kurt put Helga on a train to see her grandparents in Eisenach in the east. Although Helga did not know it, it was the last time she would see them.

Helga's grandfather, Friedrich Karl Robert Hofmeier, was a lieutenant general in the Prussian Army. In a photograph taken the year of his retirement, he slices the air with a steely gaze from under the brim of his officer's cap. A handlebar mustache defines his face: it is nearly as wide as his head is tall. The mustache, famously worn by Franz Ferdinand, archduke of Austria-Este, was a symbol of the upper class.

Lieutenant General Hofmeier spent his life in military service and was recognized many times for bravery in battle. He earned the Iron Cross First Class and the Iron Cross Second Class, the equivalent of the U.S. Silver Star and Bronze Star.

While the German Army of the late 1800s was a federal militia with mandatory service, the Prussians were an army of volunteers. They swore allegiance to the king; his army was considered the school of the nation. As Helga's father wrote in his memoir, "To wear the king's coat was to most everyone an honor; to serve in the same unit with his father the greatest wish. . . . a man who had served was to be trusted, and was proud to enjoy that trust."

The military regularly paraded past the castle in uniform on horseback, in honor of the German kaiser and the Prussian king. Officers were rarely seen out of uniform in public except on vacation or at sporting events. Many wore the uniform at home. Prussian officers were historically drawn from among the land-owning nobility, the *Junkers* ("country squires"). Stories were told, far and wide, about their bravery. Heading into what turned out to be his last battle, Prince Leopold I prayed for victory against the Saxons: "O Lord God, let me not be disgraced in my old days. Or if Thou wilt not help me, do not help these scoundrels, but leave us to try it ourselves."

The elder Hofmeier's promotions through the ranks brought so many moves that Kurt felt unable to make lasting friendships. His parents had always had many social obligations. As a child, he felt close to his mother, but the everyday work of childrearing was left to nannies. In the summer, he and his siblings and cousins were sent with servants to shepherd them to the Berlin estate of his maternal grandmother, Henriette Maria Louise Charlotte Einbeck.

The lieutenant general had retired in April 1914 but apparently was unable to sit twiddling his thumbs with World War I at stake, and within a year had returned to service as Artillery Commander for the 8th Replacement Field Artillery Brigade.

Despite his apparent ferocity on the battlefield, at home Lieutenant General Hofmeier was something of a papa bear who enjoyed playing with his grandchildren and collected handmade clocks. His wife, Paula Adelheid Charlotte Ramm Hofmeier, ruled the roost—despite being thirteen years his junior. She managed the house as well as their many social engagements (always ensuring that the correct people were paired together at the dinner table).

Lieutenant General Hofmeier was meticulous about his handlebar mustache, carefully washing it every day when he washed his face. When Helga came to visit, she found him quite pleasant. She was fascinated watching him part the mustache in the middle and use two tiny brushes to comb it on both sides until it was shiny and smooth. Then he pinched each end of the *schnurrbart* and twirled it into a half curl.

He seemed happy to play with her but had his own ideas about games. When she suggested a children's card game, he said it was *langweilig* ("boring") and taught her a more sophisticated French game, Bezique.

Their home was alive with timepieces, more than two dozen in varying sizes from grandfather clocks to cuckoos. Each one needed to be wound every day and sounded on the hour. Most of the clocks clicked and chimed and buzzed in the guest bedroom—where Helga slept. Midnight was a particularly sleepless event for Helga when all of the clocks went off, sounding their bells twelve times in a cacophony of offbeat syncopation.

The Nazi party grew in size and velocity. A 1932 Nazi party election rally in Helga's birthplace, Frankfurt am Main, drew thousands. Inside the town's largest auditorium, hand-painted slogans read: "Death to Marxism," "Join the Hitler Youth," and "Germany will live." Anti-Nazi rallies were held in Berlin and elsewhere, often organized by the Communist Party.

By the end of 1932, unemployed Germans reached 630,000: many of them began to voice their dissatisfaction on the streets of Berlin. Now there were more brown-uniformed Nazi party members on the streets, and the Nazi version of the German flag dotted the sidewalks in front of homes and businesses. Sometimes, there was a public fight when Nazis tried to drag a Jewish family out of their home.

Helga was eight years old when Hitler was appointed Chancellor of Germany in 1933. The next day, known Communists were rounded up and arrested at gunpoint and chained to walls with their hands above their heads. The Nazi flag with its thick, black swastika, was unfurled above the Frankfurt am Main town hall. The formal persecution and mass expulsion of Jews began. Across Germany, Nazis stormed into bookstores and schools and confiscated books they deemed "un-German," piling them in the streets and setting them afire.

All children at least ten years old were expected to join the Hitler Youth Club, *Hitler Jugend.* Once a week they donned the special uniform, much like the Boy Scouts and Girl Scouts in the United States. Then they gathered together under a group leader to sing patriotic songs and listen to special presentations extolling the virtues of serving their community, their country. Teenagers were expected—if not required—to volunteer as workers in a neighborhood family, with priority given to farmers and families with at least four children. Upon turning sixteen, girls and boys were approached and given the name of a family chosen for them. The teenage "volunteer" would move into the home and work for one year in exchange for room and board. If the family could afford to, it might give a small amount of money as well. Girls were assigned household tasks and catered to the mother; boys repaired household items, managed small carpentry tasks, and were given farm chores. Wealthy parents usually found the ways and means to have their children excused, sending their sons to college and demanding that their daughters were needed at home.

In the cities, the boys of the Hitler Jugend were encouraged to loot Jewish stores and beat up Jewish people in the streets. Homes of Jewish people were forcibly entered in a supposed search for subversive material. The raids became looting episodes in which lawless gangs stole the personal belongings of innocent people. Fierce protests in Berlin initially resulted in some material being returned but soon died down in the force of Nazi suppression. The National Socialist Party, which had fewer than sixty members in 1920, would grow to more than eight million by the end of World War II.

We trace Leonore's whereabouts that summer from her letters, which began in Hamburg where she visited relatives. At the end of the summer of 1932, she wrote from the international seaport in Genoa, Italy, as she prepared to board a ship headed for Japan. When the ship docked in Colombo two weeks later, Leonore managed to send a letter to Helga. By the third week of October, Leonore wrote Helga from Tokyo. On December 10, 1932, she married Fritz Kiderlen in Tokyo. Leonore's letters from Tokyo to Helga in Germany continued for three years until, at last, the couple arranged for Helga's passage to Japan.

When Helga learned to read for herself, she dove into her mother's handwritten letters, which were long and full of details about everyday life. They were cheerful and conversational, as if the child were sitting nearby, and laced with motherly advice such as, "Be careful with the silver." Birthdays and Christian holidays were occasions for giving silver, and by the age of six, a proper German girl already possessed the first engraved pieces of her collection. In Helga's family, a girl could expect to end up with a twenty-four-piece place setting of sterling silver—in case she married a man with a large family.

"I know you are too small now, but later on you will be thankful you have the silver," her mother wrote. "It can be a lot of work, too, to have beautiful things, because they have to be cared for. Don't bring it with you; let's keep it over there for when you are older." She would have given different instructions had she foreseen the ruins Allied bombers would make of Europe's finest cities, including Munich.

Leonore inquires about the cold temperatures in Germany, and gently advises her daughter to be on her best behavior with the children she will be traveling with to Japan. Coaching Helga to keep up her schoolwork, Leonore describes a German school she and her husband visited in Omori, a suburb of Tokyo. "The school is small, with three classrooms, a gym with a shower room and separate toilets for boys and girls, a reading room, and a huge blackboard in the room where chemistry, physics, and geography are taught."

The Christmas letter of 1934 describes making Christmas cookies and suggests that "maybe we can do it together next year." It was a clue of what was to come. The child who had learned to live without her mother for three years now faced the possibility of a sudden reunion.

One cold Sunday before Helga's upcoming oceanic voyage, Helga's aunt and uncle took her to one of the large graveyards in Munich for an annual memorial service. It was difficult to get a grave at that time in Munich: war, poverty, and disease had left so many dead with so little ground. Cremation was becoming more popular, despite the protests of the Catholics. Helga held her Uncle Lückchen's hand as the beautiful songs and heartfelt prayers rang through her nine-year-old heart. It was a poignant reminder that when family members are gone, something of them still remains. If you can just hold on to it.

Uncle Lückchen (Albert Witzel) picks up
Helga from ice skating. Munich. 1933.

Chapter Two

The Voyage

IT WAS A WINTRY DAY LATE IN **1934** when Helga's aunt, uncle, and grandmother gathered around the dinner table and explained that soon she would board an ocean liner that would deliver her to her estranged mother and her new stepfather. She was a mere nine years old. That day set a pattern that imposed itself on her life for decades to come: unpredictable news that required her to leave everything behind and start anew. Early on she learned to be sure-footed in foreign territories.

Helga didn't want to leave her family and friends in their close-knit Munich neighborhood and at first felt betrayed that everyone had hatched such a drastic plan without consulting her. But eventually she made her peace with the news. She reasoned that she wanted to see her mother and she had never been to another country. Besides, she had been raised as an obedient child and knew that she had no choice in the matter.

She would travel with Wilhelm and Charlotte Bunten, a fine German couple, and their three children: Rosewita, Liselotte, and Wolfgang, the toddling baby brother. The idea of going so far with strangers was frightening, but Helga's uncle explained that Mr. Bunten was a business associate of Helga's new stepfather, and Mrs. Bunten wrote Helga a friendly letter, introducing herself and letting her know they would take very good care of her.

It was a voyage made by an increasing number of Europeans before Hitler came to power and after. They admired the artistry and technological wizardry of the Japanese people and saw the feudal system of Japan as similar to their own culture. Japan was happy to court European commerce and civil engineering. Political reforms of the late 1800s had turned Japan's medieval culture into an industrial society with sophisticated transportation lines created by U.S. engineers and a navy modeled after the powerful Royal Navy of the United Kingdom. Japan maintained an open-door policy for Germans, whether Jewish or gentile. Immediately after World War I, increasing numbers of Europeans moved to Japan following the collapse of the German economy and the rise of Nazism. At one point before World War II officially began, a Japanese ambassador issued tens of thousands of visas to allow Jewish people to hide there.

Pulling out a world map, Helga's uncle pointed to the cities she would pass on the month-long voyage. Uncle Lückchen would accompany her on the train from Munich to Milano, where he would leave her with the Buntens, arriving from Berlin. The last train would be from Milano to the Italian port of Genoa, where Helga and the Buntens would board the freighter *Kulmerland*. They would sail through half the world: through the Suez Canal, past India, Thailand, Shanghai, and then on to Tokyo. Helga's aunt and grandmother joined in the conversation, attempting to smooth over any unease the child felt. Later, Helga overheard her uncle saying that her father would be sending payments to the Kiderlens in Tokyo, where the Deutschmarks would be exchanged for yen.

Before leaving Munich, Helga penned one last letter to her mother and sent paper bookmarks that she had decorated with embroidered shapes of Christmas candles, butterflies, the sun, the moon. "Omi put the holes in it for me—she copied some of the ones you could buy in the stores—and I put the needle through," she explained.

With half a million cubic feet, the *Kulmerland* could carry hundreds of passengers and 100 tons of cargo; Helga recalls only a few dozen passengers when she was aboard. Operating under the

Hamburg-America shipping company, the *Kulmerland's* officers were German and the crew Filipino. The merchant ship, named for a part of Prussia that was home to the Hofmeier ancestors, was powered by six huge steam boilers and appealed to Helga's family as capable of providing safe passage through waters that were potentially dangerous both politically and geographically.

Helga held tight to the metal deck railing as they sailed past Corsica and the great city of Rome. It was just after New Year's 1935, about the same time that pilot Amelia Earhart became the first person to fly from Honolulu to California. (Earhart would famously become the first woman to fly solo across the Atlantic Ocean. But her record-setting would end in 1937 when she disappeared over the Pacific Ocean while attempting to pilot solo around the world.)

As land disappeared and the ocean opened up, Helga steadied her footing and drew her face deeper into the fur lining of the jacket her aunt and uncle had given her. She could not help but think of who she was leaving behind and who she was going toward. Fingering the gold bracelet her mother had sent "to my dear Helgchen," Helga set her mind that no matter what happened, she would not worry about things she could not control.

The voyage was often stormy, but rarely was Helga afraid. The ocean spread out before them— sometimes indigo, sometimes emerald color, depending on the angle of the sun. She did not grow tired of watching the waves dance, feeling the salty spray on her face, and sometimes catching sight of dolphins leaping high as water rushed up on each side of the ship. At night, against the black-blue sky, the stars twinkled with a dazzling intensity she had never known.

Helga felt very grown up, strolling into the ship's dining room for meals: breakfast at eight o'clock in the morning; at midmorning a cup of hot bullion and a little sandwich; at one o'clock the main meal; afternoon tea, coffee and pastries, with milk and chocolates for children; and a light dinner at the end of the day.

Accommodations were a bit crowded but comfortable. Mr. and Mrs. Bunten slept in one room with their smallest child; Helga and the two girls slept in an adjacent bedroom, each with her own little bed. The family shared one private bath, which would have been a luxury on cargo ships at the time. One of the Bunten girls was a year older than Helga, the other a year younger. The girls had already made the voyage from Germany to Japan at least once, and were proud to show their new friend the shuffleboard court and the room where, once a day, the children could watch an hour-long movie of a funny European clown. Sometimes they were allowed to tour the belly of the ship, where huge machines pumped water through boilers for the steam-operated engines. Remembering that voyage, Helga would long recall the sparkling clean engine room.

Each day Helga followed their progress, tracing the route with her finger on a map the Buntens had brought. From the Mediterranean they passed Greece and Libya and slowed the pace through the Suez Canal. Passing through the long, manmade corridor—120 miles long and 700 feet wide—she noticed a wall and on top of the wall, lanky camels carrying their riders. From Egypt's Red Sea, they returned to the high seas and steamed toward Asia.

Now and then they had "Shore Days," where contact could be made with the locals. In one village, the people of the marketplaces were unlike anything Helga had seen in Germany: many men wore white shirts and white skirts and tall, white hats; many of the women wore layers of long black fabric around their bodies, shoulders and heads, making them look mysterious and austere. At some ports smaller ships approached and waited alongside as huge cranes lifted wooden supply boxes onto them.

From every port Helga sent postcards to her loved ones in Munich and her mother and new stepfather in Tokyo. The year 1935 was a turning point in world history, one full of uprisings and build up to war. In Germany Hitler announced compulsory military conscription, and suddenly Great Britain and the United States noticed that Nazi Germany had an army of 300,000 men in the Wehrmacht and 2,500 war planes in the Luftwaffe. The world watched and held its breath as

Nazi Germany began to methodically expand its borders into adjacent lands.

The *Kulmerland* sailed through the Arabian Sea and on to Ceylon (now Sri Lanka), a critical port at the southern tip of India. Great Britain had attempted to colonize parts of the island since the late 1700s, causing bloody reprisals. When the *Kulmerland* docked in the winter of 1935, the uprisings in Colombo prevented the passengers from going ashore—how Helga wanted to see the elephants she had heard were there! Instead, she gave thanks for the little ivory elephants hanging on the bracelet her mother had sent and watched oil being pumped into the ship's fuel tanks while a vendor climbed the rope ladder and sold tea and small hand-carved animals. Within a few years, Ceylon would become a key part of Allied naval operations in World War II.

The waters became warmer from Sri Lanka through the Bay of Bengal and were dotted with jellyfish as big as a table. Helga saw her first palm trees, their fingerlike fronds gently swaying in the breeze. She happily put away her winter clothes, donned her new sundresses and enjoyed the warmth. On the deck, people stretched out in chairs, talking and relaxing, usually wearing a hat of some kind, and often a shawl or afghan as well, to shield against the wind and the glaring sun.

Leonore's January 20, 1935, letter bursts with excitement. "If this letter reaches you, you have done almost half of your cruise and you will be in the land of monkeys that play on the beach near Singapore. How do you like the ocean cruise? Is it very shaky? I hope you didn't get seasick. I hope there was a lot of laughter in your cabin."

Sunset on the ship was a magnificent event. Helga and the Buntens, along with many other passengers, liked to stand or sit on deck and watch the splendor, which was more vast than anything the girl had ever imagined. From her Munich neighborhood, the sun disappeared over the typical European skyscape of the era: four-and five-story stone buildings with chimneys and smokestacks that, in winter, obscured the view with rising smoke.

In the Manila marketplace, people sat on a dirt floor trading and chewing betel plant leaves that they seemed never to either swallow or spit out. Some of the passengers went in a group into the jungle, where Helga and the Buntens saw many different kinds of exotic birds. Some of the local people, their mouths red from betel leaves, held bananas in the air below the trees, teasing monkeys to come close. Playful yet wise to the ways of humans, the monkeys hung out of reach on a lower branch, watched carefully, then swooped down to grab the banana and fly back to the safety of foliage.

Leonore traced her daughter's route meticulously, sending letters of anticipation to the ports where Helga would soon arrive. On January 30, she wrote, "We can hardly believe that you are coming closer and closer; if you receive this greeting, you have been already in Manila and seen the young women with the beautiful dresses." Helga and the Buntens *had* seen them: women sitting on floors with piles of cigar tobacco in front of them, patiently rolling the damp tobacco into cigars. To Helga, the odor was nearly overwhelming.

When they arrived in Hong Kong, the ship docked but the passengers were advised not to go ashore. Instead, slender young men jumped into rowboats and rowed near the huge ship to display their wares: jewelry, handmade shawls, and trinkets. Helga always thought the men looked hungry. If a passenger decided to buy from the floating merchants, a rope ladder was let down, allowing them to climb up the side of the ship to the railing—but not aboard. From the railing, purchases were made through a ship's purser, who passed money and goods back and forth and negotiated the proper change. Sometimes passengers tossed coins into the water and watched the young men dive for them. When found, a coin would be waved triumphantly in the air with a smile and a shout of gratitude.

Reaching Shanghai, the ship docked. Leaving the safety of the boat with the Buntens, tottering down the gangplank and into one of the world's oldest cities, Helga experienced for the first time what it was to be the racial minority. So many people of yellowish skin and black hair moved in the streets, and she felt very tall. A thriving market town for nearly a millennium, Shanghai was one of the largest cities in the world when Helga arrived, with three million people. Tables and wooden bins were packed tightly together and overflowing with fresh-caught fish, filleted and whole; bananas, grapes, and many fruits and vegetables foreign to her; live exotic birds in wooden cages; teapots of every kind; hand-painted china teacups; wooden calligraphy brushes made of animal hair.

The Buntens and Helga changed ships, boarding the smaller Japanese *Haruna Maru* from Shanghai to Yokohama. This allowed them to arrive in Japan as quickly as possible, within a month of leaving Italy. As Leonore wrote in her letter, "The *Kulmerland* won't arrive until March 6, and we don't want to wait that long to see you." It would have been difficult to determine the actual arrival date and whether her daughter was aboard a German ship. The whereabouts of large ships on the high seas between World War I and World War II was just barely unclassified. Any foreigner inquiring about the arrival of a German ship might well be asked, "Why do you want to know?"

Before boarding the *Haruna Maru* in Shanghai, Mr. Bunten telegraphed the Kiderlens their expected arrival time in Yokohama, the largest city in Japan after Tokyo. Leonore worried as her daughter's ship came closer whether the rough seas would make her daughter seasick and wanted very much to be on time for Helga's arrival. Coming into the Yokohama harbor, the *Haruna Maru* glided past local fishermen in traditional "junk" boats, in the same construction that has been used since the 1200s. It was a prominent, international port city with the largest Chinatown population of any city outside China.

Some memories remain imprinted on the soul, no matter how much time passes. For the rest of Helga's life she would recall the sight of her mother and new stepfather standing on the dock. Only nine years old, she had been on the ship for a month, passing through 6,000 miles of ocean. The emotions that arose in Helga—laying eyes on her mother—brought a strange ache. Three years ago when her mother disappeared in the night, Helga had refused to cry. Instead, she focused on loving the family she had, the family who remained. She maintained a stalwart disposition, as a proper German girl should. But a person can only refuse grief for so long: it will have its day. Powerful new feelings now pushed past a protective layer around Helga's heart and threaded their way towards the soft center. For an instant, she was overcome as grief—long held back—mixed with love. Then she recovered and threw her arm up to wave at them. Fritz waved back, but curiously, Leonore's arms were occupied. At first, Helga didn't comprehend what lay in her mother's arms. When she recognized it as a cat, she was surprised: the only people Helga had known to have cats were farmers, who needed them to catch mice.

Although Helga couldn't see it, Mount Fujiyama, sacred to the Japanese, towered in the distance, its white cone rising more than 12,000 feet into the air. As she rode in the back of her stepfather's leather-upholstered Crossley touring car through narrow side streets in the Tokyo suburbs, everything seemed strange to Helga, but she was soothed by her mother's voice, talking excitedly and describing the life they would share together.

Two of her mother's other two cats slunk out to inspect her. The cats had their own bedroom, complete with special bowls for food and water, cozy beds and soft rugs to cushion them from the hard floors.

Fritz was polite and friendly and showed his new daughter a small room prepared especially for her. Helga sat on the little bed and studied the straw-mat floor and translucent paper doors and windows. All she had ever known was hardwood, stone, brick, and glass.

A paper house! she thought to herself.

Helga in Karuizawa. 1936.

Chapter Three

Beginning Anew in Japan

THERE WAS VERY LITTLE ROOM FOR PERSONAL ITEMS IN THE LUGGAGE Helga had brought halfway around the world, but she had squeezed in her birthday ring and her birthday angel. The wooden birthday ring had holes for sixteen large, white candles—the same kind used to decorate live Christmas trees in Germany—and a birthday cake would be placed in the middle of the ring. On March 11, a few weeks after setting foot in Japan, Helga leaned toward the lit candles, made a wish from the depths of her ten-year-old heart, and blew. The mother she had not seen for so long and the man who now was her stepfather watched with satisfaction. All would be well.

Beside the cake stood her blond-haired birthday angel holding a gold-painted trumpet to her lips, announcing Helga's birthday. The angels were also a German tradition: sometimes the figurines were wooden, sometimes porcelain or china, but the little angel always carried something special. It might be a birthday cake, a specially wrapped present, or a musical instrument. The story of Hansel and Gretel, told through a children's opera popular in Germany at the time, was another reminder that a child's angels were always nearby on important occasions. In the opera, as in Grimm's fairy tale, Hansel and Gretel were brother and sister whose impoverished parents could not feed them. Rather than watch them starve, the parents led the children into the woods and left them there. Lost, tired, and hungry, the abandoned children lay down to sleep. Here, Engelbert Humperdinck's fairy-tale opera (written in the late 1800s) becomes magical. Fourteen angels surround the children and guard them while they sleep. The children awake to a great, wonderful light and soon find their parents, who have finally found food.

The child could still picture the winged guardian angels on stage when her grandmother took her to the Hansel and Gretel opera in Munich. Was there such a thing as guardian angels? She surveyed her situation. She was unsure what to expect from her mother: Leonore's letters from Japan, although cheerful, sometimes mentioned feeling sickly and staying in bed for days at a time. But without fail, she would make a plea for intimacy with her daughter. "In your honor tomorrow, I will drink a glass of wine at the noon meal to toast you. Just think, my dear Helgchen, if our thoughts cross, that is a very dear feeling in my heart and yours."

From the moment Helga left, Herzeltäntchen, began writing to her dear Helga. She addressed the letters "care of Rudolf Ratjen" who was affiliated with the Mercedes dealership that employed Helga's stepfather. When Helga turned 83, she still had boxes of postcards and letters from her Herzeltäntchen through 1939: after that, World War II made the mail impossible to deliver.

Rudolf Ratjen had moved to Japan in the early 1900s with the Delacamp company, spent time in a Japanese internment camp during World War I, set up business in Tokyo and married a Japanese woman. After the war he built up his own commerce company, representing Mercedes, Deutsche Grammophon (which had already built a recording studio in Tokyo), a German machinery company, a German sparkling wine they proudly, if erroneously, called champagne, and products from many other homeland companies. Rudolf Ratjen and Company, Import-Export Representatives, set up shop in Tokyo and developed satellite offices in Osaka, Japan, and Mukden, China.

Unlike many European immigrants, Leonore had not managed to expand her horizons in Japan. The few friends she made were mostly older German women. A free spirit who disliked conformity, she confided to Helga her disinterest in the conversations of German women she met. They seemed to speak only of their husbands' business, or the affairs of the National Socialist German Workers' Party. German men were expected to join the *Nationalsozialistische Deutsche Arbeiterpartei* even in Japan. Women's groups also were formed, but Leonore ignored the social pressure to join.

Adolf Hitler became chancellor in January 1933, but he was initially viewed by the old guard as a crude and incompetent leader. Many hoped he would just go away. History would show that the Nazis opened two concentration camps that year, one at Dachau and one outside Berlin, but hardly anyone knew about them at the time. International news sources were few and far between, and word of mouth traveled slowly. Few people on earth could have predicted that in a few years Hitler would command German troops to invade Poland—launching World War II.

Helga had never heard her parents speak ill of Jewish people, and she had played with Jewish children when she lived in Munich. Neither was "the Jewish question" a topic Helga overheard anyone speaking about. Leonore found members of the National Socialist Party an uncivilized sort, much like Japanese boys. *Ungezogen* is what she called Japanese boys. "They have no manners," she told Helga, "and they are treated like gods. The little boys are never punished and get away with anything. The little girls are all very well behaved."

Japanese girls acted like servants, as far as Helga could see. Whenever she was out with her mother, she saw little girls with a younger sibling strapped on their backs. If a girl completed her household chores and was sent out to play, her younger sibling would first be tied onto to her back. Leonore did not understand why the Japanese did not have strollers like the Europeans. "The babies come everywhere, even in the theater," she complained. "Sometimes they scream, but the Japanese don't care."

Her objections did not help Helga, who struggled to adjust to life in Japan. In Germany she could walk with friends to school; she played in a park across the street from her house. When she spoke, everyone understood her. She missed the baby she thought of as her little brother, the son of her aunt and uncle. Her aunt wrote her that, "for the longest time he walked around calling your name."

Longing for her homeland, nevertheless Helga found herself admiring the Japanese people, especially their extreme level of politeness and stoicism. This she understood. They did not show their feelings in public. If a Japanese person was upset, he or she would simply bow and walk away. Just like in Germany, the feelings would be dealt with later, in private.

They lived near the Uehara train station, not far from Tokyo Bay. She could almost walk to the Meiji shrine, with its large iris garden named for an honored emperor. Their postal address was 816, Shibuya, Yoyogi Honcho, Shibu Yaku, Tokyo, Japan—but it was not a designation that would ever allow a stranger to find it. House numbers were not consecutive, and even local Japanese could not locate an address by its house number. Only taxi drivers seemed to be able to navigate the curious system.

Their house was small compared to the homes Helga had known in Germany, but she adjusted quickly. In no time, she had grown accustomed to the shojis: room dividers made of rice paper and framed in wood. Some shojis were sliding doors, or sliding walls, and some were windows. There were no doors that "opened" European style. Traditionally, eating and visiting in Japan takes place seated on pillows on straw tatami mats. Rooms are measured by how many mats they can hold: a six tatami room is roughly nine-by-twelve feet. For the Japanese, housekeeping was simple: if humidity was high, the mats were taken outside to air dry in the sun. Fritz had Europeanized the house by covering the tatamis with Oriental rugs and bringing in European furniture: bookcases, stuffed chairs, a small dining room table for six.

Friedrich ("Fritz") Kiderlen was the perfect stepfather: a soft-spoken man who apparently enjoyed saying "yes" to Helga. While *Vati* was a name reserved only for her biological father, she called Fritz *Vatl*—dear little father. Making household decisions, setting child-rearing rules were left to Leonore. And yet it is not accurate to say that Fritz was a soft man entirely. For one thing, he had the nerve to own and drive a

Crossley every weekday to the Mercedes Benz showroom, where he was a salesman. The leather seats in the Crossley folded down to make room for sleeping, and before Helga arrived, Fritz and Leonore used it as a camper. For a quick respite from the city they made a weekend drive into the woods to enjoy a quiet night under the stars and sleep in the car (always with one or more of Leonore's beloved cats).

Following the great Japanese earthquake of 1923, Fritz's uncle, Rudolf Ratjen, had opened the Tokyo Mercedes dealership. When he offered Fritz a job, it was sufficient reason for him to leave his impoverished homeland. The frugal Fritz bought an affordable car upon arriving in Tokyo, and his boss never stopped teasing him about not driving a Mercedes. "The Mercedes is a wonderful car," Fritz agreed. "If I could afford one, I would have it."

Leonore and Fritz neither publicized nor tried to hide the fact that he was not Helga's biological father. To register Helga in school, Leonore and Fritz were required to use the name Hofmeier on the child's immigration papers, but she became known as Helga Ki, short for Kiderlen. Young as she was, Helga understood that names signified identity and kinship: in Munich, she had been known as Helga Witzel, her uncle's last name.

The first week of school, Vatl escorted ten-year-old Helga, and from then on she went alone. The routes at the time did not allow Helga to travel in a direct route, which would have been due east and then south. Instead, she took three trains, first riding north and then heading south. Six and a half million people lived in Tokyo, and many of them used the trains every day. The Japanese train system was designed for passengers to step aboard on one side and hop off on the opposite side.

To get to school, Helga walked twenty minutes to the Uehara train station and stepped up onto a train jam-packed with people. She rode the train north for ten minutes. When the train was approaching her stop, Helga made sure she was in place to allow the crowd to push her body toward the door. She jumped off at Shinjuku, which was already on its way to becoming the busiest train station in the world.

From Shinjuku, Helga climbed onto a train that reversed her course, heading down the east side of the Meiji Shrine and south toward the coastal town of Shinagawa. After that twenty-minute ride, she changed trains again and rode another ten minutes south to Omori. From the Omori station, it was a twenty-minute walk to school.

"Don't talk to strangers," her parents had warned, and she didn't. "Keep your mind focused on where you are going, and avoid looking around at everything else, which will distract you." It was advice she heeded for years to come.

Leonore urged Helga to accept life in Japan. "You must get used to life here," she said. "School starts in a few weeks." The school in Omori was one of a long line of government-sponsored schools for German children in Japan; the first had been built in 1904. Teachers and curricula were German, and the school followed the German school calendar year, beginning classes each year after Easter. It was a classical education and included Latin. The only Japanese person on staff was the *housemeister* who cleaned the three buildings, maintained the landscaping, and rang the school bell signaling students to come and go. Conveniently, he and his wife lived next door.

There was one main building for academics, with a special room for physics and chemistry. Classes were also held in the gymnasium, where small chairs and benches were set up when it wasn't in use for athletics. The gym was equipped with a basketball court, a large sandbox for high-jump landings, as well as a leather "horse" for acrobatics.

When a teacher entered the room, he or she stretched out the right arm and intoned "Heil Hitler," to which the children responded by standing and doing the same. Only one teacher did not salute Hitler. "Herr Beck," the British, Oxford-educated teacher, had apparently become stranded in Japan as tensions mounted between countries. When he came into the room in the mornings, instead of saluting the *führer,* he gave a cheerful "Good morning!" He was quite the individual, sometimes sitting on top of his desk with his feet in a chair instead of standing behind the desk like other teachers. Despite his friendliness and his occasional guitar playing in class, he was a strict teacher and demanded that the students work hard.

Helga became her mother's best friend and constant companion. She carried a German-to-Japanese pocket dictionary and soon was able to translate just about anything her mother needed to say to a local shopkeeper or neighbor. The two of them often went into the busy metropolis of downtown Tokyo, a sea of tall buildings with western architecture. Most people traveled by train, and pedestrians and bicyclists outnumbered cars and buses. Those who could afford it took taxis, which were large sedans built by Nissan. There were dozens of venues for live theater and music, and one street was devoted to foreign motion pictures, including Hollywood films. Hearing English spoken in the American and British films, Helga's use of the language grew by leaps and bounds.

Western clothing—slacks, skirts, button-down shirts—was worn, but it was not unusual to see women strolling in long silk kimonos, some of them carrying rice-paper parasols to shield the sun. Tokyo was dotted with parks and sacred shrines where, in the springtime, the air filled with falling cherry blossoms.

Helga was surprised to see that homemakers and maids hung laundry on clotheslines strung in trees. Weren't people embarrassed to have their underwear sailing in the wind for all to see? She was shocked to see Japanese men on the streets wearing nothing but *fundoshi*, a traditional thonglike undergarment, their chests, legs, and bare buttocks exposed. The word comes from a Japanese expression, "tighten your loincloth," the English equivalent of "roll up your sleeves." Sometimes two large men wearing *fundoshi* would be walking with a heavy stick between them, carrying a heavy object on the pole. While the clothing was considered manly and athletic in Japan, it was disorienting to a properly raised German child.

Vendors filled the streets and walked around with flowers in hand or wooden carts full of fresh grocery items. Others had makeshift outdoor kitchens, with a small hibachi grill they could set down anywhere to deep fry or cook a hot noodle dish prepared on the spot. She had never seen people eating on the street. There were delicate handmade porcelain teacups and teapots, and intricate Japanese drawings. Merchants took the time to speak politely to Helga and in time taught her the Japanese names for the items they were selling. That way they could ask her in Japanese if she wanted to buy their wares.

Customs, even those that Germany and Japan held in common, were vastly different. Teatime European-style meant sitting at tables sipping black Indian tea with cream and sugar; teatime for the Japanese meant perching on pillows on the floor drinking hot green tea. Women of both cultures carried white handkerchiefs, but Helga noticed that in Tokyo many of the children had runny noses and used their hankies frequently; she did not know why.

She was well aware that she was a guest in their country. "You are not here to do as you please," her mother instructed. The first time her mother took her to a Japanese home, she learned to remove her shoes and put on the slippers provided. She learned not to sit down until told to sit. When the hostess presented Helga with a small gift, she immediately opened it, only to hear gasps: *"Ooooh!"* Then her mother said, "I forgot to tell you you're not supposed to open a gift until you get home."

To open a gift in front of everyone was considered an emotional intrusion. "The Japanese don't want to see your reaction," her mother explained. "Did you notice the Japanese woman at the party who laughed? She lowered her head and covered her mouth with her hand. To laugh in public is not refined."

Tokyo was already an international city and an important node in the world economy. Local shops and restaurants reflected a wide variety of tastes, from Eastern (Okinawan, Chinese, Korean, Thai) to European. At the international foods store, Helga and Leonore could buy cheese from France, butter from Denmark, coffee from Brazil, and the strange, new cuisine offerings from America, like cornflakes. Customary niceties were observed, especially by shopkeepers: women would put their hands on their knees and bow deeply in greeting; men would bow their heads. Japanese merchants in the more elegant shops, such as jewelry, knew English and would use it. All the merchants were curious about their customers.

All of the food was fresh: canned food was something that soldiers ate. Every week the "meat man" from the local butcher shop stopped at each house to take orders of beef, chicken, and pork. Later in the week he delivered it—always trying to time his deliveries after ice deliveries.

The Kiderlens' kitchen was also equipped with a gas stove that Leonore used, sometimes letting Helga cook with her. Food was stored in a pantry in the kitchen, where a light bulb was always left burning to keep food from molding in the high humidity. The wooden icebox was a kind of cabinet with three tin-lined cubicles: milk, meat, butter, and cheese were stored in the main compartment, and above and below was an ice compartment. Several times a week, the iceman came in his horse-drawn cart. He cut rectangular sections of ice to fit the upper and lower compartments, which kept the food in the middle cool. Below the icebox was a small pot that caught the melted ice water.

For the most part, Helga enjoyed Japanese food: her favorite dish was hot rice with marinated eel on top and a spicy sauce. She did not like Japanese desserts, which often are filled with sweet beans, so she was always grateful for her mother's desserts. Leonore was a good baker and made perfect German cakes and German Christmas cookies. She made wonderful rice pudding and a chocolate pudding that was as beautiful as it was delicious.

Japanese children from the neighborhood would come to the house and ask for Helga to play with them. After all, children hardly need language to play. Plastic was a fairly new invention that was only used in industrial setting and hadn't yet debuted in consumer goods, so children made their own toys. If they were lucky, they had a rubber ball. If they could find enough rubber bands, they would make a long chain of them to use as a jump rope. Rubber-band chains were also held steady as a limbo line, for children to lean backward and "do the limbo" underneath. The limbo line was lowered in increments until only the most limber children had passed under without either falling backward or touching the line.

Dolls were ceremonial icons, not playthings, for Japanese girls.

Not so for Helga. She adored her dolls and spent a great deal of time dressing and undressing them, putting them in her little doll buggy, and taking them for walks.

For Japanese girls, Girls' Day, also called Dolls' Day, fell on March 3. *Hina Matsuri,* as the Japanese called it, was a time to display ceremonial dolls that are replicas of an emperor, empress, court ladies, guardians with swords and knives, musicians, and the king and queen's servants who dressed them (it could take hours to simply prepare the hair of an empress). Behind the royal couple stood a gold-paper screen, and there might be a lacquered table with flowers on it. The dolls were passed on through generations in each family. The year Helga turned thirteen, her parents gave her a full set of fifteen Hina dolls, along with the miniature furnishings of the dolls' imperial home. (Along with other treasured Japanese mementos, this much loved doll set would be completely lost when six feet of storm surge from Hurricane Ivan flooded Helga's Florida home sixty-seven years later.)

February 11 was National Foundation Day in Japan, when all stores would be closed. It was also Fritz Kiderlen's birthday. "This is in special honor of me," he would say with a smile. "Everyone has the day off from work!"

During the spring equinox, the observant visited their relatives' graves to clean and decorate them. It was an old custom from Germany as well, never to leave a grave bare. There would be fresh flowers, cut or potted, when the season permitted and always some kind of fresh greenery, even in winter.

May 5 was *Tangu Nan Sekko,* a national holiday in Japan celebrating boys. Families proudly displayed banners with carp on them: the image of a large carp signaled an older son, a smaller carp signaled a younger son. The carp, a spirited fish, full of energy to swim upstream, symbolized the strong spirit and prowess envisioned for boys on Boys' Day. In their home, a family would display rare family knives, helmets, and armory: the tools and protectors of men.

The fall festival, Festival for Children, was called *Shichigosan.* It celebrated children who were seven, five, and three. "In Japanese, *Shichi* is seven, *go* is five, and *san* is three," Helga's mother explained. Since it was a cultural observation and not a national holiday, fathers were mostly left out of the celebration because they were at work. But mothers dressed their children in ceremonial silk robes and walked to the neighborhood Buddhist temple.

Although the temple doors were always open, Helga did not go inside on Japanese holidays, but she had wandered in on other days. The custom for entering the temple was first to remove one's shoes outside the door and put on the slippers provided. A large rectangular basin of water, with a cup that hung from its little overhead roof, also stood outside the door. As a gesture of cleanliness and purity, the devoted dipped a cup of water from the basin, rinsed the mouth, rinsed the hands, and spit into a neighboring spittoon.

Chrysanthemums, fully blooming in November, adorned the temple on Culture Day. Many of them had been trained to grow downward on wires, these cascades reminiscent of a waterfall. Fireworks exploded in the air as blue, red, and yellow sparks fell earthward. Special foods, fried over hibachi grills, were always part of the celebrations.

Not long after Helga arrived, Vatl bought a larger, older house in the same area and ordered renovations. By 1937, they had moved in and hired a live-in maid who had lived in a fishing village along the coast near Tokyo. Fusako was a few years older than Helga and made wonderful miso soup that Helga loved. As an only child, she was happy to have the older girl for company—and to practice Japanese with her. At a deeper level, Helga intuitively understood that she and this Japanese girl had much in common: removed from their birth families, they were both orphans of a sort. Years later, Helga would describe Fusako as "the most kind, correct, disciplined, honest and true person I have known."

Helga in Karuizawa. 1938.

Chapter Four

Karuizawa Summers

FRITZ'S OLDER BROTHER, HEINZ KIDERLEN, ENJOYED high-level connections in Tokyo. Heinz had served on the German naval vessel *Deutschland* under Paul Wenneker, who was captain of the ship from 1938 to 1940 and later became admiral of the German navy. "I have a little brother," Heinz told Wenneker. "If you ever have a place for him, remember the name of Friedrich Kiderlen." Heinz also eventually rose to the rank of admiral.

Wenneker was described by a Japanese official as the "smooth and tactful attaché of the German Embassy in Tokyo, spreading the Nazi doctrine in the manner common to all German diplomatic missions at that time."

When Fritz moved to Tokyo, he began preliminary discussions with the German embassy about the possibility of working there, and Helga became friends with Wenneker's daughter, Utta.

In the summer of 1938, Helga began to spend the summers in Karuizawa (alternately spelled Karuisawa), a tourist town a two-hour train ride northwest of Tokyo. It was described by Issac Shapiro in his autobiography, *Edokko*, as a resort for foreigners. "Karuizawa was policed by the *kempeitai*, Japan's dreaded gendarmes or military policemen," he writes. "They were stern and ruthless. They were there to make sure that the foreigners didn't spy or break the rules in any way or do anything that was the least bit provocative. They had the authority to enter any home and arrest people, without a warrant, merely on suspicion.

They wore Japanese army uniforms with armbands that said, in red on white, *kempeitai*."

Spies were not uncommon in Karuizawa's international wartime atmosphere. One of them, as history would reveal, was Richard Sorge (also spelled Zorge), a German communist and a spy for the Soviet Union. Because spying on Nazis in Germany would have been dangerous and next to impossible, Sorge posed as a German journalist in Japan. There he joined the Nazi party, toasted the führer with absolute credibility, and built an intelligence-gathering network between 1933 and 1934. Sorge worked closely with Eugen Ott, the military attaché at the German embassy from 1934 through 1940. Ott then became the German ambassador to Japan and Wenneker took his place as the naval attaché. In both of Ott's high-level positions, Sorge apparently regularly checked intelligence he had gathered against the information in Ott's office.

Helga was schoolmates and friends with Ursula Ott, daughter of Eugen Ott. "Ulla," as her friends called her, was a year younger than Helga and lived in a fortress of formality. The embassy was not so much a home as a compound of beautifully appointed buildings where international affairs were conducted and history was made. There were many rooms, large and small, even tennis courts, for banquets and parties attended by famous German musicians and tennis players. Anyone who wished to enter was stopped by security guards at the gate. No one was searched, but their business had better have been prearranged and preapproved.

In 1938 Helga spent several weeks with Ott, his wife, Helma, and Ulla, in their summer home in Karuizawa. There, Helga was introduced to Richard Sorge, the soon-to-be-revealed Soviet spy. Testimony presented at his trial a few years later suggested that Sorge had notified Stalin that the Germans planned to attack the Soviet Union in the summer of 1941—advice that Stalin ignored, much to the detriment of his country. Richard Sorge was hanged on November 7, 1944. Twenty years would pass before the Soviet Union would officially acknowledge Sorge as its own. Helga's passing acquaintance with one of the world's greatest spies was one of the many ways that matters of life-and-death unceasingly circled around her young life. Somehow, through it all, she kept a bright spirit and a genuine curiosity about the world.

According to Issac Shapiro, Jewish people who had been incarcerated and tortured by Nazis in Germany found refuge in Karuizawa. He describes the German community there as "concentrated in a small village where they could more easily be watched by the Gestapo . . . [therefore, people] remained segregated and had little or no social contact with stateless émigrés like ourselves, especially Jews."

Helga remembers the commercial area of Karuizawa as having an international flair, with tourist shops that catered to European and American tastes, evening concerts, plays, and movies. Fritz leased a cottage with a large terrace overlooking the hillside, then rented a truck to haul their furniture, dishes, and other household necessities. Helga was twelve and the Japanese maid, Fusako, was only sixteen, so Fritz took Fusako's older sister with them to deliver the furniture and prepare the cottage for the summer. He and Leonore had already explained that Helga would be spending the majority of her summer in Karuizawa without them, with her parents only occasionally staying at the cottage. The fresh air and companionship of the other children will be good for you," they told her.

Helga was introduced to the mysteries of womanhood one day on an errand for an older girl. She accompanied her Karuizawa girlfriend, Ingrid, to the local store to fetch an item for Ingrid's big sister. They were to come home with "vanishing crème" but neither girl knew what it was. Helga went first to the German-to-English dictionary to look up the word: "to make disappear." The two girls pedaled their bicycles into town, wondering what Ingrid's sister was going to make vanish. They never did find out.

European teenagers in Japan did the same thing that American kids did: hung out at the local drugstore. In a corner of Brett's pharmacy, high stools were positioned around a counter where teenagers could order a soda, talk, play cards and play Ping-Pong at a nearby table. They were tolerated as long as they weren't too loud. Helga learned one day that womanly affairs were much more of a mystery to her girl-friend than to her. "A boy kissed me," her friend said. She was nearly in tears.

"What's wrong with that?" Helga asked.

"I'm afraid I'm pregnant," the girl wept.

"Did you do anything else?"

"No."

Helga shook her head slowly. "I don't think you can get pregnant that way."

Leonore often had bad days where she did not feel like leaving her room. For the most part Helga spent the summer in the Karuizawa cottage with either Fusako or Fusako's sister. It was a quiet resort where the men played golf and the women and children played tennis and swam in the swimming pool. (Emperor Akihito and Empress Michiko of Japan met while playing tennis there.) Helga and her friends picked blueberries that grew abundantly along the path to the volcanic hot springs at Asama Mountain, an active volcano for more than a thousand years. Sometimes Fritz rode a bicycle beside her; sometimes she rode her bicycle to other children's cottages. They would push their bikes up the steep roads snaking along the volcanic slopes, then whiz downhill, bearing down hard on the pedal brakes.

Helga's weekly letters to her mother (which survived World War II, repatriation, and Hurricane Ivan in 2004) reveal much about her brave heart. It is hard to believe that these letters were written by a thirteen-year-old girl.

26 July 1938
Karuizawa

My dear little Mother –

Your lovely letter just arrived so I want to answer right away.

You don't need to worry about the cooking at all. Both mornings and evenings I eat just as if I were at home and

Fusako always cooks something yummy for lunch. I'm certainly not starving. Anyway, Fusako keeps everything in order. She does it all on her own and everything is clean. Our neighbor, Frau Buhre, is astounded! It was really dirty here, especially tracking the dirt in. But it will eventually all be pretty. A new stove for heating has arrived since we have no chimney. I can still use a small area rag-rug.

I don't like your plan very much either. If you don't want to come up here, then I'll just have to do it all ourselves. I would, of course, much rather have had you up here, and I think you'd begin to feel better here. Frau Oetmann just drove back to Tokyo, and that trip will probably be too much for her, too. On the first night here, I had a terrible headache and a 101 temperature. I was shivering in spite of the warm cotton batted kimono.

It's pouring right now and it's so foggy that I can't even see 10 meters away. Yesterday, Ingrid Buhre and I went to the swimming pool. The water was pretty cold, and we lay in the warm sun for a while. I bought a season ticket that cost me three yen. You can swim and lay around in the sun whenever you want. Otherwise you have to pay 50 sen every time you go in. You can take great walks here. I recently walked to the mossy spring with Ingrid—the little river eventually runs into the sea. It's so cool and gorgeous there—pine trees, birches, chestnut trees—just like in Germany!

Vatl has probably already told you that one of the duvets for the down quilts did not arrive. There is a striped duvet, but it's the one used for the mattress futon. I did find one duvet for Vatl, but just can't find the other one.

Right now, I'm in the process of lining all the cabinets with white paper. We only have one small mirror, from the bathroom, for the whole house. And I've only found one egg cup and no tea cups. I'm drinking out of the pickle jar.

The Buhres are no problem at all. Ingrid and I play

together every day, she here or me at her house. Sometimes we ride our bicycles. It's not hard, usually straight or up little hills. If we see a big hill coming, we pedal fast downhill so it's not so hard to go back up the next one. I'm always careful when I see a car, and usually just get off my bike as one passes.

Goodbye for now, its already quarter past nine. I've chatted long enough—just like you and I always do, Mother.

Think about your plan very carefully again. You know that I'm much happier when you are here—but if it's just too much for you, then we'll just do it your way.

Please write soon. Many fat kisses to you—and to the old grouch (Vatl), as well. Tell him he needs to change his attitude a bit. He was wonderful when he was here. Tell him hello and don't yell at him too much!

Your little babydoll
[Helga is 13]

1 August 1938
Karuizawa

Dear little Mother –

Frau Schmidt got here in good shape yesterday, as did the trunk and another stove. Many thanks for your letter and the 50 yen. I am happy to get the money, I was broke. I bought dishes and asked around about petroleum fuel for the stove. It's still available and costs 4 yen a can, but it's not standard oil. Should I buy two cans anyway?

Frau Schmidt brought me a book and some playing cards. I'm always playing Solitaire because Bezique is much harder. Mrs. Schmidt and I went down to the little town this morning. She thinks its heavenly. I've been invited to Inge Lietzmann's birthday party Thursday. I have to get her a gift. There's a lot to choose from up here. Yesterday I went to church with Inge— the pastor got mad because not many people were there, so we both walked out early.

The white blouse fits good, but the white bra is too big in the back. Please bring the hammock with you when you come. Frau Schmidt thinks the down quilt is too warm, so she is using a blanket she brought; she only uses one pillow. There were already two good mattresses in the house when I got here. I took one and the other is on the chaise lounge. I bought a new, all white, futon for 8.30 yen. It fits my mattress just fine. I haven't bought tablecloths yet. I want to wait until you get here. It's fine without one for the time being. Bring little place-mats with you—we can always use those.

There isn't a coffee pot, so I make coffee by putting coffee grounds in a piece of netting and pour the hot water over the top. It works fine. There are no enamel cans here. I don't need the white shorts anymore. I have plenty others here. I saw Hella Janson the other day and asked if her sister Erika was coming up. Hella said that because her Dad was here, Erika couldn't come until next week. The blue curtains are really sweet—Frau Schmidt is altering them to fit our windows.

How is my little Wutsche? Bring all the cats with you when you come! It will all work. Please come soon, with the old grouch and all the cats! I have my fingers crossed.

Your babydoll
[Helga is 13]

5 August 1938
Karuizawa

My dear little Mother –

Thanks for your letter. All the delicious goodies also all arrived. It has been pouring every day since last Sunday. Today is the first clear day and so the metal worker came today. They don't have the white rocks to build a chimney with here, so I ordered sheet metal. The workman is going to repair the stove and that, along with the sheet metal and the connecting pipe, will cost us 4.50 yen. I don't think that's too expensive. I pay 6 sen for icebox ice, 750 grams of eggs are 70 sen, milk is 10 sen, and all the vegetables fluctuate in price. I write everything down and still have about 40 yen and that will suffice until Vatl arrives.

We always eat well. Every morning I have milk and puffed rice, an egg, bread with jam and cheese and a tomato. Frau Schmidt doesn't like jam. She eats only tomatoes and bread, butter and eggs—that's her passion! Sometimes I buy breakfast rolls at Fujiya and toast them over charcoal. At noon we eat vegetables with onions (I know you hate them!), potatoes, and either meat or fish. We have tea and cake every afternoon. Fusako buys her own cake because she doesn't like ours. At night we sometimes eat the noon leftovers, but we usually just have cold sandwiches. We can get liverwurst up here—it's good, but not as good as Lohmeyers! So you see, you don't have to worry about me eating enough!

Please bring the iron up, as I sometimes have to iron a bit. And don't forget the hammocks. The sun umbrella would be great, but we don't really need it. The sun isn't that strong and we usually sit on the veranda anyway.

We don't need the petroleum heating stove yet, but if we come here in January, we'll need it for sure. I'm buying just one can of petrol. I also need coat hangers.

I got your letter this morning, along with the pajamas and the dress. Thanks so much. The pajamas fit good, the pants are a little long, but who cares? I can use the dress. I wore the red dirndl to Inga Lietzmann's party—most girls all wear them. Eight of us were at the party and had a great time. I'll tell you all about it when you get here.

I can't get it into my head that you don't want to come up here. I haven't told anyone, not even Frau Schmidt, because I think that you'll eventually come. I could do it alone, but you know that it's so much better when you are here! Think about it again.

Fusako is constantly cleaning all day. I borrowed a Latin book from Ingrid and we're doing our vocabulary words now.

We don't even think about swimming these days. It has rained constantly and everything is swimming. The tunnel is repaired, but the road is still a work in progress. Hella just came by and asked if I wanted to go to Kutsukake with her, but Frau Schmidt said you didn't want me to go out traveling alone and that I needed to wait until you got here. I invited Erika over for next week.

So I close—but you think about coming here!

Love and kisses from your babydoll.

Oh—I'm invited over to the Buntens tomorrow.

[Helga is 13]

Helga and her friends loved to take long hikes. No matter where they trekked, they happened upon the home of a Japanese person offering refreshments to passers-by. A small hand-painted sign alerted hikers to come inside, where they could get hot green tea with a fresh *nori* roll. Rather than take up household space, they sat on a rock in the shade enjoying their repast. Hot tea was served in both hot weather and cold, following the Japanese belief that hot tea can cool the body.

On those woodland hikes, they saw many houses with a small silk-worm operation. The rocky volcanic soil was not fertile for growing crops, but they could grow silk. Disease in the worms had crushed Europe's silk industry in the late 1800s, creating worldwide demand just as Japan opened up its borders for trade in the early 1900s. Raw-silk production in Japan was now soaring to new heights.

White and yellow cocoons were hatched in a crude incubator, then placed on a net that had been stretched over a bamboo rack. Birds were kept away so they wouldn't eat the worms. Silkworms ate only one thing: leaves from mulberry trees. A woman would tuck her baby into the back of her dress, leaving a little head peering over her shoulder as she tended the family silkworm farm. Mulberry leaves were picked each day and crushed to make a powdered food for the newly hatched worms, which looked like tiny black strings. Feedings were at regular intervals six times a day, sprinkling a precise amount of mulberry dust over the worms on the net. Too much or too little and they would die. The worms devoured food, grew quickly, and soon could be fed chopped leaves, then eventually whole leaves. The feeding periods, called *rei*, lasted from three to six days, followed by *min*, periods of resting and sleeping. After about a month, each worm would begin spinning a mile-long silk thread from its mouth.

Television wouldn't regularly broadcast until the late 1940s, so the first thought after dinner was: Let's go finish our chapter! They read English and American novels, including *Gone with the Wind*. They read powerful German authors like Friedrich Schiller and Goethe.

When they moved into the larger house in Uehara, the young Fusako was brought in as a full-time live-in maid. As everyone knows, a German household must be kept a certain way, and Leonore trained her in the proper German methods. The dining table needed to be covered with a freshly laundered linen cloth. Silver place settings were part of everyday life and needed regular polishing to prevent blackening in the Tokyo humidity. Kitchen knives were crafted from carbon steel and were sharpened by rubbing with a powder compound and then burnished against a wine cork. The iron stove was scrubbed at the end of each day and buffed with black polish.

At one period while Paul Wenneker was traveling out of the country, his daughter Utta instructed their driver to pick up Helga on the way to school. Riding with Utta in the back of the Wennekers' luxury sedan was quite a treat from the usual early-morning train ride and afforded Helga the indulgence of sleeping past dawn. She continued to take the public train home.

Leonore and Helga were often invited to Japanese tea parties, and while some European men married Japanese women, the sexes and cultures in Japan remained largely separated. Also, with Hitler running

Germany and Nazi influence heavy in parts of Japan, Jewish people were careful to avoid contact with anyone who might be a Nazi sympathizer—which meant virtually every German.

It was said that at least 1,000 Germans lived in Tokyo by the 1930s. "The German House," located a few blocks from the German embassy, drew officials and businessmen seeking a German lunch with German beer. More than a restaurant, it was a cultural enclave with a library of German books and a performance room where children performed in plays celebrating German customs and culture. At Christmastime the women held a bazaar and sold embroidered linens and home-baked goods.

And yet, the traditions of the Japanese, Shintoists, and Buddhists did touch Helga's life. She saw the *kadomatsu* arrangements of pine boughs and hollow bamboo set out for the New Year (*Oshogatsu*) as invitations and tributes to spirits that could bring about a prosperous new year, an abundant harvest. The Kiderlens observed the Japanese tradition of removing shoes before entering the home and pulling on slippers left inside the sliding door. Fusako lived in a small servant's quarters behind the house, with a bed, toilet, shower, and an outdoor cooking space for her little hibachi grill. Sometimes Helga watched Fusako grill and prepare vegetables and fish with spices, and she enjoyed eating with her in the little servant area.

Fritz bought Helga a Japanese *tansu*, an ingenious set of small wooden compartments that stack and lock together and that from the front looks like a cabinet. Here she kept her dolls, hair ribbons, socks, her silk slips, and silk underwear. Twice a year a Japanese dressmaker who specialized in European styles came to the house, measuring each family member, creating new garments and mending old ones. Nothing was thrown away; even socks and silk stockings were mended.

Purity was a cultural standard for the Japanese, and each day hours were devoted to cleaning the home, body, and clothes. Kimonos, made from about twelve yards of cloth, were hand washed in wooden buckets, then a bamboo pole was slid through the big sleeves and hung between posts or tree branches behind the house.

There were public baths, separated by gender, and most Japanese homes also had an outdoor bath, ofuro, for the family. Preparing and taking a bath was labor intensive; baths were taken several times a week, not every day. The typical Japanese bath was an oval-shaped wooden barrel with a small oven at one end. The tub was filled with water, then a fire made in the adjacent oven. A lid on the oven opened to allow inserting wood for the fire.

For the Japanese, the process of bathing was hierarchical and ceremonial. First the husband, the master of the house, stepped into the tub. After he had soaked, he stepped out of the tub to soap up and rinse off, then returned to the tub to soak again. After the father went the wife, then the children, and finally the servants stepped into the bath.

The toilet was always its own room, either outside or on an outside wall. A bathroom was for bathing: a toilet was always a separate room with a window that opened to the outside. Two men came once a week to empty the toilet; they sold the contents to nearby farmers for fertilizer. Helga recognized the Japanese toilet as similar to the public facilities in Germany. Inside was an oval-shaped hole in the floor that was covered with a porcelain hood. The Kiderlens bathed Japanese style, but they also had an indoor bathroom with sinks and a shower.

Most Jewish children attended Yokohama International School. Helga attended a private school for German children with at least one German (Aryan) parent, either German-Japanese or German-Jewish. The school observed the same customs, calendar and curriculum as schools in Germany. Classes were held Monday through Friday with a half day on Saturday morning. The school year ran in intervals, beginning immediately after Easter and including a month-long summer vacation and a three-week Christmas vacation. One day a week, the afternoon segment of classes was omitted to allow the children outdoor activities. If it was cold enough, they skated in the park on the frozen pond just like they had in Germany. The Lutheran pastor came twice a week to the school to teach Bible study, and a priest came now and then to teach the handful of Catholic kids.

By 1939 Helga was a winsome fourteen-year-old who spoke

German, English, and Japanese; studied Latin in school; played with dolls; and enjoyed tennis, hiking, bicycling, and board games. Shanghai Millionaire was a popular board game, a forerunner of Monopoly. (Players roll dice, buy properties they land on, collect and pay rent, but all on well-known streets of Shanghai.) In the evenings, Helga played card games with Fusako.

Leonore leaned on her daughter for companionship. Leonore and Helga were a busy pair, tending to household duties as well as a small flower garden. They walked regularly to Lohmeyer's, a butcher shop that specialized in smoked meats and catered to Germans. Popular movies from Germany, France, and the United States were readily available in local theaters, and they enjoyed late matinees featuring the hottest stars of the day: Fred Astaire, Ginger Rogers, Katherine Hepburn, and adorable child star Shirley Temple. Sometimes Fritz would join them after work and treat everyone to dinner at their favorite restaurant where the Hungarian maître d' spoke very good German. They ordered potato chips served hot and fresh from the oven with schnitzel, thin-sliced veal breaded and fried with a little butter on it.

Despite Fusako's help, Leonore's health deteriorated. Once a month when her menstrual time came around, she suffered from severe cramps and headaches. When Leonore felt ill, she called the school to report that Helga was sick and couldn't come to classes that day, and Helga undertook the obligation to stay home from school to comfort her mother.

But the march of war cannot be ignored and soon reached Helga's quiet life in Japan. The German air force attacked Poland in September 1939, starting World War II. Within weeks Helga's stepfather was brought into the embassy to work directly under Paul Wenneker and Eugen Ott. Ott had been sent to Tokyo in 1934 as military attaché at the German Embassy.

The German navy, the *Kriegsmarine*, depended on regular shipments from supply ships operating between Europe and Japan. As purchasing agent, it was Fritz Kiderlen's job to pay contractors. We do not know how Kiderlen felt about working in a capacity that, in serving his country, essentially served the Nazi regime.

Every neighborhood had a small round building that served as a one-man police station that was staffed 24 hours a day. Whenever Helga walked by, the policeman bowed Japanese-style and bid her good morning or goodnight. She understood that the policeman was as much a spy as a guardian. She knew that her maid conversed with him regularly. While everyone got along perfectly well, there was a growing sense of "us against them."

"Now that we are connected to the embassy, they will watch us," Vatl told Helga. "But we must be careful what we say in public." The happy climate in Japan was turning upside-down, and Helga's life was about to change.

An American B-25 bomber lifts off from the aircraft
carrier *Hornet* for the April, 1942, raid on Tokyo.

Chapter Five

An Imminent Strike

HELGA'S LIFE WAS PUNCTUATED WITH PRIVILEGE AND INDEPENDENCE. She rose before dawn while the house was quiet and got herself off to school. Because her morning rustlings inadvertently disturbed Leonore's sleep, Helga volunteered to sleep in the *kura*, a cement-block structure behind their house in Uehara. Typically, *kuras* were a luxury of larger homes and used to store the many decorations used by Japanese to celebrate holidays and seasonal changes. Originally, Fritz and Leonore thought the maid would stay there, but Fusako simply said *kuras* were not for sleeping, and chose a three-tatami room next to the kitchen.

Helga, however, loved the isolation of the *kura*, and at thirteen it had become her private living quarters. The sliding-glass door and diminutive window were buttressed with iron shutters, allowing it to be locked tight from the outside. It must have looked like a little prison, but Helga never thought of it that way. The window in the one-room building overlooked their flower garden and small swimming pool. When the Tokyo heat and humidity made sleeping impossible, Helga slipped into the water and cooled off. She slept on a futon mattress in a narrow closet; when she grew so that her feet and head pressed against either end, she simply pulled the mattress out into the room every night. Each morning she folded it into the closet, Japanese style. There was a *tansu* with its stacking drawers, a sink with hot and cold running water, and a little mirror above the sink. On school days she made herself breakfast, walked to the Uehara train station, caught three trains to Omori, and walked fifteen minutes to school—reversing the trip at the end of each school day.

As 1939 closed its doors, traditional Christmas carols rang out for peace on earth—a hopeless cry. Japan faced internal struggles: its government was unstable, and its prime minister had been assassinated. Japan had withdrawn from the League of Nations. Imperial Japan's attempted military domination of the Chinese Republic had gone on for more than two years. The major players in the Second Sino-Japanese War would soon become the Axis and Allied forces of World War II. Poland's attempts to defend itself against Luftwaffe bombings were shattered when Hitler approved dropping more than five hundred tons of bombs a day. For Poland, surrender was the only option. German tanks rolled through continental Europe as Hitler's speeches made clear a plan for world domination. In the spring of 1940, Axis and Allied countries were bombing not only each other's military installations but also their cities. Three hundred German planes bombed Paris, and French planes attacked Munich, where much of Helga's family lived.

Helga was fifteen years old. As she understood it, Hitler wanted more land; Hitler wanted Poland to be like Germany, part of the National Socialist party, and the Polish people didn't want that, so a war was started. Munich, where Helga had spent the first part of her childhood, was now the heart of Nazism.

Life was neither here nor there. Everyone was in motion, and families struggled to find normalcy amidst impending disaster. For several summers Helga attended a Hitler Youth Camp about an hour's walk from Hakone, a little village in the mountains outside Tokyo. "My mother didn't like the Nazis, but she couldn't say, 'No, my daughter can't go.' It was dangerous," Helga said, reflecting on the camp. "So I went to the summer camps and such, but I didn't see it as political. I was [at that point] seventeen, eighteen years old: I saw it as social. In the morning we got up early, went outside to do exercises, raise the Nazi flag, sing a song to it, go to breakfast. We had morning classes, afternoon classes, then a late lunch."

Helga wrote faithfully to her father and stepmother back in Berlin, and Kurt and Edith Hofmeier replied with long letters packed with details of family life. Helga learned that she gained a new brother, Fritz, in 1936. On August 2, 1939, Kurt wrote:

> Ferch über Potsdam, Burgstrasse 2
>
> My dear child –
> It's been just too long since I have written you a real letter. We won't discuss how that came about; there are many reasons. I had always hoped that we would see each other again this year and we all would have been thrilled. But nothing came of it, so I wanted to send you a good long letter.

Kurt summarizes his recent career advances, including being named as medical administrator of the Children's Hospital in Berlin in the fall of 1934, writing a book in 1937 that qualified him as a professor and lecturer at the University of Berlin, and being named Chief Administrator of the Children's Hospital Kaiser Auguste Victoria House, "an institution that is known around the world."

As a member of the official German delegation to the 1937 International Pediatrician Convention in Rome, he observed:

> Lots of military exercises followed, as big changes are a concern for everyone. Last year was also entirely full of hushed political tensions that left no one untouched. In spite of this, we've been able to record successes that we certainly hadn't thought possible before. All are working with a passion that few people outside of Germany could even begin to understand. There is never enough manpower, all plans are being accelerated and everything is taking place at an unheard of pace. It's not always about the timeframe, but right now, if we want to take a lead and keep it, we have no other choice. It can't continue this way with Poland.

His administrative duties, along with maintaining his own private practice, created twelve- to fourteen-hour workdays, without a break or time to go home for lunch. He has very little time for family.

Kurt's second wife, Edith, also wrote Helga regularly. Her letter dated June 20, 1940, paints a picture of war beginning to brush against the lives of an upper class German family who traveled internationally and placed a high value on education. It also shows Edith's love for the stepdaughter she rarely saw and her congenial attitude toward Leonore:

> Your mother is exactly correct when she says that French is a basic building block to all education. When I was in Rome for an International Pediatrician convention, I thanked my lucky stars that I knew a bit of French. I was able to understand a bit of both Italian and Spanish through my French. One of the directors of the convention was so nice to me. She didn't know a word of German and I don't know Italian, so we just conversed in French. We were also able to speak French with another delightful couple we met who were from Portugal. I'm really mad at myself for not knowing more about speaking foreign languages—they get you farther in life, they are much easier to learn when you are young, and you never know who you're going to marry. I have to master different languages now that your dear father travels internationally so much. He prefers to travel with his wife, so I have to learn to converse so I don't disgrace him when we travel.

Clearly, Kurt wants to see his daughter more: he advises her that Germany offers the best education, lifestyle and climate:

> You have to see how you can get back here. I hope that won't take too long. How are your studies going? I don't have a very good opinion of school there. I think that you need to have several more years of study in Germany, as it is, of course,

completely different here than in a foreign school. In a few years' time you'll also have to deal with the career question. So it's time for you to come back so we can discuss it all. I'm certain that your mother has made some plans, but I want to have a say in them, as well.

Hitler released the Luftwaffe to destroy London, and the globe was formally divided in the Tripartite Pact. Its signers recognized two spheres of influence: Japan acknowledged "the leadership of Germany and Italy in the establishment of a new order in Europe," while Japan was granted lordship over "Greater East Asia." The Axis Powers (Germany, Italy, and Japan) agreed to defend each other for the next ten years. The Japanese ambassador to Germany, Saburo Kurusu, signed the document on behalf of Imperial Japan.

Nightly bombings of Europe's cities and innocent civilians continued without mercy. Buckingham Palace, cathedrals, art galleries, orphanages—no area was sacred. By November 1940 the bombings had spread to other European cities. In the beginning, the technology of Allied aircraft was so inferior to the German Luftwaffe that the Allied casualty rate on its own raids was as high as 75 percent.

Anyone could plainly see the shell-shocked Dutch women and children on Tokyo streets, one of many tragic byproducts of war. "We suddenly got all these people," Helga recalled, fifty years later. "Most of them couldn't even speak German; they spoke Dutch. More than two hundred women and children came. Suddenly, the school was packed. They built a small building for the kindergarteners because there were so many little ones that came from Dutch East Indies."

But Helga's naiveté was blossoming into independence. While she still spent much of her time with her family, more of her free time now involved group sports and organized activities. She enjoyed academics as well as the rigorous acrobatics, gymnastics, and sports held twice a week in school. "I loved sports but I was not that good at it," she said. "I won a few pins . . . but I usually came in third. I was an excellent skier: at the Hitler youth ski camp I came in third in the slalom competition, and that was when there were no ski lifts. You had to climb up the mountain with your skis: either carrying them or walking with them apart, making a wide V, or side-stepping. Then you would ski down."

While the world's greatest powers faced off, people attempted to live as normally as possible. The Kiderlens' lives, connected with the German embassy, were luxurious compared to the lifestyles of the rest of the country. In addition to having Helga as a helpmate and Fusako as a housemaid, Leonore often had use for yet additional assistance. When Fritz heard about a German teenager who needed work and housing, he brought her into the household. The girl and her mother had suffered a year-long internment in a camp in Sumatra. Many prisoners of war were taken in the early 1940s, when the Japanese squared off against the Dutch and British for control of Sumatra's oil resources.

The Kiderlens paid the teenager a small amount each week and gave her weekends off. This allowed the Kiderlens to have weekends together as a family and the girl to afford the train ride to visit her mother elsewhere in Tokyo. Before the year was out, the girl and her mother moved to Kobe, where they had found relatives. Fusako remained as the Kiderlens' maid.

Helga had plenty of friends, but since they lived in different parts in and around the huge city of Tokyo, they mainly saw each other in school. Sleepovers were rare, because on weekends families spent time together. On a Saturday or Sunday the Kiderlens often drove or took the train to a nice resort area or into the country to visit old temples surrounded with blooming flowers: Nikko with its famous red lacquered bridge; the lake known as Chusenji; Kegon, a popular waterfall; and Kamakura with a stunning statue of Buddha. At Shigasaki they got a hotel, and Helga learned to swim underwater when the waves swelled close.

Radio broadcasts of Japanese music and propaganda failed to catch Helga's attention, but she loved playing 78 RPM records. In the German tradition, the music most often sounding from the Kiderlens' phonograph was classical: Richard Wagner, Richard Strauss, Franz Liszt,

Gustav Mahler. But they also enjoyed popular American bandleaders like Glenn Miller and Benny Goodman. Helga enjoyed the luxury of owning one of the first portable record players. The turntable was powered by an ingenious wind-up hand crank with a wooden handle; the whole business folded neatly into a little suitcase. Helga hardly left the house without it, taking it to the park, to the lake, in the boat.

War seared the globe. Jewish people in Eastern Europe were forced to wear a yellow cloth star as identification and were attacked and murdered without provocation. In April German tanks entered Athens, forcing Greece to surrender. Hitler's propaganda minister Goebbels pitched the führer as "a genius . . . building a new world." As Germany planned to invade the Soviet Union, Goebbels wrote in his diary, "Once we have won, who is going to question our methods?" In June, the entire male Jewish population of Gorzhdy, Lithuania, was exterminated by Nazis. U.S. President Roosevelt pledged to support the Soviet Union.

And yet a civilized life continued for certain people, evidenced by Edith's letter of February 15, 1941. She thanks her stepdaughter for chocolates she sent to them in their Berlin neighborhood, Dahlem, and congratulates Helga on her confirmation into the only Lutheran Church in Tokyo. "I hope you have a grand celebration, one that you can remember for the rest of your life," Edith writes. "I hope you like the ring. We looked for it with much love and think the stone is especially nice. I wonder what kind of dress you'll be wearing, white or black. Please take lots of pictures and send us some."

Edith inquires whether Helga received a German textbook that she shipped, adding, "The bookstores had not been allowed to ship books for such a long time, so I now hope that you can get back to your French lessons."

When Kurt visited a patient in Halberstadt, Edith accompanied him. Picking up a local newspaper, she found, much to her surprise, a photograph of Helga and Ursula Ott. The picture was political propaganda, meant to illustrate levels of cooperation between Japan and Germany and to assure the public that all was well. Ursula was the daughter of German ambassador Eugen Ott, whom Kurt had known when Ott was a lieutenant colonel in the German military in Zehlendorf.

Berlin was under constant military strike from Allied forces, and bombings, particularly in Zehlendorf, were now endangering residential areas. Edith writes that their children "have been scattered to the winds." Like many European families, Kurt and Edith sent their children to live with a variety of farm families in the country. Edith mentions her Polish maid and her little trips to the country. "If those English return with their oppressive manner, I will leave again, although I am reluctant to leave Vati in the air-raid shelter alone," she wrote, "although I have fixed it up quite nicely with bedding and all kinds of things. The children always slept well there at night, waking only when the bombs fell especially close to us."

As yet there had been no strikes against the Japanese homeland, but everyone knew a strike was imminent. "When we heard the Japanese had attacked Pearl Harbor, we said, 'Now the Americans are going to attack us,'" Helga said, looking back on that time. "Europe was at war. The world was at war. It was to be expected. But we didn't know how or when the attack would come, and there was no place to go. Japan didn't have any air-raid shelters."

Women's leagues had formed among Japanese and German women to do what they could: knit socks and sweaters, sew a decorative blessing on the headscarves of Japanese soldiers. The customary handkerchief worn over the forehead was sent house to house for each woman to sew on a cross stitch, then be blessed at the temple to protect the soldier. Japanese women also were trained to assist in the event of an air strike, some to haul water and form water-supply lines in the worst-case scenario.

The Kiderlens began to organize and pack their things in anticipation of moving out of the danger zone that was Tokyo to the relative safety of Hakone, a small mountain village. "If the navy moves to Hakone, be prepared to go with them," Fritz was told.

"We wanted to deliver the first good news that we'd had in World

War II," said pilot Jimmy Doolittle, who led the U.S. invasion of Japanese air space in 1942. A World War I flight instructor, in 1929 Doolittle had been the first pilot to take off, fly, and land an airplane using instruments alone, with no visual outside the cockpit. After the Japanese attacked Pearl Harbor, Doolittle was recalled to active duty, made lieutenant colonel, and assigned to the first retaliatory air raid on Japan.

The U.S. was determined to attempt an air raid over Tokyo, targeting steel plants, oil refineries, oil tank farms, ammunition dumps, dockyards, munitions plants, and airplane factories. The Japanese would be forced to keep their own aircraft at home, in defense of the home islands.

Each B-25 carried three 500-pound bombs and one bundle of incendiaries. The specially constructed incendiaries were long tubes bundled together to fit in the bomb bay and designed to separate and scatter over a wide area after release. After dropping their payload, the planes were to turn in a southerly direction, get out to sea as quickly as possible, and after being out of sight of land, turn again and take a westerly course to China.

On April 2, 1942, when the U.S. aircraft carrier *Hornet* set out across the Pacific, virtually no one aboard knew where it was going. They powered west for ten days and were joined by the flagship USS *Enterprise*, along with a full escort of cruisers and destroyers.

Tokyo lay sleeping on April 18 when a Japanese patrol boat spotted the American ships and radioed warnings home. The USS *Nashville* sank the picket boat and the *Hornet's* crews leaped into action to get the planes ready for take-off. None of the sixteen B-25 pilots had ever taken off from an aircraft carrier before, but within an hour they took to the air, each carrying one ton of high-velocity bombs. They were more than 600 miles from the Japanese coast—and 200 miles farther out to sea than planned.

Six hours later the planes began arriving over Japan, flying single file just above the water. Encountering only light antiaircraft fire from the shocked Japanese, they were unhindered in their mission. Before they could drop their bombs, the planes pulled up to about 1,500 feet to avoid being hit by the fragments.

It was easy to see that the damage would exceed the most optimistic expectations. U.S. Army Air Forces reports detailed the mission. The first trio of planes covered northern Tokyo, the second covered central Tokyo, the third flight covered southern Tokyo and north-central Tokyo Bay, and the fourth trio covered southern Kanagawa, the city of Yokohama, and the Yokosuka Navy yard. A fifth flight went around to the south of Tokyo and on to Nagoya, where one plane bombed Nagoya, one Osaka, and one Kobe. Using only sixteen planes, the Americans made it seem like a massive invasion was taking place.

Helga was in particularly high spirits as she sat in school that day. As soon as classes let out, which, as usual on Saturday, was at one o'clock, she would go to the German embassy for Ulla Ott's birthday party. The morning was quite normal—until the eerie blast of Tokyo air-raid sirens exploded into the quiet of the classroom. The children did not move. They had been trained for this moment: wait for instructions to come over the loudspeakers in the building.

This time, though, the alarm did not signal a test air raid: this was the real thing. "Everyone get ready quickly and go home the fastest way you know," the students were told. "The planes are coming!"

It was a ten-minute walk to the train station. "I did not feel panic, only excitement," Helga said, remembering that day decades later.

At the station, six trains stood motionless with their doors open. Omori was always busy, with trains coming and going, so the sight of the quiet cars with their mouths open was odd. Nearby, Japanese women hurriedly tied their kimonos high, baring their knees, and set to work filling buckets with water in hopes of extinguishing likely fires from the bombings. Other women joined them, assembling in lines and passing wooden buckets from a water spigot on the train platform. They worked quickly, pausing only for a heartbeat to quickly peer into the sky.

Everyone watched the sky. First came the airborne sound: *MMM-MMM*, the deadly purr of the B-25.

"They couldn't be from America: American planes cannot fly so far from home," one of Helga's friends called.

"They don't look Japanese," someone said.

The planes roared past in the noonday sun, flying low enough that Helga and her friends could see the Army Air Forces insignia.

"Americans!" a boy yelled. "But they're leaving!"

The danger had passed. Or so it seemed. "To the ice cream shop!" Helga suggested, ignoring the panic. Up the stairs the classmates flew, out of the train station and to the main street level. The streets were strangely quiet.

Children have a way of bypassing horror, of finding joy wherever it can be found, and that is why, when Doolittle's bombers returned, Helga was enjoying an ice cream with her friends.

Rapid-fire shots from antiaircraft guns rang out from where they were mounted on the roof of a nearby building. The guns aimed into the sky at the B-25 bombers that were clearly returning.

Helga and her friends dashed out of the ice cream shop and into a nearby butcher shop owned by a German. She wanted to use the phone. If she could call home, she could figure out what to do. But the shop was empty, so Helga and her friends made their way across the nearly deserted street and down to the train station. Passengers were being guided on board the trains, even though none of the trains were moving. Helga jumped aboard the train that went to the embassy. She could feel her heart pounding against her ribcage, her panic a decided contrast to the Japanese people sitting silently around her, looking down at their laps.

The train started, moved a short distance down the track, then stopped. All the lights went out. No one moved. No one spoke. After what seemed an eternity—five minutes in reality—the lights went back on, and the Japanese train passengers were sitting quietly, still looking down at their laps. Their faces registered almost nothing, even when the train finally started heading down the tracks to its destination.

Their train rushed into the more urban, more populated part of Tokyo. The guards at the gate of the embassy compound knew Helga by now and had seen her name on the guest list for the party. She was let inside, where she told Mrs. Ott what she had just been through.

"Don't worry," Mrs. Ott said, apparently relaying the propagandized viewpoint of the events. "The planes are gone now. One crashed, and the others had to land someplace they did not expect to land. But the Americans bombed a school, and a few children died."

After the party, Helga found her stepfather's office in the embassy complex. He offered her tea and pastries and they chatted without too much fanfare, then walked home together. The Doolittle Raid had destroyed dozens of industrial targets in Tokyo, taking the lives of uncounted civilians unlucky enough to be within range of the bombs and incendiaries. But its greatest success lay in demonstrating to Japan and to the world that the United States had the capacity to drop bombs halfway around the globe. With the Doolittle Raid, the U.S. raised a fist and flexed its muscles.

Three years later the U.S. would return to lay waste to one of the world's greatest cities.

As the Japanese continued to fight across Asia and
the Pacific, civilians struggled to maintain some
semblance of normal day-to-day life.

Chapter Six

Surrender Is Verboten

ALTHOUGH HUMILIATING FOR JAPAN, THE DOOLITTLE RAID did little to damage the Japanese war machine. What hurt Japan was the expansion of its own military aggression. In addition to the ongoing war with China and India, each month Japan invaded, attacked, and tried to defend itself in an increasing number of islands and small nations in the Pacific. Eventually, Japanese forces in the Pacific suffered a series of defeats at Midway, Milne Bay, and Guadalcanal.

The fear of being bombed hummed in the air. Leonore made black curtains for each window of the home to keep indoor lights from shining through. "So that from the sky they can't see where people are living and bomb them," she explained to her daughter. Meanwhile in Washington, D.C., the United States Army was methodically plotting out Tokyo's most densely populated neighborhoods. "The planes flew over for almost two years before they finally began bombing," Helga said.

Since all able-bodied Japanese men were serving in the military, a civilian defense program was created to minimize casualties in the event of an air attack. Women made up the bulk of the civil defense organizations and were trained to combat fires and to help each other. People set up rain barrels in front of their houses for use to fight fires if necessary. Although the civilian defense groups were well run, they would be overwhelmed by what was to come.

Leonore made increasing requests for Helga to stay home. Perhaps she worried about the child's safety, perhaps she sought the comfort of Helga's companionship. Either way, the numerous absences from school took a toll on the girl's educational progress. Despite being an enthusiastic student and a quick learner, Helga had barely passed what would have been her junior year of high school. "I went to school when I could, but sometimes my mother would call the school and say she needed me home," Helga said. "I don't know *why* my mother felt she needed me home, but she did." Helga came to the sad conclusion that she could not keep up her schoolwork and told her teacher she was needed at home and must drop out.

December 1, 1942, was Helga's last day in school; the Omori school lasted less than a year after Helga left. German schools had existed in Japan since at least 1904, when the port of Kobe drew workers to Yokohama. But now there were increasing dangers as well as distrust of all Germans, and school was closed "for safety reasons." Makeshift classes were offered a few weeks later in German communities in the tourist towns of Karuizawa and Hakone but with little consistency.

As New Year's Eve approached, Fritz took Helga to the Shiga Kogen resort in the Japanese Alps. Joining a group of German friends, they celebrated New Year's Eve with dinner, dancing, and snow skiing followed by hot springs soaks. It was a welcome relief from the atmosphere of war preparations throughout Japan.

From the quantity of letters Helga wrote to her mother from Karuizawa—one a week—it appears that the eighteen-year-old was now living alone in the little Karuizawa bungalow for much of the spring, summer, and early fall. At the end of September, she would depart along with most other resort guests to avoid the heavy snows of winter.

Upon arrival each spring in Karuizawa, Helga and Fusako would carry their food and other supplies, sometimes a piece of furniture, up the steep hill to the humble rental house. Several times a week when Helga ventured out for more food and cooking items, she carried her parcels up the hill herself.

Something was always missing—the teapot, cookware, stovepipe—anything made of metal in particular. In the following letter, Helga updates her mother on the replacement efforts, and describes the blueberry bushes growing in the volcano nearby and the berries the shrubs yielded that she would pick and carry home.

September 19, 1943

Dear Mutti,

You cannot buy any stoves here. . . . I guess I will have to ask someone to construct one. He has to come here and measure and it takes a few weeks. The paper then goes to the embassy and to the Gaimusho, the local Ministry of Foreign Affairs (just for a stove, I don't know why). If they allow it, then I can get the tin. Also it depends on the length of the pipe whether you can get it, but the stove will be 60 yen. Another woman in the area did not buy a stove but is going to have a fireplace put in; in her house she had the fundamental iron facilities there before she moved in.

It became complicated to make any changes in the house. I talked to six or seven people about stoves to see what they had to say. Maybe we could put the pipe through the bedroom to heat the bedroom as well. I think at one time people had a stove like that. There is a stove in the ceiling, which is only covered in the big bedroom with a piece of tin. Let me know what you think is best.

I am still looking for a kettle to boil tea water. The weather is beautiful; someday maybe I can get a box of apples, which I will send to you in Tokyo; the blueberries I will carry myself. It is amazing what blooms in the lava fields. In the spring we have the most gorgeous azalea bushes, the most gorgeous pink. This volcano once in a while would spit a little bit, cause a little bit of dust that would go all the way to Tokyo sometimes, with the wind carrying it.

I hope that Vatl can pick me up with the car because I have so much stuff so please answer me as soon as you can.

[Helga is 18]

When Helga returned home that fall, she was forced to tell her parents something was wrong with her health. "There is a little lump," she said, "I can push it in and it will pop up again." The local doctor pronounced Helga's condition a hernia.

Recovering from surgery, teenaged Helga enjoyed being the center of attention. She was fed and nursed and cajoled. She could forget about the sad state of the world. From the Catholic hospital in Yokohama, Helga's letter to her mother is full of spunk.

> The Navy doctor, Schroeder, is so nice to me, but he doesn't have much time. It seems to be getting very cold outside but here I don't feel it, even though I sleep with the window open to the disgust of all the nurses who say that is dangerous. They are very nice and spoil me, even the head nurse. The nurses are all Catholic nuns; I tried my best English with them, and they try to make me laugh. When a patient starts to feel better, they come and knock on the door all day long. They tell me jokes, but I cannot laugh because of the hernia surgery. . . .

There was no such thing as dating in Helga's world, but it had nothing to do with being in the midst of World War II or living in Japan. Following old European custom, teenagers went out in groups or had home parties with both parents present. Not only were the parents in the house, but quite often they also attended the teenager's party. And so it was especially odd when a couple of German soldiers kidnapped Helga from her hospital bed and took her out for a little fun in Yokohama.

Completely bored with the hospital, the sailors had been hospitalized for nine months while recovering from an explosion that rocked

Yokohama harbor. On November 30, 1942, flames erupted on the German tanker *Uckermark*, setting off secondary explosions that created an oily burning hell across the harbor water. Three German ships caught fire and sank into the sea that night. Nearly sixty men perished; of those who swam to safety, most suffered grave burns and severe poisoning from swallowing oily sea water.

The night they kidnapped beautiful Helga and took her to a movie in downtown Yokohama must have been heaven for them all: a brief respite from the horrors of war and the emotional and physical pain of their wounds. After the movie, they returned Helga safely to her hospital room.

In Helga's own words:

Girls did not go on dates: girls and boys just saw each other in a social environment. We could hike or play tennis or go to someone's house.

None of us wore makeup. Our custom was to be clean looking and normal looking. If a girl tried to put on rouge, everyone would be very critical and say, "Who's she trying to impress?"

I had several marriage offers. There were not that many girls there. Always old men would look at me, but I was so shy and I had no clue.

There was a German man who had grown up in Havana and was educated in Germany then wound up in Karuizawa. He had a PhD and was trying to get home to Cuba but got stuck in Japan. He was about ten years older than I was. I met him in the fall just before going back to Tokyo. I was at a party with a friend, and these two men came up to us and said, "What are girls like you doing at a place like this?" They thought we shouldn't be there. Maybe the hostess didn't have a very good reputation. So we went outside and stood and talked a little bit.

I met him again on the tennis court and we got to talking

and went for an ice cream. When I had the hernia surgery, he came and brought beautiful flowers and said he had missed me. He came often to visit us in Tokyo, and told me several times that he wanted to marry me but wanted to wait until I was twenty-one years old.

November 24, 1943

Dear Mutti,

Thank you for the cookies, I am feeling much better. Tomorrow they are taking out the thread from the stitches. I am getting daily constipation with nothing happening. I only had one success. They gave me enemas, and now they are giving me a salt drink. I am hoping that helps. They are also giving me a spa with a certain salt in the water.

I don't sleep well in spite of sleeping pill, and also I can't sleep during the day, but I am always sleepy. It is noisy and people come in my room. Otherwise everyone is very wonderful and I eat well and have a good appetite.

One of my beaus came yesterday. He is quite [a bit] older than I am, and he hung on to me for awhile and said, "I would marry you if you were not so young; let's wait until you are 21." He is a teacher at a Japanese university who teaches German and humanities. . . .

[Helga is 18]

Across Europe and Asia, the world's great powers were bombing civilian targets as well as military installations. Prisoner-of-war camps sprang up here and there. The Omori district, where Helga had attended school, would soon house an infamous POW camp set up on an artificial island in Tokyo Bay. One day as beautiful eighteen-year-old Helga strode near an American prisoner of war working on a street crew in Tokyo, she heard a long, appreciative whistle. Instantly, a Japanese guard raised his gun and brought the butt down on the head of his prisoner. There was no sound from the American soldier as blood began to pour from his skull and he returned to his work. Helga was also struck: with shock that any man would be so familiar with a proper German woman walking down the street—Americans were so crass!—and yet she found herself admiring the strong internal spunk and spirit of the American soldier, who must have known the price he would pay. She picked up her pace and in perfect Japanese, said to the guard, "You don't need to do that," and hurried past.

Since cities were targets, all hopes for safety lay in the countryside. Mothers of every nationality passed their children and their jewelry to relatives—and, if necessary, acquaintances and strangers— to get them to the safety of a rural area. Soldiers in every homeland knocked on the doors of townspeople and demanded a woman hand over her family heirlooms and metal household items for the war effort.

"Surrender is forbidden," Hitler told his army when they were completely surrounded by Russian forces in Stalingrad. "The Sixth Army will hold their positions to the last man and the last round, and by their heroic endurance will make an unforgettable contribution to the establishment of a defensive front and the salvation of the western world."

In the Pacific, Japan was coming apart at the seams. The possibility of evacuation was in the back of everyone's mind, but returning to Germany was nearly impossible through the normal sea-faring routes. Instead, desperate souls attempted the dangerous journey home through Siberia. Many Germans were relocating to the mountain towns of Hakone and Karuizawa in hopes of escaping the looming air strikes. The Japanese allowed the German navy access to the port of Yokohama where their ships were docked, serviced, and restocked with supplies.

By the summer of 1944, the Japanese were running out of oil and steel reserves and unable to force imports. Hungry factory workers worked to new levels of fatigue. The civilian population too was underfed and quickly running out of basic supplies, including clothing. By November 1944 the U.S. embargo of scrap-iron exports that began in 1941 finally forced shortages in Japan.

Production in its factories spiraled downward from absenteeism, sickness, and air-raid alerts. Steel mills were short on ore and coke, munitions plants could not get steel or aluminum. Japanese war production was losing steam, including for high priority items like air-craft engines. Combat air missions were reduced.

In June 1944 Allied forces landed in Normandy, and the United States began massive bombing of Japan that summer. By late 1944 most of Japan's warships sat immobilized for lack of fuel. Japan's econ-omy, strangled from import cut-offs, was about to be finished off by B-29 bombers. On November 24, 1944, twenty-four B-29s bombed the Nakajima aircraft factory near Tokyo.

The official U.S. War Department report issued in 1946 concluded that Japan's military capabilities were already economically demolished at the end of 1944 and would have remained so without the horrific bombings carried out by the United States the following year.

Otto Ratjen, another of Fritz's uncles, had been bombed out. Helga and Vatl walked for miles pushing a little cart to help him collect what survived of his belongings and to move him in with them. "Poor man; he couldn't hear. He was nearly seventy, and he was in shock. So we walked to where his house had been to take him to Hakone so he could get away from the city. It was impossible to drive. There was so much debris: fallen electrical lines, pieces of wood, windows."

Uehara, where the Kiderlens lived, was also a likely target, so in late 1944 they began to move their belongings, as well as Uncle Otto, to a small vacation house they rented in Hakone. Sometimes when Helga's parents returned to Uehara, Helga stayed behind with the maid and the cats and a wire-haired fox terrier they had accumulated along the way.

Hakone historically catered to tourists and had several large hotels such as the Fujiya that catered to Westerners. The naval office of the German Embassy had already moved to Hakone, and the rest of the embassy staff continued to make the move between 1943 and 1944: a good thing, because the German embassy in Tokyo would be com-pletely destroyed by May 1945 bombings.

Isaac Shapiro gives an eyewitness account of U.S. bombings on

Japan in his autobiography, *Edokko: Growing Up a Foreigner in Wartime Japan.* "My fourteenth birthday, January 5, 1945, fell on a Friday, and I woke up to the sound of bombs falling all around us. By the time I was dressed, I could see the flames in the distance. Looking up, I saw Japanese fighters flying up to meet the B-29 Superfortresses. I saw one of them go down in a blaze of fire, even as anti-aircraft guns were blazing." A shell from a 12mm U.S. cannon fell through their roof. Minutes later, two air-raid wardens arrived and demanded the Shapiros turn the shell over, which they did.

By the end of January, trams and subways were no longer running, many shops and cafés had closed.

U.S. forces landed on Iwo Jima in February, 1945. The B-29s, nicknamed "Superfortress," had four engines and an operational range of 3,200 nautical miles. In February and early March 1945, urban areas of Tokyo were attacked three times by more than 150 B-29s in each attack. Fusako, the Kiderlens' maid, wept when she told them that her older sister in a Tokyo fishing village had burned to death when flames caught her paper house.

Life continued in the shadow of war, but there was no getting away from it. Helmets were distributed to as many citizens as possible. "Everybody was supposed to have a helmet on when they were outside; that was the law," Helga said. "Women had to wear funny-looking pants called *mompe* over their kimonos. They were like a skirt but with two openings for legs so you could run. And that became the fashion. The helmets had a string that went under your chin, and when people got on the trains, they wore the hat hanging down the back of their necks with the string around their necks. When the train got crowded, we would get shoved into a helmet or squashed between two helmets."

Wearing a mompe, women could walk fast and jump into the foxholes that had been dug across the city. The shallow, rectangular holes offered no shelter from above but allowed people a sunken area where they could squat down together and hide.

Each night at the dinner table, Fritz updated Leonore and Helga on the latest news reports from the German embassy. Helga also got news from an illegal shortwave radio that she kept under her bed.

"Somebody came to the house now and then to check to be sure we did not have a shortwave radio—and to confiscate it if you did," Helga said. "I always hid mine under the bed. I knew where on the dial to find the German ships, and I always listened to hear the news. They talked about letters from home, they gave out greetings to different families back home, and from families to men on the ship. 'We miss him,' people would say. 'We wish him well.' They played a German song, gave a little bit of political news, like: Hitler is celebrating this birthday, or there's nothing new on the eastern front now, but the Russians have suffered losses in their attack of such-and-such city. The news was always on the side of the Germans. For Hitler's birthday, we all had to go down to the German navy installation, sit outside, and listen to a German official who said we wish Hitler well on his birthday and we hope he has the energy to keep this up and win the war." They were not told that in March 1945, General Patton's Third Army had crossed the Rhine.

Sometimes Helga would hear a woman speaking very good English, addressing American soldiers on ships nearby. "Good morning," the velvety voice would say, then proceed to precisely describe Allied military maneuvers that had failed and bemoan the number of Allied soldiers wounded or dead. "You are in such a bad situation," the woman would say. "Wouldn't you rather be home?" Perhaps as many as a dozen English-speaking women made propaganda broadcasts to demoralize Allied troops. "Tokyo Rose" they called her generically. Her words sometimes hit their mark, but the men continued to listen because her comments gave them clues as to what the Japanese knew—and how effective Allied maneuvers had been.

The forest surrounding the Hakone mountain resort was controlled by the Japanese government, but arrangements were made to allow each German household in the area to take one tree in December for their Christmas tree. Members of the little German community learned to reach out to each other; no one was a stranger. Helga still remembers the nice man who would always come around to split the

Kiderlens' tree into pieces for them. One German family began baking German bread and giving it to the neighbors. When they arrived once a month or so, Helga invited them in and made coffee for them. Sometimes the Kiderlens were given a sack of green coffee beans and Helga tried to roast them herself, but she had an extreme dislike for the strong smell as she stood over them stirring and shaking them so they would be evenly roasted. One man was a shoe repairman and stitched together the family's ripped shoes. "They were glad to help and they were glad to come to someone's home for a couple of hours and have a beer or coffee or whatever could be found to share," Helga recalled. "To have a cup of coffee was really a special thing."

German women and girls knitted socks for the German soldiers, and sold shawls and other handmade items to raise money for the soldiers. "I remember being told that the reason we were fighting Poland was that the Polish people had started shooting at Germans along the border, so the Germans went in and shot back," Helga said. "It was a long time before I knew it had actually happened the other way around."

It was a time in world history when tight circles were drawn around everyone's lives. The Kiderlens kept to themselves and never went into Tokyo. "It was a strange feeling," Helga said. "We felt lucky to be friends with the Japanese. We felt fairly safe. But all around us, people were suspected of spying for the enemy and being thrown in jail. You had to be very careful about whom you associated with and what you said. I learned to keep my mount shut and quietly do my thing."

German submarines docked in the port of Kobe, and from time to time German sailors wandered up to Hakone. Often they lived in the Miyanoshita Hot Springs Hotel and went roaming in the forest. Inevitably they found the Kiderlens, made quick friends, and offered to pitch in with chores. It is easy to imagine a war-weary sailor stumbling on the compelling sight of beautiful brown-haired Helga. Each man inevitably offered his own unique skill set. One man repaired their shoes, another brought extra wood; sometimes the sailors shared their rations, which were better than what the Kiderlens could get.

More than one sailor's heart was stirred by the mere sight of Helga, who was tall, well-proportioned, radiant, and at nineteen years of age had never been kissed. One day when Helga was cleaning the Hakone house in preparation for moving more belongings there, a handsome German sailor appeared. "His submarine was based in Kobe," Helga remembered, more than sixty years later. "He was two years older than I was. I was up there alone and this sailor came up, and he said, 'What are you doing here?' He was there for ten days. We got to know each other a little bit, then he went back to Kobe and we corresponded after that. He was the first man that I ever kissed. We talked about marriage, but he said we must go home to Germany first. He said he had nothing to offer me yet— the world was at war, and so many people had lost everything. He wanted time to find a place to live and a job in Germany." But Helga would soon make a decision that ended her romance with the German sailor.

Nowadays it takes a strong imagination to picture the news blackout that figured into everyday life in 1945—before personal computers, before cell phones, before the World Wide Web. Sometimes when Helga was in Tokyo, she looked for a newspaper, but it was hard to find one. Before the bombing, sometimes she could find a copy of the *Tokyo Advertiser,* printed in English, which Fritz's uncle would read to them. Occasionally she found a copy of *Stars and Stripes,* the U.S. Department of Defense's independent daily military newspaper, which had its Pacific debut in 1945. Although American and European movies had been popular in Tokyo for twenty years, they were no longer shown.

Food rationing began in April 1941; by 1944 the average person in Japan had precious little access to food, unless they lived on a farm. "It was rough, the eating," Helga said. "We could get fish and rice, but even that was rationed."

Food shortages were so serious that hoarding food was a criminal offense. An innocent person simply trying to get food for his or her family might be turned in by his neighbor, and the general public was on high alert that no one would get more food than anyone else. One day while Helga was riding the train in Tokyo, she noticed a young

Japanese girl sitting across from her wearing a kimono.

"I thought that she looked pregnant," Helga said. "She had a big belly and she looked like she was feeling sickly. But when she stood up, I realized she had dropped something and was trying to pick it up. When the train stopped at the next station, the police boarded and opened her kimono. Out came a sack with rice. Somebody must have turned her in. While they arrested her, everybody stayed in their seat. This is typical Japanese: they don't get involved; they just let things unfold. Then the police took her away."

Isaac Shapiro's autobiography describes heart-breaking hunger. "We got up from the table hungry after each meal . . . mostly, all of us craved meat. . . . When there was a shortage of rice, we bought soybeans, and we ate them in every form, for every meal, until we couldn't stomach them anymore. And then, suddenly, they were no longer available. We ate cauliflower leaves instead."

Whenever possible, each country raided the other's ships for supplies. When Germans raided American ships, American products filtered into the Kiderlen household: Colgate toothpaste, Quaker Oats, canned meat. Sometimes they got Australian sausages to add to soups and bread. Sometimes there were sardines or corned beef from South America. Helga took care not to eat too much and to share food with her friends when she could. Eggs were a precious commodity and only available from local stores, so Helga would take a can of meat and trade it for a few eggs. And yet, the worst was yet to come.

The formal Japanese surrender, aboard the U.S.S. *Missouri*.
September 2, 1945.

Chapter Seven

Christmas Trees Falling

CONTROL OF THE AIR WAS ESSENTIAL, and the American attack of March 1945 was plotted around Japan's weakness in night-fighting and anti-aircraft.

Firebombs were the current weapon of choice, and the phenomenon of the firestorm was a newly-discovered after-effect. When Allies firebombed Hamburg in August 1943, the result was a hurricane of fire, sucking oxygen from the air and mercilessly killing thousands of civilians by flame and asphyxiation. Firebombings continued, including on the beautiful city of Dresden in February 1945. From the German point of view, Allies were unfairly targeting their cultural history: the centuries of art, literature, and architecture that Dresden had housed. More than 3,900 tons of firebombs and explosives were dropped on Dresden during a two-day period, destroying fifteen square miles and killing as many as 25,000 innocent civilians.

When U.S. forces unleashed their firepower over Tokyo, Japanese civilians were defenseless. They tried to create firebreaks by tearing down more than 615,000 homes and buildings along selected streets or using natural barriers. In the end, it did not matter: incendiaries were dropped on both sides of the breaks.

Shortages of steel, concrete, and other construction materials made building air-raid shelters impossible. Each family was given the obligation of creating its own hole to hide in, covered with the only available resources: bamboo and a little dirt. Wherever possible tunnels were dug into hillsides.

Holes were also hand dug in municipal areas of Tokyo. When there was an air raid, Japanese policemen would stand by these holes and direct passers-by to get in. As many people as could possibly fit would squeeze together in the fire holes and wait until there were no more foreign planes in the air and the air raid siren went quiet.

Helga had a different idea. "I'm not getting into that grave," she told herself, and when the policeman tried to get her to dive in, she flashed her pass for the German embassy, and he waved her past.

The first week of March, U.S. bombers flew low over Tokyo, setting off searchlights and antiaircraft guns. War-weary Tokyo residents went to bed hungry on March 9, the distant wailing of air-raid sirens lulling them to sleep. As they slept, typically wet winter weather made a surprise change to mild temperatures and gusty winds.

The next day was Helga's twentieth birthday.

As the sun rose upon Tokyo Bay that day, 324 American B-29 bombers began their mission, though fewer took part in the actual bombing. Gen. Earl Johnson, 9th Bomb Group, noted, "When my crew got to . . . the entrance to Tokyo Bay, I could see the city of Tokyo was all lit up but, of course, by the time we got to 'bombs away,' most of the lights had been turned off, and one could see flashes of antiaircraft guns on the ground. But . . . they weren't hitting anything."

Lt. Robert Copeland, a copilot in the 500th Bomb Group, described the plan in his diary: "We're going in at between 7,000 and 7,800 feet. 150 of the . . . ships taking part in the strike will be ahead of us so there should be some large fires when we get there. We're carrying 40 M–18 incendiary clusters. No guns will be carried."

The first wave of bombers had launched from Guam, Saipan, and the Tinian Islands. No guns were needed. The firebombs, dropped amidst heavy winds, created an instant inferno. Before dawn on March 9 and 10, some 279 B-29s attacked Tokyo's most densely populated areas with more than 1,600 tons of firebombs. Each plane dropped 180 oil-gel sticks, less than a meter long, on the tightly knit neighborhoods. Then two waves of planes emptied their bays of a lethal cargo: napalm.

Covering fifteen urban miles, they flew as low as 500 feet. Supposedly, the bombers' primary target was the industrial district near Tokyo Bay, where workers' wooden homes were densely packed around factories. The winds that morning were outrageously high. All the ingredients were there for creating a perfect firestorm.

Methodically, the planes came in waves, dropping their cargo and marking the target. The second wave of planes flew lower, circling and criss-crossing, leaving great rings of fire behind. Soon other waves of planes came to drop their incendiaries inside the previous marker circles.

Underground tunnels had been built as emergency shelters in the event of air attack, but when the bombing started, it all happened so fast that many people were simply roasted alive. Those who were at home initially planned to stay there and heroically fight the fire. But how could they, when a single house might be hit by ten firebombs?

Incendiaries have an initial delay before exploding, allowing time to eat through the roof of the wooden buildings. The flaming cylinders splashed along rooftops, setting fire to everything they touched. The ground, which had been covered with soft cherry blossoms, turned into an inferno.

French news reporter Robert Guillain gave a powerful eyewitness account in his book, *I Saw Tokyo Burning: An Eyewitness Narrative from Pearl Harbor to Hiroshima*:

> They set to work at once sowing the sky with fire. Bursts of light flashed everywhere in the darkness . . . then fell back to earth in whistling bouquets of jagged flame. . . . A huge borealis grew [from] the gradual, raid-by-raid unrolling of the carpet-bombing. The bright light dispelled the night and B-29s were visible here and there in the sky. For the first time, they flew low or middling high in staggered levels. Their long, glinting wings, sharp as blades, could be seen through the columns of smoke rising from the city, suddenly reflecting the fire from the furnace below. . . .

Around midnight, the first Superfortresses dropped hundreds of clusters of the incendiary cylinders the people called "Molotov flower baskets." . . .

From the ground, the incendiaries looked like little burning Christmas trees—until the wind caught them and blew fire in every direction. Then the fires spread and merged. When the M-69s reached the ground and detonated, they released 100-foot streams of fire, sending flames rampaging through densely packed wooden homes. Even the asphalt boiled in the 1,800-degree heat.

Clutching their belongings, people crowded into any clear space they could, but then their bundles and clothing caught fire. The open holes that had been dug for emergency shelter filled with people; the next day, their charred remains were found. Whole families died in the holes they had dug under their wooden houses, which caught fire and collapsed. Many people had stayed heroically put as the bombs dropped, faithfully obeying the order to go into the holes they had dug.

"As they fell, cylinders scattered a flaming dew that skittered along the roofs, setting fire to everything it splashed and spreading a wash of dancing flames everywhere," wrote Guillain.

As civilians attempted to hand pump water through hoses that were too short to reach their targets, roofs collapsed under the impact of bombs. Houses ignited like paper lanterns and burned from the center out. Flames from a distant cluster of homes whipped through the air and suddenly sprang up nearby; hurricanes of fire sent burning planks flying. Screaming families ran through the streets carrying their children and dragging crates or mattresses. The traditional style of strapping a baby to a mother's back in an *onbuhimo* made of gauze, cotton, or wool became a death trap. Many mothers who finally managed to get to one of the few air-raid shelters in the city uncovered their babies to breastfeed them only to find they had already died from heat and smoke inhalation.

Hooded garments, supposedly fireproof, had earlier been distributed but caught fire and burned people from the head down. As fireballs flew onto heads, anyone near a river or canal jumped in, only to boil to death. People also began burning from their feet up or burst into flames as fiery wind entered their lungs. Telegraph poles and overhead trolley wires fell in tangles across streets. No one could get close enough to fight the fire.

The bombing continued for three godless hours.

Coaxing Helga to talk about that March 1945 day is not easy. "Those three hours went very quickly," she says initially. "We lost the whole house. Though it worked out fine, really. Nobody was badly hurt or burned in our family." But in time, Helga begins to remember, and tell, the details.

"We had just gotten back from Hakone and had left my uncle there," Helga recalls. "Then I rode my bike to the embassy to pick up rations. It was the day for butter. I got six pounds, some for a German neighbor and the rest a ration to last us several months. I put all that butter in a cardboard box in the *kura*." They were all getting ready for bed when suddenly they heard the roar of B-29 bombers, followed by a strange whistling sound—*zzzzt, zzzzt, zzzzt*—as the incendiaries fell. Then came the disgusting stench. Helga ran outside in time to see the U.S. Army Air Forces insignia visible amidst the scorch marks on the belly of the bombers, strangely illuminated from the fiery sky.

"When the firebombs fell to ground, they began to burn everything nearby. "They had a strange smell," Helga recalled. "Little pieces of fire were flying all around. It was like being inside a big bonfire. I was alone outside, and these fire pieces would get into my hair so I went inside to get an old scarf to bandage my hair. All of a sudden, part of the house was burning, and the air was so hot it felt like my skin and clothes might catch fire. I told my parents, 'I'm going in to get the cat,' and I went in, got a towel, put it around the cat and ran to the pool with her. We had little steps to go into the pool, and I got under the water and put her under also. She did not like that. She scratched and fought me and then jumped away.

"All three of us tried to take something out of house, but the smoke was everywhere, and you couldn't see. It was the night before my twentieth birthday. The wind was so strong in one direction that all the houses on one side of ours were burning, and all the houses on the other were not burning. I ran back into the house and got a few suitcases—one that had our passports and such. Then I put them in the *kura* and quickly got into the pool to wet myself down again so I wouldn't burn. I went into the house several times, running up the stairs to get our belongings and then each time getting back into the water, but I couldn't get all everything because the house was burning too much.

"The air was all smoke and fire, and there was the noise of planes overhead and the noise of the wind, and suddenly I saw my stepfather. He said, 'We are in the front! You should get out front! What are you doing?'

"'There are two more suitcases I'm trying to get,' I told him. He had been trying to get things out of the front of the house. So together we went in and got some things. The smoke was so bad. It would clear for a moment and you would think it was going to stay clear, and you would run in the house, and all of a sudden you couldn't see where you were going. It was a tricky thing. We also had a little garage, where the car was and some other things were stored, but the things in the garage had started to melt and couldn't be touched. My stepfather had already taken the car out of the garage so it wouldn't burn, but after that, it never started again."

By the time the bombing had stopped, Helga had lost track of her parents in the fire and smoke. For a moment she thought of calling for help, but who would have heard her? She spent the night alone, in the toxic air, huddled by the little pool. She didn't want to venture far from the water, in case there were more fires. On the eve of her twentieth birthday, Helga tried to take heart in the only good thing she could think of: that she had tried to rescue her mother's last remaining pet. The other three had died or disappeared when the bombings began.

It was a very long night, the dark and quiet punctured occasionally with cries in the distance. Helga was afraid to imagine what morning would bring.

Dawn came, under cover. It was as if the sun itself dared not shine on the horrors that lay on the little island. As diffused light mingled with the grey air, Helga picked her way through the blackened rubble to the front of the charred and burned house. Her parents were sitting there, quietly eating pineapple slices out of a can.

That moment marked the end of her childhood. She understood, once and for all, that she was alone in the world.

Neighbors had given Fritz their house keys before fleeing to the mountains just days earlier. Helga, Fritz, and Leonore walked to the neighbors' house, carrying what they could. Thankfully, the house was intact. They fell on the beds and tried to rest and recoup their senses. Helga was especially exhausted from all the running up and down stairs to retrieve their belongings. After a few moments of rest, Helga and her parents headed to the bathroom to try to remove the smoke and stench.

Fritz walked to a nearby hill to get an overview of the houses below, to gauge wind direction, and decide what to do next. As he watched flames finish off his house along with the rest of the neighborhood, he pulled out a cigarette and lit it. The house was a rental, but they had built the swimming pool, *kura*, and garage on the landlord's property and thus the Kiderlens owned them.

As Fritz took in the cigarette and the brutal realities of the morning, he was struck on the shoulder. He turned to see a Japanese policeman glaring at him.

"No smoking during an air raid," the policeman ordered.

Fritz exhaled, looked him in the eye, and said, "I am watching my house burn." He continued smoking his cigarette.

That morning, Helga's twentieth birthday, sirens had sounded the all-clear around 5 a.m. Remarkably, the lost cat appeared, sitting by their burned house. The concrete *kura*, just a few feet away, was un-scathed—but its iron doors were still too hot to open. When the iron finally cooled and they got inside, they found their silver spoons, forks, and knives all melted together. All of the butter Helga had brought from the embassy had dissolved, and the whole building, her little house, smelled like rancid butter for ever after. It would be years before

Helga could stomach eating butter again.

She found her wristwatch on the ground the next day amidst smoke and ash. "It wasn't working, but I opened up the back with my fingernail and blew out some of the dust and dampness and put in my pocket. The next day when I took it out of my pocket, it was working again. It was a German watch. I had it for almost another year before it quit working. To this day, I'm not dressed until I have my wristwatch on."

The following day one of Helga's friends came by to see if she was all right. He had tried to ride his bicycle through Tokyo but found it impossible because of the countless bodies strewn throughout the streets. There was still a light wind blowing and some of the bodies, reduced to ashes, were simply scattering like sand. In many areas, passage was entirely blocked by whole incinerated crowds.

"I was lucky," Helga said. "I always thought I would come out all right. I did as I was told, and nothing ever happened to me. When we did go out, to get to Hakone, it was horrible. We saw men crying. We saw some people dead, some people still moving while they were dying . . . you feel you must help, but sometimes nothing can be done. I have seen people die; you help if you can, but if you can't help, you must go on your way."

In a period of ten days starting March 9, more than 9,000 tons of bombs were dropped on Tokyo, Nagoya, Osaka, and Kobe, destroying 31 square miles. In April an extensive program of sowing minefields in channels and harbors at night was added. A total of 104,000 tons of bombs were directed at 66 urban areas. The official death toll of 100,000 was overwhelmingly civilians.

In Germany, Patton's Third Army plowed through the Rhineland. Helga was alone in Hakone on April 30 when her shortwave radio announced that Hitler had committed suicide in his underground fortress. Germany surrendered May 7; the war in Europe officially ended.

"That's how I heard that Hitler's villa had been taken and that he had killed himself and that somebody declared that the war was over and the Russians were coming into Berlin. Then the bad times really started for Germany," Helga said. "My father's family had been living in Berlin but moved to Strasbourg, and I had no idea where anyone was. It was a hard time, not knowing what had happened to the people back home."

Some Japanese people were furious at the Germans for giving up, for forsaking them. One day in town, Helga got an earful from a shopkeeper. "You are not holding to the promise!" he yelled. "Your Hitler is a bad man who did not keep his word! Where are the Germans when you need them?" As he continued shaking his hands in the air and spewing at her, Helga felt hot tears rise and turned away, leaving the man to his fury.

The Tokyo bombings continued without mercy. "Everyone was just waiting for an invasion," Helga remembers. It came. On May 23, more than 500 giant B-29 Superfortress bombers unleashed another 4,500 tons of bombs on Tokyo, obliterating the commercial center and railway yards and the Ginza entertainment district. Two days later, on May 25, a second strike of 502 Superfortress planes rained down some 4,000 tons of explosives. Together these two B-29 raids destroyed 56 square miles of the Japanese capital.

"One day we had a problem with a plane attacking the train," Helga remembers, in a typical pragmatic understatement. "It was one of those little planes that takes off from a ship, something smaller than a B-29. They came and flew real low; we could almost see the pilot's face. Then they started shooting. We all got on the floor of the train and lay down; then we heard the machine gun shooting. The train stopped and we all had to get out, and I saw that one man was bleeding from some part of his body. We didn't want to stay on the platform because they could shoot us there, so many of us walked into the fields and tried to hide under a tree. That was a shock."

Tokyo fire bombings killed many more people than did the bombing of Hiroshima and Nagasaki. Army Air Force Gen. Curtis LeMay boasted that the U.S. was "driving [the Japanese] back to the Stone Age." That summer was one of the most awful in history. Isaac Shapiro describes his mother spending the night more than once on the roof with a broom, batting at sparks to keep them from catching the house on fire. In July some 42,700 tons of bombs were dropped on Japan. With the activation of the Eighth Air Force on Okinawa, plans called for the bombings to increase to 115,000 tons per month. There was no need. "By the time the atomic bombs were dropped, we had nearly run out of strategic targets in Japan," wrote Henry C. Huglin, Commander of the 9th Bombardment Group.

On August 6 and August 9, 1945, the first two atomic bombs to be used for military purposes were dropped on Hiroshima and Nagasaki respectively. One hundred thousand people were killed, 6 square miles or over 50 percent of the built-up areas of the two cities were destroyed. Japan had now suffered nine months of direct air attack.

"After that, the American planes still flew overhead every day, but there were no more bombings," Helga said.

Along with most of Tokyo, the Kiderlens' home was in cinders. The concrete *kura* had withstood the heat and flames and had kept some of their belongings safe. The three of them sought refuge in the rental house in Hakone. It was a very dark time: very little food, no money, many of their clothes and precious items destroyed—and constant air attacks. Occasionally during that summer of Superfortress bombings, Helga took the train to the rubble of their property to stay in the *kura* and spend a few days cleaning, organizing, and preparing to move more items to Hakone. Fusako stayed with Helga and the two of them tried to move quietly, to disturb no one, but their presence was duly noted.

One hot summer day, a Japanese policeman brought a letter to the door. Helga bowed, thanked him in Japanese, and disappeared into the privacy of the *kura* to read the contents. Per the terms of the surrender, which now controlled Japan, all Germans had to leave Japan and return to Germany.

Helga recalled, "This letter had the names and ages of everyone in our family and told us to report to certain places. It said we could take back only so many pounds of belongings. My mother was sick and had not yet recovered. The first ship would leave in January and take all the German soldiers. The second ship would leave in August and would take all the diplomats and German people who had their own companies. Since we were with the embassy, we were assigned to the second ship."

On the train back to Hakone, the letter safely tucked in her pocketbook, Helga pondered the future with an uncertain feeling. It was August 15, 1945. She had been away from her beloved Germany for ten years. She missed Germany, her loved ones there, the food, the social life. But the Germany she had grown up in was gone. Many of its great cities lay in charred ruins. But if she didn't go to Germany, where would she go? What would happen next?

Anyone who had a radio kept it on as much as possible to as not to miss a war news broadcast. Isaac Shapiro and his family were among those listening; their radio was a simple, prewar battery-powered receiver encased in a small wooden box. As he recalls, a news broadcast was interrupted to call everyone's attention to an upcoming special announcement from His Majesty, the emperor. At the appointed time, the announcer asked everyone to stand while the national anthem was played.

Helga was on the train when a strange voice came over the loudspeakers. No one had ever heard this voice before, and it spoke in such an old, formal form of Japanese that many people could not understand what was being said. The court language was complicated, using "thee" and "thou" for pronouns and other forms of words that were virtually unknown to modern-day Japanese people. The broadcast went on for about ten minutes.

"To our good and loyal subjects . . . we have decided to effect a settlement to the present situation by resorting to an extraordinary measure. . . ." Helga's knowledge of German and Latin as well as Japanese helped her piece together enough of the message to comprehend: Hirohito the emperor of Japan, was informing his people that Japan had accepted the Allied terms of surrender. Her translation was: "We must give in before everyone is killed."

It was a painful moment for the emperor and his people. In 1926 when he became emperor of Japan, it was the world's ninth largest economy, after Italy. He had hoped for *tennozan*—a great victory—but instead his first speech broadcast to the people of Japan was the emperor's reading of the Imperial Rescript on the Termination of War. It is hard to imagine the feelings aboard the USS *Missouri* as it floated in Tokyo Bay while Japanese Foreign Minister Mamoru Shigemitsu signed the surrender document two weeks later.

While the emperor's voice rang through the train, there was no reaction, despite the oddity that in twenty years of ruling Japan, no one had ever *heard* the emperor's voice and despite the fact that most Japanese opposed the surrender. Everyone sat still, their eyes closed or looking at their laps.

"I got off at Miyanoshita, a fancy hotel, just like I always did," Helga remembered. "The German ambassador lived there since the embassy had been bombed. I found him and told him: 'I heard the emperor speaking, I didn't understand half of it.' And he said, 'Yes, the war is over now.'"

She began trudging up the mountain, away from the unmoving trains, heading for Hakone. When she passed a group of Japanese young people on the path, they pelted her with rocks, calling her dirty names in Japanese and yelling, "You betrayed us!" Picking up her pace, she turned from the path and cut into the woods to avoid harassment—or worse. When at last Helga reached the outskirts of her neighborhood, found a Japanese neighbor and asked him, "What is going to happen now?"

"I'm sorry, I don't have much time," he said, rushing past.

"That's OK," she continued, "I just want to know where we stand."

"I don't know what's going to happen, but everybody will be notified," he called. "Stay put until you receive further instructions."

She walked home and told her parents what she had heard. Her parents had not been listening to the radio, and would not have understood the archaic language even if they had heard it.

"Then Vatl went to the neighbor's houses to see what they had to say, but most people didn't know yet," Helga said. "So we waited to see what would happen."

They did not have to wait long.

In Helga's own words:

I was taught to accept things as they are and to respect life; we did not run around naked in the house, and we had a certain shame that you don't take your clothes off in front of your father or mother. You're taught that from when you are small on. But the Japanese didn't have that shame because it's a natural thing, and lots of little kids run around naked. Even in France, there were lots of bathers without a bathing suit, except women and girls wear a bikini bottom, so you get used to that. It's a natural thing and you don't think about it. We don't do it but they do, and we don't have to do what they're doing.

The Japanese didn't have heat in their houses; they had a little hibachi with charcoal that they used to warm their hands. At night, they sat in the hot bathtub, and then they went to bed.

I saw some cruelty there. One man decided to get rid of his cat and he took a shovel and cut its head off. It was an attitude of: What we don't need we get rid of. I always hoped I wouldn't be an enemy of theirs.

I also saw many kindnesses, especially pampering the boys. The girls learn to cater to the boys.

The firebombing destruction in Tokyo was very terrible and still very bad looking when I left; only a few restaurants had opened downtown. There was no place to stay because I had the *kura* packed with things I was trying to keep, and of course it stunk with melted butter. Also my parents couldn't get transportation but up there in Hakone where they were, nothing was destroyed.

After the bombing, people were afraid to leave the few things they had saved; they were afraid someone would get it. We cut trees and made posts and put blankets over the top to keep it from the rain, or we would put a piece of tin over it—whatever we could find from the house to make a little place fairly dry.

Because of the war, things were more expensive. We had a food shortage and food was rationed. Now you can get imported food regardless of summer or winter, but in Germany and Japan we lived by the crops. In the big cities of Japan there were so many foreigners that they had international food shops, small shops. You just walked down the street and picked what you needed. . . .

Then in March, the big bombing. They said they wanted to come at night and fly lower to more effectively destroy. And that is what they did to us, and they did it well. Before, they were too high up and couldn't focus. Then they dropped the firebombs and set everything on fire.

It was part of war. In World War I they had started bombing and shooting at people in cities. With this war it was the same thing; Russians go down the street in their big cars and with their big cannons that they would shoot.

The populations are always involved. Soldiers cannot tell who is civilian and who is a soldier, so they just shoot everything, and if you are lucky you get away. I was lucky. Many of our friends were lucky. It was only from above. If they had landed with their tanks who knows what would have happened. They bombed and then they invaded.

I didn't think about getting hurt. You do what you can, you make a few plans: if something happens, we will meet at these people's house. You know you can lose each other, so everybody does something to save some things that are your own and to not get hurt. I just went into the house as soon as the fire came closer to save the cat. I knew I had to wet myself down so the fire wouldn't burn me as easily. That's the first thing you learn: to go in the water if you can, if there is a fire close by. I had a few suitcases packed.

How close was the fire? The neighbor's house was burning, and the people behind us, their house started to burn, and the separate garage we built, *that* started to burn, and then our house. The roofs didn't burn, but the heat was so intense the paint would come off; it was like a firestorm: the wind was blowing maybe thirty miles an hour and the fire was blowing around. We didn't have the proper water to put out the fire.

In our *kura* I had closed all the doors. I had just picked up the butter ration from the embassy. I did all the shopping on my bicycle for the families that lived in our area, so I had about twenty pounds of butter in a cooler, and this rancid butter, the smell of that was awful.

People later cleared the streets. I had a bicycle and it had been behind the garage and didn't melt. I could ride it, but it didn't ride well; the wheels were not completely round after that.

The main train station where we used to change trains they had heavily bombed, so you couldn't get from one place to another. Some things were still smoldering. The next day I found my parents, and we walked up a paved street to a neighbor's place and tried to rest.

What did people do for food and shelter? We had to go to someone's house that hadn't been bombed. They didn't have much food in the house . . . we had a few cans that we had already put there, and we ate out of the can—canned pineapple and canned beans and canned tomatoes and canned meats.

I don't want to be in a firestorm again. Fire is a bad thing. The smell afterwards, you can't get it out of your mind; you dream about this because it smells so bad. I am afraid of fire now. Although I enjoy a fire in a fireplace. . . .

Helga in Hakone. 1947.

Chapter Eight

The Dai Ichi Hotel

THE DUST HAD BARELY SETTLED ON THE RUINS OF TOKYO when Gen. Douglas MacArthur moved into the Dai Ichi Life Insurance Building and settled his wife and son into the U.S. Embassy a few blocks away. MacArthur was chauffeured to the Dai Ichi Building each day in a black 1941 Cadillac limousine flying his five-star flag and flanked by military police motorcycles. From his sixth-floor office he could gaze across a broad boulevard and look down on the palace of Japan's wartime emperor, Hirohito.

To his credit, MacArthur left much of the local Japanese government intact, easing the occupation and the transition from war to peace. And there was no need for political power-mongering: he brought with him enough soldiers to bring the total number of U.S. troops in Japan to 430,000—most of them in the Tokyo-Yokohama area. After five years of embargoes, food shortages, and constant bombings, the population of Tokyo had halved, to 3.5 million. Assessing the physical damage, the U.S. estimated that 30 percent of the entire urban population of Japan lost their homes and many of their possessions. More than 2.5 million buildings and homes were destroyed.

The *U.S. Initial Post-Surrender Policy for Japan* gave MacArthur the power to enforce the terms of surrender but directed him to exercise authority indirectly through the state wherever possible. He was given extensive responsibilities beyond the Japanese home islands, including the repatriation of Japanese troops from areas they held at the end of the war. MacArthur insisted only Japanese ships be used—he wanted to avoid the sight of U.S. military ships carrying hundreds of thousands of Japanese soldiers who would look like prisoners. But since the Allies had sunk most of Japan's merchant fleet, the process took many months. MacArthur was also directed to deal with the widespread malnutrition that plagued postwar Japan, and in the spring and summer of 1946 he ordered thousands of tons of emergency food supplies from military supplies to be distributed to the Japanese people. Other American goods also flooded Japan: often soldiers threw pieces of candy and single cigarettes to Japanese people and children on the streets. But many Japanese children had never seen a cigarette and would pick one up and try to eat it.

Not everything the Americans did was good. It is said that all is fair in war. But stealing is wrong, and that is the opinion Germans and Japanese took as they watched American soldiers storm through their homes. The soldiers took the family silver, the women's jewelry, and anything else they wanted.

"We saw the Americans coming," Helga recalled. "A few of our young men climbed the mountain near us and said, 'The Americans have landed!' They came with ships and flat boats and motorboats. They landed on the coast below us, so we were scared: Are they coming for us? Then we saw them driving on the streets. We thought the Americans would arrive in Cadillacs, but they were dirty and tired, and they came in filthy old Jeeps and many of them were walking. If we saw them going by, we didn't go out of the house."

Wondering what to hide first, she suddenly realized that she owned a piece of Germany that could get her in very big trouble. A small framed photograph of Hitler hung on the wall over the desk where she did her homework. She never thought much about it—until the moment when she imagined American soldiers finding it. American soldiers, who were so proud of defeating Germany. Then she remembered her navy blue skirts and white shirts—her Hitler youth uniform. She had completed the uniform by tying a black scarf around her neck and weaving it together in a knot—a symbol of unity.

Gathering the uniform and the picture of Hitler, she placed them in a small sack and walked to Hakone Lake. She found the heaviest rock she could lift, placed it in the sack, and put the bag of contraband in a rowboat. In case someone was watching, she rowed leisurely. At the middle of the large lake, she glanced around and tossed the sack overboard. Watching the bubbles rise as the thing sunk out of sight into the water's depths, she took a deep breath and let it out slowly. The pink of sunset blushed across the sky. The day was ending and she had made herself safe. For now.

As it turned out, the Kiderlens' house was not searched. In downtown Tokyo, signs and street names in the area were reappointed in English alongside the Japanese, and many buildings that had survived the war were largely requisitioned as offices and barracks for U.S. soldiers. However, local people had no idea what the soldiers were talking about if they referred to the American name for a Japanese street.

According to documents from the time, the Hattori Building in the popular Ginza shopping district became the Eighth Army Post Exchange, stocked with American consumer goods. The Tokyo Takarazuka performance hall became the Ernie Pyle Theater, memorializing the much-loved American war correspondent who had been killed on Ie Shima in April 1945.

It came as a shock when an American man arrived at the Kiderlens' house in Hakone, accompanied by one of Helga's friends. It was the fall of 1945, when American troops occupied both Japan and Germany. "Can you give him a cup of coffee?" her friend asked.

"What do you think this is?" Helga demanded, unable to extend hospitality to one of the occupiers. She eyed the soldier and pictured her beloved Germany, now a wasteland. "You take him somewhere else and get his coffee."

About two blocks from MacArthur's headquarters in the Dai Ichi Building stood the Dai Ichi Hotel in Shinbashi. Built in anticipation of the 1940 Olympics, the Dai Ichi Hotel featured air conditioners, elevators and 636 rooms. During the war it had housed Japanese Field Grade officers (majors, lt. colonels, colonels) and now continued to serve as home for U.S. officers.

In interviews for this book, Helga held the Kiderlens' repatriation papers, issued in German and dated September 7, 1945. Each document resembles a passport and has a photograph attached. Leonore appears much older than her forty-three years. She looks piercingly into the camera lens, her deep-set eyes unmistakably sad. Her head is slightly cocked to the right, and below her beautiful high cheekbones her lips are parted as if she is asking, " What is happening and why is all of this necessary?"

Among the many photographs of Helga, there is only one in which she looks less than regal, less than vivacious: the photo on her repatriation passport paper. Her long brown hair is done up in the traditional European style, forming a soft round crown around her face, and she is looking to the left—as if refusing to look straight into the camera. Her expression is brave—and terrified. Although the papers were delivered in 1945, the Kiderlens' trip back to Germany occurred two difficult years later.

Strong and independent, Helga decided that the best course of action for herself and her family was for her to find a way out of repatriation. Getting a job with the forces in power would be a good idea, and no sooner had the thought entered her mind than the opportunity arose. Helga's life sometimes went that way: faced with an undesirable outcome, she thought of a way out, and that way out soon arose in front of her.

The civic infrastructure—transportation, food, water, sewage—was nonexistent or challenged. There was very little transportation in Tokyo for a while, other than U.S. military Jeeps and a few charcoal-burning vehicles in Tokyo. Helga soon realized that contamination from eight months of toxic bombs and incendiaries had poisoned the water supplies and food gardens. She learned not to eat out. Using the bathroom was a primitive event. "Except for the office and business areas of Tokyo, there were no sewers, so outdoor toilets were built into the small homes. Every Monday, wagons with oxen were used to remove the waste."

Sometimes, she tagged along with a girlfriend to Miyanoshita, one of the most upscale resorts. Helga enjoyed swimming, and she was curious about the American officers. She was aware that several men in the CIC department acted like members of the FBI. "They kept quite a bit of lookout over us," she recalled.

One day when Helga took the train from Hakone to Tokyo, she ran into her girlfriend Barbara.

"What are you doing these days?" Barbara wanted to know. "My girlfriend has many connections with Americans; won't you come with me to a party? You won't have to stay long, and you can take the train home."

It is easy to imagine Helga's enjoyment and ease—perhaps even a sense of relief—to be at a lovely party with food catered by Japanese cooks and to be waited on and recognized as the beautiful, intelligent, multilingual woman she was. Barbara and Helga spoke Japanese to the Japanese servants when they needed something, English to the Americans to be social, and German to each other.

An American officer, Col. Joe Muldoon, sat next to Helga and began asking questions: What are you doing here? How old are you? You can't be very old . . . about sixteen?"

"I am almost twenty," Helga replied, head held high.

"You speak English, Japanese, and German," he noted. "We could use someone like you to run the snack bar in the Dai Ichi Hotel."

"What's a snack bar?" she wondered out loud. "What's a snack?"

The job offer included a free room at the Dai Ichi Hotel, making the arrangement rather irresistible. The Dai Ichi housed U.S. commissioned officers, military attachés, and military contractors. In addition to a full-service dining room, the hotel offered drinks, sandwiches, and pie slices from a snack bar in the basement. From five o'clock p.m. until midnight, Dai Ichi guests could stop by to have a snack.

"I thought it was a strange hour because it was open during the time that dinner was served upstairs," Helga said.

Helga was living in the *kura* by herself most of the time now. She was grateful for the job and the accommodations since living in the

hotel eased what would have been an undesirable transportation bur-
den: leaving downtown Tokyo at midnight to catch a train.

The Dai Ichi Hotel was described by Maj. W. T. Gillham in a letter
home written November 7, 1945. He observed the lack of a private
bath but was grateful simply to have hot and cold running water with
showers just down the hall. "The hotel is about on a par with an average good commercial American hotel, but is one of Japan's best," he
wrote. "The mess here is excellent, and every night we get a beer ration
for a quart of Japanese beer, which is excellent. We also have a bar in
the basement, where beer and whiskey can be purchased in limited
amounts."

Helga supervised the snack bar, where an elderly Japanese man as-
sisted her, making sandwiches and serving beer, wine, and other alcoholic beverages from the little station. Next to the snack bar was a
locked storage compartment for alcohol. Every supply that came into
the snack bar storeroom was under strictly defined usage and had to be
properly accounted for—every ounce of alcohol, every slice of meat,
every piece of bread. Customers, who were for the most part American
male officers, had to hand over a ration slip in exchange for a drink or
a snack. A man couldn't just waltz up to the snack bar and ask for six
bottles of whiskey.

"Men often tried to seduce me to give them more whiskey," Helga
laughs, "but I always said in a very nice way, 'I'm sorry but I have instructions not to do that. You can take it up with my supervisor if you
like.'"

Twenty-four loaves of sliced white bread came into the storeroom
at once. "I had to know how many slices were in each package and
use only two slices for one sandwich," Helga remembers. "A ham-and-
cheese sandwich had one slice of ham, one slice of cheese, mayonnaise,
and mustard; then it was cut sideways."

Each night, she supervised her Japanese assistant to wash napkins,
silverware, and everything else that was used that night and returned it
to its storage place. They also counted all the food before closing shop.
Every night two American servicemen came by at 11:50 p.m. to check

on Helga as she finished counting money and supplies.

One night at midnight as Helga and her assistant were closing up, they realized that a sandwich was missing. When her supervisors came by, she could smell them as they came down the hall. "They loved coming by to see me, but they were drunk half the time," she says. The soldiers tried to chat with Helga, but she explained that she was busy trying to account for a missing sandwich. She showed them her receipts.

"Don't worry," they said, "we'll find the person who took that sandwich." Helga and her Japanese assistant stayed in the snack bar until they were too sleepy to stay awake any longer; then he went home, and she went upstairs to her hotel room. But she still worried. "I was responsible for accounting for the supplies," Helga remembers, "but I knew that the Japanese people who worked with me would get in trouble if it wasn't found."

When she returned to the snack bar, something had appeared on the counter, covered with a napkin: the missing sandwich. The elderly Japanese assistant appeared. He was always on time for work, always dependable, had never caused any trouble at all. But on this day he was crying.

"I have a sick wife at home," he confessed. "I wanted to bring her something that would give her some strength."

Helga listened to his pleas, then wrapped up the sandwich and gave it to him.

"Go home, and don't come back tomorrow. I'll find out first if you are still working here," she advised. The man was grateful, but he continued. "Have you ever seen what is thrown away from the dining room after dinner? Food that is still steaming hot is thrown in the trash can. And people are starving all across this country."

When Helga's boss came to her to investigate, she told him, "You can fire me. But you shouldn't fire this man. He has a sick wife. He is starving. What would you do?"

Helga's helper returned the next day—and no more questions were asked and no more food went missing.

During this time, Helga briefly took up smoking cigarettes, following the growing trend in the world. Wartime brings cheaper cigarettes and more accessibility to cigarettes.

A chance meeting with General MacArthur remains indelible. Helga strode into the Dai Ichi Insurance Building, U.S. occupation headquarters, to convince authorities to take her off the repatriation list. With Germany in cinders and everything she had known there irreversibly changed, she saw opportunity for herself in the United States.

"I went into the headquarters building to go in the CIC and was waiting for the elevator. When the elevator door opened, there stood General MacArthur with a couple of other uniformed men. He was a tall, very handsome man . . . a very interesting-looking man. He acknowledged me and said good morning. I noticed that he wasn't wearing a necktie. I learned that he never wore a necktie. Even when he met the emperor of Japan, he wore his shirt open at the neck. I felt that was sloppy."

One night when an American officer demanded she hand over another bottle of whiskey, Helga politely explained in English, "Your rations are used for today."

But he wasn't about to take *No* for answer. Attempting to bully the tall young German girl, he raised his voice and asked, "Who won the war?! Give me the alcohol!"

"Go talk to your superior about it," she answered, not intimidated.

"Why don't we go out some night?" he asked, changing his tune. "We could go to dinner."

"Even if I did, that wouldn't get you the bottle of whiskey." Helga had no problem standing her ground.

During the eight months she worked at the Dai Ichi snack bar, Helga saw many favors dangled before her by the hopeful. She turned down all but one.

"The only thing I ever accepted was an invitation to visit the war tribunal court," she said. "An American criminal lawyer came to the snack bar from time to time. I had noticed him because when he came in, he bought thirty sandwiches at a time, so I said to him, 'You have a lot of parties.' He said, 'Don't tell anyone. These go to Japanese families who have children and live near the courthouse.'"

One day he gave me a slip of paper and invited me to watch the tribunals. The day I sat in that courtroom, that was the first time I understood what had happened with the Nazis and the Jews in Germany and Poland and all of those places. I had no idea until that day."

All went well for Helga and her job at the Dai Ichi for about eight months. Suddenly one day she was called to an officer's desk. "We have to let you go," he said.

"Why?"

"Because we have seen your immigration papers, and you stated that you were a member of the Hitler Youth. That is true?"

"Yes, what's that got to do with my job?"

"We can't be associated with Nazis."

Helga tried to explain. "I was so young; everyone in school was expected to join. It was impossible to refuse. Can't you give me another chance? I think I've done well."

"Yes," he agreed. "You've done a great job, and we hate to see you go."

Helga reluctantly accepted her last paycheck from the U.S. government and returned to the little *kura* amidst the cinders of her family's burned-down home. There were no jobs in Tokyo; there was hardly any food in Tokyo. If she had had the money and the means to go to the movies, now run by Americans, she might have seen a newsreel from Universal Studios: one of the few sources of worldwide news. A June 1946 news clip notes "acute shortages . . . crowds by the hundreds gather at stores. . . . buy tickets to travel to other areas of the country where they hope to buy food. . . . Many Japanese are destitute . . . living in dirt . . . they try to create shelters from war rubble."

Helga was unaware of what had happened in Germany, especially in Eisenach where her grandfather had taken refuge. In the final months of World War II, the leaders of Eisenach refused to surrender to American occupation. An all-night artillery attack in April 1945 silenced the resistance. In the ensuing weeks and months, thousands of people were forced into labor camps, barracks, ruins and shelters. Lieutenant General Hofmeier died in Eisenach the following January.

Leonore and Fritz had moved permanently into the Hakone house after the Uehara house was razed in the March, 1945 firebombings. Fritz visited Helga in the *kura*, coming only occasionally when he was working in Tokyo as a postwar volunteer. Living in the burned-out *kura*, Helga was now very much alone in the world. But the upcoming news of her mother's health crisis would soon force her into action, and in trying to help her mother, Helga would open a new door for herself. And so it was with her search for a telephone.

Helga's photo for her affidavit of identity. Being officially
stateless, she had no passport. She used her affidavit of
identity to enter the United States. Tokyo. 1947.

Chapter Nine

Nazi Go Home

HELGA'S INTERACTIONS WITH AMERICANS WERE INFREQUENT but she made a point to be cordial and, when possible, helpful. One summer day late in '47, Helga and a girlfriend rented a rowboat and rowed around Hakone Lake. Beaching the boat in a little cove, they walked the shore and climbed the black volcanic rocks not far from a road. Startled by the sound of yelling nearby, they spotted an American Jeep with four young GIs waving energetically and in apparent need of help.

The sight of the U.S. flag brought back the memory of Army Air Forces insignia snarling at her from the belly of low-flying bombers that only months before had destroyed Tokyo. But Helga and her friend climbed across the road to see if they could offer some assistance to the soldiers.

"Do you speak English?" was always the first question.

The men had taken the Jeep for a pleasure ride and now it was broken, making them late returning to the base.

"I know a mechanic a few miles down the road," Helga offered. "We can show you." She and her friend returned to their little boat and began rowing alongside the road while three GIs pushed the Jeep and one steered. When they finally reached the little town, Helga acted as translator between the Japanese mechanic and the American soldiers so they could discuss what to do next.

Ever conscientious and not particularly trusting of Americans, Helga told the mechanic in Japanese to contact her if the men did not pay for the repairs. "I didn't have any money, but I figured I could pay the mechanic with some canned food," she said.

Not only did the GIs pay their bill, but they apparently convinced the mechanic to tell them where the beautiful and smart German girl lived, for later that evening they returned with a large box of C-Rations—better than money. "They were so nice," she recalled. "They even took their hats off when they came into the house." A few days later, a letter of gratitude arrived from the men's commander to Helga in the little Hakone shack. Providing his contact information, the commander offered to help with anything she might need in the future.

It felt good to have an American ace in her pocket as she faced double bureaucracies in the attempt to avoid repatriation for herself and her parents.

Helga asked the Americans another favor. Feeding her beloved fox terrier was now nearly impossible. Many people in the Tokyo area were living on less than 1,000 calories a day. While some canned dog food was still available on a few store shelves, Helga realized she could not buy it. The dog was living on a few grains of leftover rice and minimal scraps from his meals and was getting weaker and more sickly every day. She had heard the bitter comments the last time she stood in front of the dog food in the store: "How could anyone afford to buy dog food when we cannot feed our children?" She feared that someone would kill the dog and eat him. The decision was not easy, but Helga finally drew the obvious conclusion. There was an American soldier who regularly stopped to see her in the Hakone house to see if she needed help with heavy lifting and difficult chores. She had seen the pistol he wore. One day she explained her dilemma. "Under the circumstances, I cannot feed or care for him anymore. Would you please…take him away…and shoot him." Several hours later, the soldier returned and without a word handed her the dog's leather collar. It was but one of many heartbreaking decisions Helga would soon make.

Leonore was now so ill that she needed to be in an intensive care unit, not facing a month-long voyage in third-class passage in the hull of a military ship. Looking back, Helga realized that anyone could have seen this coming. Years earlier, Leonore's letters from Japan to Helga in Germany sometimes mentioned feeling sick and staying in bed. When Helga had first arrived in Japan, her mother seemed healthy. But a year later when the family moved to the larger house, Leonore worked very hard to keep it in the perfect German style and to train her Japanese maid in the German ways. It was then that Helga first knew her mother had "a female problem," bleeding between her menstrual periods.

When Helga was still in school in Japan, sometimes she would come home to find her mother in the darkened bedroom. "Please don't open the curtains," Leonore would plead, for any light was blindingly painful. There were some good days, but as time went on they were outweighed by bad days. After the move to Hakone, Leonore had an unusual bout of heavy bleeding.

Now, Leonore had been bleeding for months without appropriate medical care. Wartime Tokyo was hardly the time or place to find a German-speaking gynecologist, and Leonore refused to be seen by a Japanese doctor. One day she was so sick that Fritz took her to a German-Japanese hospital in Yokohama, where it doctors performed emergency surgery on Leonore.

By the time Fritz was able to get in touch with a German general practitioner, Leonore was so weak, she could not get out of bed.

"You must find an American doctor specializing in woman's care," the doctor advised. "Your wife needs additional surgery if her life is to be spared."

In postwar Japan, Fritz was at a loss as to how to help Leonore until a chance meeting with American soldiers. A Jeep carrying four U.S. officers sped past Fritz as he walked down the street in Hakone, then screeched to a halt and backed up. "Who are you? Where are you going?" one officer asked. Another man asked directions to get over the pass and down to the water.

In perfect English, Fritz gladly gave the Americans directions, then explained that he had lived in Japan since 1923, first working for Mercedes and then for the German embassy. "We are waiting to be repatriated, but I am concerned because my wife is very ill. She needs a special operation. "

"I'm a doctor," said one of the Americans, showing Fritz his ID. "May I visit your wife? I will see if I can help."

The American doctor arranged for a military ambulance to arrive at the Kiderlens' house the next day to rush Leonore to the Catholic hospital in Yokohama. There, doctors confirmed a growth in Frau Kiderlen's uterus that was as large as a baby's head. Furthermore, she had lost too much blood over the years and was too weak to undergo the necessary hysterectomy. They kept Leonore three weeks under constant nursing care before they determined she was strong enough for such an invasive operation. Leonore survived the surgery but afterward, the large incision refused to heal.

Helga learned that authorities planned to send Leonore from the Yokohama hospital directly to the repatriation ship. It was a poignant picture of the depth of anti-German sentiment, that "the Americans" wanted this poor, sick, middle-aged German housewife sent back to her country of origin as soon as possible, despite being deathly ill. Helga sprang into action.

She consulted a Japanese attorney friend who advised her to call a particular U.S. office in Tokyo. She would notify the authorities that her mother would never survive the trip to Germany (where she would be forced into a camp with minimal access to health care). Helga would convince the Americans revoke her mother's repatriation orders and allow her passage to the United States.

Her next obstacle was to find an American who would let her use the telephone book and telephone to make the call—the U.S. government had a separate telephone communications service in Tokyo and did not use the Japanese utility

She walked through the American neighborhoods in Tokyo looking for someone who would let her use a telephone. The only thing in Helga's mind was that this single phone call might save her mother's life. Surely the Americans would understand.

In a rare admission of fear, Helga looks back on that time and says,

"It was very scary, not knowing what would happen." As bad as it was, help was on the way. The American doctor Fritz had encountered earlier was pulling strings to have Leonore's name removed from the ship's passenger list so she could have time to heal. There was no doubt that his actions saved Leonore's life. (Fritz later visited several U.S. military offices to try to locate that doctor to thank him. Finally, he succeeded in finding a mailing address that he used to send a heartfelt letter of thanks for the kindness the Americans had showed.)

"I had to announce to the American authorities that we are not going to be on this ship. And, I thought somehow I could find a way to avoid repatriation for myself," Helga said. In typical Helga fashion, she cleared one hurdle after the other.

She walked into an American neighborhood and rang a doorbell. "My mother is sick. If I could just use your telephone . . . I have cash and can pay."

The house she chose happened to be the residence of Col. Albert Watson, an American Army officer. Mrs. Watson was cordial and warm as she listened to Helga's story. "Sure, make your call," she said, and helped Helga put the call through the Japanese phone system to the American phone line.

Helga reached the office responsible for the repatriation of Germans and explained that the Kiderlens were not going and why.

Mrs. Watson was at her side to help if she needed. She must have been impressed by the young woman's confidence. Mrs. Watson also had a question of her own. "Where do you live?" The twenty-one-year-old explained that she lived just a five-minute walk away, in her family's *kura*.

"Visit me again tomorrow when my husband is home," said Mrs. Watson, whose mind was churning. Colonel and Mrs. Watson had two rambunctious boys, John and Albert, and Colonel Watson's work and social obligations as an American officer in Tokyo kept their lives more than busy.

The next day Helga returned as instructed. Colonel Watson was serious and to the point, as might have been expected: "Have you ever thought of going to America?" he asked.

"I don't think that's possible," Helga answered. "We are supposed to return to Germany." But the colonel's question alerted the girl that a different future for her was suddenly a possibility.

"I can arrange to bring you to America with my family."

Quick-thinking Helga stalled for time. "I'll have to speak to my parents."

"But you're twenty-one years old?"

"I wouldn't do anything if my parents were against it."

Sitting in the little concrete shed behind her family's burned-out home, Helga considered the larger scene. They had lived in an ashen aftermath for nearly two years. Nothing that a human being needed—food, medicine, bathrooms, clean water, hygienic supplies—was available anywhere. No one in her family had a job. Mutti was gravely ill and would be put on a repatriation ship as soon as doctors would allow it. But the Germany they had known was forever gone. Worse, the world had become anti-German. Mutti and Vatl would be sent to a repatriation camp, which might be the same disgusting concentration camps where the Jews had been held. Her own father's letters were no longer written from his fine Berlin home. Kurt Hofmeier and his family considered themselves lucky to be squeezed into the attic of family friends.

Years later, Helga's sister-in-law, Dorothee Hofmeier, corroborated Kurt's tragic stories with her own sad recollections. (Dorothee married Helga's half-brother, Hans Melchior Hofmeier —Kurt's son from his second marriage). "My father was the director of an X-ray clinic in Stuttgart," Dorothee wrote. "I remember the end of the war in 1945. As the director, my father had to formally surrender the hospital to the Americans. I can still see him standing in the small courtyard, fragrant with blossoms, when a soldier pulled his revolver and pointed it to my father's head and asked him if any German soldiers were hidden in his hospital. It was a huge hospital; how could he know?"

Helga had to ask herself: What good would it do anyone for me to live in a repatriation camp in bombed-out, poverty-stricken Germany?

Those postwar years in Japan must have been completely miserable, but to this day Helga will not say so. She says simply, "This whole thing with the war, I was sort of numb. In Germany there was nothing for me. When I thought about the possibility of going to America, I thought that it would be the best thing to do. From America, I could send care packages, food and necessities, to my parents. If I got papers saying I could come to the U.S. and stay with an American family and that would be security."

To pay for her passage to America, Helga signed away the next three years of her life, as the documents signed between her and Col. Watson reveal.

> October 28, 1947: We the undersigned have loaned Helga Hofmeier $306.77 for one-way passage by commercial water transportation from Yokohama to San Francisco, $50 for railroad fare from San Francisco to San Diego, California, and $15 for passport and telegram. Total: $371.77.
>
> Col. Albert Watson, Mrs. Watson

Helga signed the following agreement, created by Colonel Watson:

> I the undersigned agree to pay the above loan in the amount of $371.77 at the rate of $25 per month. I also agree to assist the Watsons in the maintenance of their home and care of their children until this indebtedness is paid.

Colonel Watson further signed an affidavit of support for Helga, which they both signed. In it, he pledged that he was a native of the United States by birth, gave the names of his parents, his age (thirty-six), listed his cash accounts and the value of his personal property: two horses, a sedan, a Jeep, investments, bonds, and life insurance:

I am a friend of Helga Hofmeier . . . who desires to enter
the U.S. for permanent residence. I hereby solemnly swear that
I will receive and care for her and at no time will I allow her to
become a charge of the United States or of any state, territory,
or subdivision thereof. I freely incur this obligation because of
friendship and the desire to assist the applicant in becoming an
American citizen.

Become an American citizen?! The idea had never crossed Helga's
mind. They had lived in Japan for ten years and not become Japanese.
She could not imagine not being a German citizen.

"I didn't know that I would lose my German citizenship," she said.
"I've always been German. There were a thousand Germans living in
Japan for many years, and they did not become citizens; they were still
Germans. I thought this would be the case everywhere in the world.
You had to live in Japan thirty years before they would consider you
for citizenship. My stepfather lived in Japan from 1923 to 1947 and he
never thought of becoming a Japanese citizen."

**"At that point I realized I was stateless: I didn't know where I
belonged." - Helga**

A strange realization dawned on Helga: she was a stateless, un-
identified alien. The German passport given to her when she left her
beloved Munich in 1935 was good for ten years and had just expired.
Tokyo was utterly destroyed, and it was hard to understand who was in
charge of the country. But she needed some kind of official identification card if she was to leave Japan.

"There was no German representation, no German power or authorities," she said, "so the Japanese made identification cards for my
parents and me, stating that we were Germans, that we had been with
the German embassy in Tokyo, and that we were living in Hakone. It
was an accepted ID because of the times." She took the Japanese ID
to the American consulate in Yokohama, showed them the agreements

between her and Colonel Watson, and soon left with an official-looking document with her photograph on it.

In her innocence, Helga did not realize at the time what a clever arrangement the colonel had created. The full picture of Helga's predicament was that she would have to work for the Watsons much longer than the two years of the signed agreement because a German immigrant at the time was required to live in the United States for five years before applying for citizenship. For spouses of the U.S. military, the requirement was only for two years.

Harsh stories were circulating about conditions on the first repatriation ship that had come in January. Uncle Otto had been herded with other German men into large holding tanks and put under constant armed guard. Women were terrified of being raped and helped each other find white wigs and scarves to cover their youthful heads.

Using the bathroom meant squatting over a hole in the floor in front of everyone. There was no privacy for anyone, which was especially hard on the women who were forced to use the bathroom while American soldiers watched and made comments that humiliated the women and riled the German men who were in earshot. The women were too afraid to complain, but the men who were unable to suppress their opposition to the conditions were physically abused in response. Conditions on arrival in Germany were also nearly inhumane.

The second ship, USS *General W. M. Black,* powered into the Yokohama port in mid-August in the sweltering heat. A spartan troop ship, the *General W. M. Black* specialized in transatlantic round-trip voyages in the 1940s, carting thousands of American soldiers across the Atlantic from New York to Europe and carrying the wounded back, as well as later participating in the Korean War and Communist China offensives. More than 500 feet long, she could carry 3,500 passengers: in 1947, many of them were German prisoners of war and German citizens being repatriated.

Helga took the train to the Yokohama hospital to visit her mother one last time and pack her few belongings: hairbrush, toothbrush, comb, nightgown.

"Finally one morning the Americans came and took my parents. I could not go with them because my mother was carried in an ambulance type of car; several people were sick or elderly and they had a special bus for them, with a nurse. So I could not have gone with them, anyway."

The next day Helga walked up the gangplank, memorizing the sight of her parents waving at her from behind the ship railing with a throng of people coming and going and moving trunks all around them.

Fifty years later, that day is crystal clear in her mind.

"A lot of American soldiers were standing around, waiting and watching to be sure nothing happened," she said. "My parents were at the railing, waving at me. I went up the gangplank, found them, and we sat down together, but there was such a chaos of people coming and going and things being loaded, it wasn't quiet enough to talk."

Ship rules mandated separation of the sexes, beginning with little boys over six years of age and including married couples. Leonore showed Helga the infirmary, where she would sleep with a half-dozen other patients on small cots. "I peeked in; it was a room with sun coming in through the little windows, and the beds looked nice and clean. It slept six people who had been ill."

Too soon, a voice announced in English: "Everyone who is not a passenger must get off the ship now." Helga hugged her parents for the last time and made her way through the fearsome crowd of people on deck. From the dock, she watched the ship in silence for several hours as American sailors prepared it for the sea voyage. As it began to creak and groan and slowly began to pull away from the pier, a young man at her side said, "We will never see them again." It was a former classmate of Helga's, Waldemar Crome, whose parents were on the same ship. Helga stood on the dock until the ship disappeared over the horizon, wondering what her parents would find in Germany. She refused to believe Waldemar was right.

Truly alone in the world for the first time, Helga sat in the *kura*, contemplating the move to the great unknown country of America. So, it is done, she thought to herself. We will see what will come next.

In Helga's own words:

It gave me such a shock when I heard my classmate say that we would never see our parents again. But it was true. I never saw my mother anymore. I never saw her again.

After my parents got on the ship, I was alone. To prepare for my trip, I had many interactions with Japanese officials, but I had never had any trouble with the Japanese people or law. You just do your best, without insulting anyone or doing anything illegal. I was always impressed by law. I always tried to behave myself. Since I could speak the language fairly well, I could always talk my way out of things.

The Watsons left in April and wrote to tell me that they were going to be living in Coronado, California, and that's where I should go. I wrote them back and told them my parents had left, and that I would find a ship to California.

I was living in Hakone on the lake in the mountains, and it was cold and hard to maintain for the winter months. Whenever I had business in Tokyo I stayed in the *kura* for a few days, and the maid stayed in the mountains.

It took four months almost. I had to go to the consulate and show them the [written] contract with the colonel and get papers to allow me to leave.

I knew a German woman about my age, Irmgard, who had come from Dutch East India with her mother and sister. One day I met her on the street in Hakone with her fiancé, an American military man who worked in the communications center, which had a radio station on the hill. He asked me if I would do him a favor. There was a big party at the communications center, and he wanted his girlfriend to come and meet all of his friends, so he wanted to know if she could spend the night with me the night of the party. I said she could stay in the *kura*, and he asked me if I would like to come to the party also.

I told him, "I don't want to go alone."

He said, "I'll get you a date. What kind of a person do you like?"

I thought for a moment and said, "If he can dance, that's good." Because so many of the men just stepped on your feet when they tried to dance.

That night Irmgard and I went to a club, to a room where people could come in and play music and read and think. We sat down, and pretty soon her fiancé came in.

"Where's my date?" I asked him. "He can't make it?"

"No, he just had to work late," he said. "He will be here. We'll wait." Then when he arrived, he said he wasn't sure if he could stay or not. He left but then he came back.

He couldn't dance but he was nice. He showed up a few days later with a Jeep and a driver and we had a nice afternoon. So we started dating. Slowly I fell deeply in love with him. I felt safe with him. I trusted him.

When I told him about the Watsons and going to the States, he was very surprised. He had to stay another nine months in Japan. I knew him for four months before I left, and the end of that time he said, "I think we could even get married; what do you think?"

I told him, "I have to look at the United States and see if I like it."

Staff Sergeant Jesse Edmonds was a Louisiana Cajun with an ideal assignment with U.S. Army Air Forces Telecommunications. His job, sending secure telegrams for the Sixteenth Communications Squadron, was easy enough, and he enjoyed the unique status of having a high security clearance.

He had been seasick the whole way from San Francisco to Yokohama, arriving on the *Chanute Victory* a few days before Christmas 1946. Growing up in Eunice, he had never been out of the state of Louisiana, let alone on the high seas until after joining the U.S. Army Air Forces straight out of high school.

As a member of Future Farmers of America in Eunice, he had never pictured himself living in a luxury hotel. And when his squadron first arrived, they had slept in tents in the snow. But life in the air force had eventually landed him in the third floor of a very nice Tokyo hotel. "Not the Waldorf Astoria, but the one right next to it," he remembered. "From where I lived, I could see the Imperial Moat."

American servicemen who flooded the streets of Tokyo were unsophisticated by European standards, but Helga eventually decided that they were a friendly lot. Besides, her girlfriend Irmgard was engaged to an American. As it happened, that man was a friend of Jesse Edmonds, and soon there was a happy conspiracy to bring Jesse and Helga together. Jesse cautiously accepted his friend's invitation to come to the club but refused to accept the blind date.

"I'd like to see what I'm getting into," he said. "Where you gonna be?"

The American Red Cross Service Club was a popular meeting place where young people could shoot pool, listen to records, and eat at the snack bar. It also happened to be located across the street from the hotel where Jesse lived. He planned to simply stroll through the club, check out the girl, and simply keep walking toward an exit if he didn't like the looks of her.

"I liked what I saw," he says, more than fifty years later. "And that's where it started. Helga was very attractive and very well-spoken. She spoke perfect English. She was more upscale and a lot better looking than the girls my friends were with—and I wasn't bad looking myself," he chuckles. "I was an enlisted man coming up in the ranks. I was intrigued with her, and apparently she was comfortable with me." The two couples finished their evening in a club on the seventh floor of the hotel where Jesse lived.

Dating was easier now that the war had been over for a year and a half: the movies had opened up again, every hotel had a clubroom, and other nightclubs also opened their doors. There were no taxis, but in those days American servicemen rode the Japanese train system for free. And for ten cents Jesse could even arrange for a military Jeep and driver from the military motor pool to take him and Helga out in the evenings.

"There weren't that many German girls in Japan in those days, and the ones that [lived there] had it made," Jesse said. "I couldn't have dated a Japanese girl; that was fraternizing [with the enemy]. But a nice-looking blond, that was fine. They didn't check ID cards in those days, and Helga could have been American for the way she looked. On the other hand, if I'd been in Germany trying to date a German girl, that would have been fraternizing. The Americans were very naïve in many ways. Nobody asked Helga for a passport: she was a white girl."

They were a handsome couple, and some folks thought they were brother and sister because their features—especially skin tone, hair color, and eye color—were similar. There was another familial similarity because like Helga, Jesse had two fathers: a biological father and the stepfather who helped raise him. Both Helga and Jesse were optimists, and their personalities quickly fell in sync.

"We clicked," Helga said. "We had similar ideas even though he was from a different culture. He wasn't crass, the way I thought Americans were. Jesse was very family-oriented, and he talked a lot about his mother and his family. I liked that. I felt that was a very important trait."

Compatibilities aside, when Helga met Jesse, she had signed away the next three years of her life to Colonel Watson. "I understood that she was going to the states," Jesse said. "She was going to California. We were both pretty steady on our feet. She knew what she wanted. And after a while, I knew what I wanted and that was that. We had six or seven months together, and by the time she left, we had committed ourselves. I don't think I got on my knees with a ring . . . but after a few months, it was accepted by both of us."

Military regulations at the time would have required Jesse to leave his post in Japan within a few months of marrying Helga if they had married in Japan. As they discussed their options for marriage and family life, this policy was foremost in their minds. Jesse wanted to fulfill his entire military obligation in Japan, roughly another year, and have an assignment in Shreveport, Louisiana, afterward.

As they discussed life in the United States, Jesse asked Helga why she wanted to live there. "I loved her answer," he said. "She said it was the American civilian women that really made a difference to her. The secretaries and nurses had befriended her, fixed her hair, put hats on her, dressed her up."

"Even if it was a bit shallow, they lived for the fun of it," Helga explained. "Everything around me was dreary and worn and used and old and tired and broken. I had always liked being feminine and pretty, and they helped me feel that way again. They liked feeling pretty and lively and feminine, and because of those women being around me, I began to feel that way again too." Military women, she noted, were not so compelling for her. "The WACs were not so nice to me. They were sharp with their looks and voices. And they were trying too hard to be like the men. They went drinking with the men. Their military training came through even on their time off."

Helga reasoned that she was young, possessed no real job skills, and had no future in either war-torn Japan or war-torn Germany.

America was Helga's only hope. Besides, she was in love with the young American. She believed him when he said that he would come for her in America. "Everyone told me I was crazy to believe him after such a short time of knowing him, but I trusted him completely."

All she had to do was get herself to the United States—and Colonel Watson's offer would be her magic-carpet ride out of Japan. She was clear-eyed about the commitment she was making, though working as a maid after growing up in aristocratic German circles was not a role she relished.

"I had learned as a child to take control of my own feelings," she said. "So I knew that is what I had to do when I agreed to let Colonel Watson sponsor my emigration to the U.S. Just as he commanded troops, I would command my feelings. I would do what had to be done, and I would do the best job I could."

In Helga's own words:

One day when I was in the *kura*, our neighbors came to tell me they were sad to see me leave, and we chitchatted. "What are you going to do now?" they wondered. I did not tell them I was going to the States. I said, "I don't know what I can do; I have to find work and move into the city somewhere."

They asked me, "Would you sell the *kura*? We would like to have the property." They came and looked at everything: we had planted trees, we put a goldfish pond on top of the upper level and a swimming pool. There was a garage, a basement, and a garden. The *kura* had been a shed, but we had fixed it up to be a room you could live in, my little room with running water.

I found a realtor to help me, and we finally came to an understanding of an amount they would pay. I had two big crates of my clothing [and other personal belongings], but all the other things I left with them. The Japanese had a law that whatever you add to is yours, but the land could not be sold. You did not own the land; you just settled on the land.

Nobody could take any money with them out of Japan. My parents had some money they couldn't take with them, so when they left it, I used that to live on, and when I left I gave the rest of it to Fusako.

The next time I went to the *kura*, the people had cut down the trees.

My neighbor paid me in yen. It was a lot of money, but there was a law in America that a German person could bring only $50 to America. I had to think: What am I going to do with all this money? What can I buy that I can take with me? Gold? Diamonds?

I was afraid of that. I didn't know anything about those things. The jeweler was next door, and he would have happily helped me. But to invest in diamonds at that age . . . I didn't know whether I would ever get rid of those things.

When I was younger, my mother gave me a [Persian] lamb coat of hers that she'd had altered for me. A fur coat is a wonderful thing because it keeps the body heat inside. In Europe you always wore a fur coat—or at least a fur collar and around the wrists. It was not a luxury as much as a necessity to keep warm.

A fur coat is always a valuable item. Women often wore a wool coat with a fox [collar] over their shoulder; it was a fashion thing. Whenever I visited Berlin, I would see the Russian people with their fur coats and fur boots and hats.

Even when I was a child, I heard people say it was not good to shoot the wild animals. Many times we went to places where they were raising foxes in cages in the snow, and their fur was so beautiful because of the snow. We went and fed them.

In my childhood storybooks, the princess wore a sable coat or wrap. The nobility had things like that.

My own coat [became] very worn over the years, and I had noticed the American women, how much they shopped and bought. Once some American women noticed me and were excited that I spoke good English. They wanted to know all about me and said, "Why don't you come out to our hotel, and we'll go out for dinner and a movie?" So when I came to their hotel, they had a big time dressing me up and taking me out. I took them to the Imperial Hotel and showed them the shops. I took them to the furrier there and said, "Here is a very nice gentleman if you want a fur coat." My mother liked to have fox fur added to the collar of her wool coat, and I had always gone with her to translate. Once or twice he had asked me to model for him, and I did.

And so the furrier remembered me now.

I said to him, "I have to leave. I was wondering if you have something for me, a valuable coat that I can afford to take with me."

He showed me several things, and one of them was a

Russian sable. It was soft and warm and wonderful. It was so light, you didn't even know you had it on. He said, "You've been good to me, you've brought me customers." And he took a couple thousand dollars off the price.

So I thought: Why not? If I can get it for that price, it is an investment. It was about ten thousand dollars.

It was still winter. I bought my sable coat and went back to the cold little place in Hakone, and I kept paying my monthly rent. I also paid for the transport of the crates. Jesse took me to the ship the day I left, and I was so glad when I finally got on the ship. I looked at the crates and my suitcase and I thought: all I own is right here.

Helga, wearing her sable coat. Aboard the
U.S. President McKinley. 1948.

Chapter Ten

A Foreign Girl

"People barely have even the most basic necessities of life. . . . All of our assets were lost in Eisenach. . . . We continue to try to remain brave. . . ." - Kurt Hofmeier, December 28, 1946

JESSE'S FACE—PLAYFUL, WITH INQUISITIVE BLUE EYES—appeared in her thoughts as Helga looked out at the wide sea as her ship headed toward America. The United States seemed even more foreign than Japan had seemed when she was last on an ocean liner. Then she was nine years old, sailing into what became the worst war zone the world had ever seen as the United States military decimated Tokyo and its people. She had endured nine continuous months of merciless firebombings. She had witnessed people dying on the street. She had survived the chaos and starvation that followed. She pushed those thoughts, those scenes, those memories, far into the back of her mind. Watching the waves rise and crash toward the hull of the ship, she worked hard to convince herself that she was not flying right into the arms of the enemy—and that America would be a place of hope and renewal for her.

In 1935 her girlish face had been ringed with rabbit fur hand-sewn onto the collar of her wool coat. On this freezing February day in 1948, her womanly curves were tucked inside a three-quarter length Russian sable. Forbidden, as all immigrants were, from bringing wealth into the country, she wore her inheritance on her back.

Her father's face appeared before her as she watched the ocean stretch and curl before the ship. Vati had written a few days after

Christmas 1946, from the university city of Tübingen. During World War II, it had been occupied by the French and escaped the massive death and destruction of active war zones.

Though overjoyed to find that his daughter had survived the war, Hofmeier was unable to hide his sadness. He and his wife were pained by the unbelievably long separation from Helga. Plus all of the news from home was bad: first the Russians moved in and took over houses, businesses, and banks. Hofmeier and his family members have lost all of their assets. Then the Americans took occupation on November 23, 1944. Noting Lieutenant General Hofmeier's death, Kurt wrote, "We can envy that he no longer has to deal with this entire tragedy and that he can now rest. You cannot imagine how difficult it was for me that I couldn't go there to comfort your old grandmother."

All of the family members had been forced to forsake their homes. They lost nearly all of their possessions and had not so much as a bed to sleep on. Hofmeier's sister, Irmi, had given up the medical clinic she founded. Uncle Gerhard had been captured, escaped and then died. Helmut lost his left foot in Normandy, recuperated in Strasburg, then was held prisoner of war for six weeks.

Helga's stepmother, Edith, risked her life to sneak through lines of occupying soldiers, gathering all of her children from the homes she had placed them in for safekeeping. She managed to find them all and bring them home to Tübingen.

Passing through French lines, Kurt Hofmeier was detained, questioned, then released. He and his family were living in the attic of a friend. He unsuccessfully looked for work as a physician and was trying to reestablish private practice as a general practitioner, but the countless people living in poverty and misery made that impossible.

"Life goes on and we continue to try to remain brave and not let things get us down," he wrote. "One day I'll get another job, and once that happens, everything will be easier." Still trying to look at the bright side, he continued, "We are able to call this little attic home; it's ours alone and we are all healthy." To hide his true location, Hofmeier instructed his daughter to send her reply in double envelopes: the outer one to a friend's address in Switzerland, from where the inner envelope would be forwarded to his actual address. While we do not know how much danger he actually faced at that point, his caution speaks for itself that he felt himself to be a wanted man.

Two years later, the doctor's journal entry from August 5, 1948, is completely dismal. From the Robert Bosch Hospital in Stuttgart he described himself as "impoverished to the ultimate degree, with few marks in my pocket, and with deep concern as to supporting my family in the next months, until the income from my office, which I opened 10 days ago, can become our livelihood."

As it turned out, Fritz and Leonore spent three months in a repatriation camp near Stuttgart before they were ordered to return to Fritz's birthplace: Hamburg. Fritz's mother lived in a small, two-bedroom apartment. Her elderly cousin lived in the second bedroom, but moved out when Fritz and Lonore arrived. For a short time, it seemed as if life might return to a semblance of normality. Fritz's knowledge of English and Japanese in addition to German eventually led to him being hired by a German friend in his export/import business. He was grateful beyond words for the opportunity to earn money again for a good day's labor. While Fritz was at work, his mother cared for Leonore; when he came home after work he relieved his mother and cared for his wife. They managed that way for the next two years, but Leonore never regained her health.

The news from Germany was nearly always heartbreaking, but Helga resisted the urge to feel guilty that she had been given a new start. She could not help the suffering her father and his family had endured. So many German people had been supplanted, so many had lost their possessions and much, if not all, of their wealth. In America, she would earn money to send to her family in Europe. She would earn money and buy food and basic necessities to send to her loved ones. She would be useful. She would make her life count.

But life in the States was as yet unimaginable. Expectations were set for her to become an American, but it hardly mattered. She would always be German, no matter what the U.S. government said. That much she knew. But so many things she could not possibly know—for example, how hard would Colonel Watson expect her to work? Helga shook her head slowly. She was accustomed to *having* a maid, not *being* one. True, they had hired her as a nanny, but she would soon find out just how much housework they expected of her.

"Do we have a passenger named Helga Hofmeier?" The voice startled her out of such faraway thoughts and brought her attention back to the deck of the ocean liner steaming westward. "Is there a Miss Helga Hofmeier? Cupid is calling for you."

She stepped back from the railing and turned to face one of the deckhands. A smiling American soldier held out a sheet of paper in his hand. "A telegram, miss. These airwaves are reserved for military, but apparently you know somebody who can get around that." He smiled as he handed her the telegram and then scooted away.

DEAREST HELGA. I LOVE YOU AND I MISS YOU. I WILL SEE YOU SOON. LOVE, JESSE.

Helga clutched the telegram wondering what would become of their budding romance. When Jesse had driven her to the dock to say good-bye, he seemed more emotional than she. Jesse owed the U.S. Army Air Forces nine more months in Japan and planned to be a career military man. He hadn't exactly asked her to marry him—it was more of a feeling between them. Would he come find her when he returned to the United States at the end of the year?

She sailed first class on the *President McKinley,* a freighter that carried four American men and two American women who were Helga's cabin mates. One of the women, who worked for the United Nations Organization, spent most of her time with the captain. Helga noticed how informally the Americans behaved, and the subjects they chose for conversation were frivolous to her. Trying to get an idea of what the country looked like, she asked her fellow passengers, "Where do you live?" Sometimes they showed her a picture of a house in a neighborhood, sometimes it was a cabin in the woods.

The food was a welcome repast from the near-starvation of postwar Tokyo. Helga relished the meals and was glad for the linen tablecloths and linen napkins that she was accustomed to. And yet Japan tugged at her heart. With each nautical mile she realized how much she would miss those years, growing into a woman in Japan. The voyage was cold and rocky and difficult physically, but she regained her sea legs quickly and never suffered from seasickness. She had hoped to go to Hawaii, but from Japan they headed north toward Alaska. Reaching the Aleutian Islands, they docked to make a freight delivery. Then they headed south again.

Helga loved to watch the humpback whales defy gravity, shooting their heavy bodies past the surface of the water, leaping into the air and crashing their full weight against the ocean surface with obvious glee. The miles at sea passed quickly enough: they left Japan on February 3 and arrived in the port of San Francisco on Valentine's Day.

An immigration officer was the first person to cross the gangplank, looking for all emigrants and collecting their papers. Helga showed him the various letters and documents she had collected from the Japanese government and from Colonel Watson. Next step was to identify her luggage. The officer opened both of the large wooden crates and peeked inside at the clothing, fine linens and china, and heavy framed photographs as he asked question after question. "What are these things you have brought with you? Where are you going? Are you traveling alone?" When she explained her destination, the officer quickly stamped her papers and moved to the next person.

A well-dressed couple in their sixties smiled and waved in her direction from the dock. Helga glanced behind her on either side but no one was waving back. She scanned the dock again: neither Colonel Watson nor his wife was in sight, but the older couple kept waving in her direction.

"Helga?" the man asked as Helga started down the gangway.

It was Colonel Watson's parents, who welcomed her with open arms and helped usher her through customs. The fact that Mr. Watson Sr. was a retired Army colonel was no doubt helpful. Helga had detailed the contents of each crate and suitcase, and the immigration officers opened only one of her suitcases, stamped her papers and let her pass through.

The Watsons arranged for her crates to be sent to the colonel's home and escorted Helga to their luxury car. They showed her around San Francisco a bit before arriving at the Hotel Canterbury on Sutter Street. The Watsons paid for Helga's private room with a private bathroom, all of which she found quite elegant. By the time she had cleaned herself up and put on a fresh dress, it was late afternoon. The plan was to meet the Watsons in the hotel dining room at six and then join them for the movie afterward. Newly released, *The Treasure of the Sierra Madre* starred Humphrey Bogart and promised to be an exciting cinematographic experience about mining for precious metals in the American West.

First, though, Helga needed a walk. Besides, the view from her room was blocked by another building. She needed to see the shops and vendors close up.

She stood in front of a flower shop, puzzled by the sight of big red hearts, when a voice sounded behind her. She jumped.

"Do you like this window? A friendly American in uniform smiled down at her, removing his officer's cap.

"Actually, I am thinking it is a strange decoration. I've never seen anything like that."

"Do you like hearts and flowers?"

"I like to look at flowers, but why are there so many hearts?

"It's Valentine's Day."

"But what does that mean?"

"You give a flower to people you love."

The more he tried to explain, the more confused she was.

"That's nice, but I have never heard of it," she said, not quite giving in to a smile. Yet she was curious about him. "What are you doing here?"

"I might ask the same of you," he said. "I am on leave. I have to go back to Fairbanks in two days; this is my vacation."

"I just arrived from Japan."

"Japan? Oh! I was in Japan last year on duty. I thought you looked familiar. Did you ever go to any parties with Japanese people who attended American colleges?"

"Yes, of course—I also thought you looked familiar."

The warmth between them grew effortlessly, two international strangers meeting in front of a flower shop on Valentine's Day.

"A beautiful girl like you should have a corsage."

"What's a corsage?" She knew many words in English from her years in Japan, but this was not one that she had ever known or needed before.

He ducked inside the flower shop and returned with a gardenia corsage, which he pinned to Helga's collar. The scent of the white flowers was intoxicatingly sweet. The two of them walked the streets, talking and getting to know each other until it was time for dinner. As he escorted Helga into the dining room, Mrs. Watson invited him to join them for dinner. [Helga, in her modesty and grace, prefers not to name the Valentine's Day soldier.]

The Watsons and the soldier chatted while the famished Helga dove into her food. After so many months of scarcity in Japan, her focus was riveted on eating. The Americans chatted about army life, and after dinner Mrs. Watson invited the soldier to join them for the movie. He proposed meeting for breakfast instead, adding that he'd like to show Helga around town.

Helga understood very little of the movie and nearly fell asleep from exhaustion. She recovered quickly, however, for she and her Valentine's date were inseparable the next day as he toured her around the city, sightseeing at the Golden Gate Bridge and in Chinatown, then stopping later to investigate an all-American sport: bowling.

"Do you like bowling?"

"What's that?"

Helga wasn't interested in trying the sport, so they ate popcorn, drank Coca-Cola, and watched the bowlers. They finished the day with a hamburger in the streetcar diner, where he told Helga about his childhood on Lake Erie, the cold winters and ice fishing, time in the woods as a boy. They traded addresses and pledged to write each other.

Arriving at the Watsons' home in Coronado, Helga was shown to her room, which she found quite acceptable.

"And these are your maid uniforms," Mrs. Watson said, gesturing into the closet in Helga's room.

Helga rose to her full height, scrutinizing the black-and-white dresses. "I have my own clothes."

"But these are the clothes that our maid always wears."

"I will wear my own clothes."

Five days after arriving, Helga wrote her mother, first describing the voyage and then getting down to business:

> I sold the *kura*, pool, and land to the neighbors, the Oinumas, for 70,000 yen. I couldn't buy any dollars and it would have been very risky, anyway, so I bought a beautiful sable fur coat for 65,000 yen—it's dark brown and I got it for half price because of my friend at the Imperial Hotel. I think I spent the money wisely.
>
> I'm happy with my teeth—the dentist tightened [the braces] every day, and he was able to remove them two days before I sailed. I still wear a night guard. The whole thing cost me 12,000 yen.
>
> I've received both my crates—the freight cost $18—and $7 customs in San Francisco. They did not search my possessions in either Yokohama or San Francisco. I had declared everything I had, so they must have thought I was honest. Everyone was very friendly.
>
> Colonel Watson's parents met me at the ship. He is a retired colonel, about 70; she is younger. For their age, they are quite peppy. They picked me up in their new black Lincoln. They gave me a tour of San Francisco that afternoon. It is a heavenly city.

In the mornings Helga cooked breakfast, first for the colonel, then for the boys; Mrs. Watson sometimes slept late or had breakfast later with her parents. By the time she had cleaned the kitchen and straightened the house, it was time to go shopping. In her first few weeks, Mrs. Watson's parents were staying in one of the guestrooms, so she shopped and cooked for six.

A landscaped peninsula full of wealthy retirees, Coronado is one of the most beautiful and most expensive places to live in the country. Helga found it much to her liking since until World War II she had enjoyed many of the finer things in life

Before long, the Watsons trusted her enough to leave the boys with her for a week while they went on a trip together. Before leaving, the colonel told Helga, "If those boys don't listen to you, you can put them over your knee."

"That's not my job," she told him. "I will tell the boys what to do, and if they don't do it, I will tell you later."

"Isn't the Germanic way of childrearing harsher than the American way?" The colonel was clearly puzzled at her reluctance to use corporal punishment on the children.

She tried to explain. "The way I was taught, if a parent said no, that's all there was to it, and if the child didn't obey, there was a punishment. Apparently I was not difficult as a child; I always did as I was told."

When the Watsons entertained, Helga served drinks and hors d'oeuvres. Once a week she vacuumed, but the regular maid washed floors, cleaned toilets, and took care of the dirty work.

She worked six days a week. On Thursdays she usually went into town and window-shopped or bought basic living supplies for her parents: bandages, wheat, butter, and wool sweaters against the terrible cold. Sometimes she took in a movie.

Her contact with men was for the most part limited to letters. The third officer of the *President McKinley* wrote her several times and came to take her to lunch one day. "Helga, I am in love with you. I can't stop thinking of you. I'm going to divorce my wife and marry you. I have a big house in San Francisco. . . ."

"I can't do that," she told him. "I am engaged."

Then there was Herbert, another gentleman she had met in Germany who also wanted to marry her, but he was in the Sudeten and, she concluded, had nothing to offer her financially.

The Valentine date wrote without fail every week, sometimes twice a week. But eventually, his interest became more personal—some would say overbearing. "I don't like it that you are taking care of those children and that house," he wrote. "I talked to my mother about this, and she said she would take you in."

"I have a contract with these people," she told him. "Besides, I am engaged."

Despite his disappointment, the Valentine's date continued to write Helga. He wanted her to know that he had made colonel, he sent her books: one on U.S. immigration, one on how to live on a budget. She found him pleasant, but she was too busy taking care of her duties to pay much attention to his entreaties. He pointed out that if she saved up her money, she could buy her way out of her contract sooner. He didn't know—and she didn't point out—that she was sending care packages to her parents in Germany.

Helga had very little money and was exhausted much of the time, taking care of the boys and managing the household. She was up at dawn and worked on her feet until long after dark. In addition to caring for the Watson family, she had her own laundry and ironing and sewing repairs to tend to. The Watsons' washing machine was broken, so Helga washed all of their clothes by hand. Moreover, the colonel's uniforms needed special attention.

When she saw an advertisement for a new washing machine, she was floored. "You dump the clothes in a tub and add water and soap," she wrote her mother. "Then you push the button. When the machine stops, the laundry is clean, rinsed, and wrung out. Your hands don't even get wet! But the beast costs over $300!"

Discovering that other maids in the Watsons' upscale neighborhood earned $60 per month, Helga asked Mrs. Watson for a raise. The bold move earned her an additional $10 monthly.

She slipped into the driver's seat of the Watsons' Jeep for her first driving lesson and found it not a difficult task. Once she had mastered the Jeep, the Watsons allowed Helga to drive their Cadillac. She practiced as often as she could and avoided heavy traffic, keeping to the quiet streets of Coronado neighborhoods.

On her day off, Helga shopped in San Diego for basic necessities to send to her parents in the repatriation camp. She purchased only those that would ship well and arrive safely for her parents to use: powdered eggs, lard or butter in a can, and canned soup were almost impossible to find, available only to soldiers and occasionally for exorbitant prices on the black market, but she continued to search for them. She worried constantly about her parents' health, whether they were hungry or cold.

She discovered a store named Goodwill, where people donated their clothes, and she shopped there every week to find warm clothing for her family in Germany. The problem was she knew her mother's taste, and the fashionable ladies' clothes were priced well above what Helga could afford. One day she came upon a white wool jacket her mother's size and proudly shipped it along with her weekly letter.

Sometimes cigarettes were considered contraband, sometimes not; what could and could not be sent varied from time to time. Helga paid close attention: she had always been one to obey the rules. Besides, if her package was opened and its full contents hadn't been accurately declared, any future shipments to her parents could be banned.

How to get more money? She studied the pearl ring and pearl broach her Valentine's date had sent her and considered selling it to buy food for her parents.

In March, she wrote her mother that she planned to marry an American soldier and stay in the United States. It is easy to imagine how the news might have struck Leonore's heart: forced to live in inhumane conditions in what amounted to a concentration camp while the conditions of surrender were enforced by Americans and Russians, she may have despised them both.

Helga's May 28 letter to her mother begins with an apology. "You are probably angry I haven't written," then moves quickly to a positive note of "heartfelt thanks for your lovely letters," and finally settles into a detailed account of recent care packages she has sent to them. The package must have been large and cost plenty to ship, holding soap powder, sugar, raisins, plums, sardines, sandwich bags, honey, yeast, chocolate syrup, and more.

She had already prepared her next shipment to them, containing Crisco, Lux laundry soap, hand lotion, dried milk, margarine, two packs of cigarettes, eye shadow, cleaning brushes, and used clothing for the boys. Mrs. Watson had given permission to send her boys' hand-me-downs to Helga's nephews in Germany.

"I don't think there will be another war any time soon," she wrote her mother. "The Russians will wait, and one day their alliance will fall apart. Do you have any thoughts about the Marshall Plan? One always tries to console oneself, thinking it's getting better in Germany, but I don't believe it."

She included a photograph of her betrothed, adding that his smile seemed forced, explaining that "he says he has nothing to be happy about since I left Japan." Then young Helga puts her foot down and makes it clear that she will marry this American regardless of her mother's support:

> Your request for information about his family is ridiculous. Jesse would never allow that, and I would never ask him. I would rather meet the family myself and make my own judgments. You have really funny ideas sometimes. I'm also not going to send you one of his letters, either. His letters are to me and not for the critique of others! If you want to see his handwriting, I'll send you the envelope from one of his letters to me. He hasn't ever questioned me about my family, even though the military is very strict about foreign relatives. He just wrote that the CIC still watches him. It started the day we first went on a public date. He works Top Secret items and has a special

pass for that called a Cryptographic Clearance. Those are only for people with clear backgrounds and without connections to foreign countries. I hope he doesn't lose it when we marry, but he says it doesn't matter. We'll just see how it works out.

Although Helga ends the letter with the usual "hugs and kisses" salutation, there is no doubt that she has put her mother on notice: *I will not tolerate your doubts about my choices.*

Leonore wasn't the only one questioning Helga about Jesse. Colonel Watson wasn't fond of the idea that she planned to marry an enlisted man.

"You should marry an officer."

"I haven't met any—unless you are planning to introduce me to a few." She gave him the smallest smile.

Helga acknowledged she would be leaving before the holiday and that Jesse would give him the money to buy out her contract. The Colonel wondered if she was truly in love with Jesse or simply enthralled with the uniform. "Have you ever seen him in civilian clothes?"

"Actually, no."

"You are a very stubborn person," the colonel said.

"As are you."

"You can do better—with your family background and your intelligence, you would make a perfect officer's wife." But when the Watsons had hosted parties, the colonel consistently steered single men away from Helga, regardless of rank. No sense in ruining a good thing.

Three of Colonel Watson's friends did have an immense impact on Helga: Colonel and Mrs. Schwenk and their infant daughter. Someone, probably Colonel Watson, snapped a photograph of Helga holding the Schwenk's baby, Cynthia Jane, as the Schwenks stand in the background. Helga's face, always sensuous, is alight. She is charmed. She either sent or planned to send the photograph to someone, because on the back, she wrote, "What do you think of my new baby, Cynthia?"

Since Jesse worked in communications, he had made several calls to call Helga from Japan, using a short-wave radio. That way, they could talk for free for as long as they wanted, but the reception was always choked with interference from other signals.

Helga and Jesse both wanted to be sure she would be happy living in the South—or at least find out if she could get along with his family.

"Both of us had heard stories about some of the foreign girls who ended up after the war in Arkansas or Louisiana under poor conditions," Jesse said. "She wanted to be sure and I wanted to be sure that if she went to Louisiana, she'd find out that people who lived there actually had bathrooms."

Since he was still in Tokyo, she was on her own to plan the trip. Boarding the first bus, and on each one afterward, she sat directly behind the driver and asked, "Please—will you tell me where I should get off to change buses? I have no idea where I am going."

It was September 1948. She got her first idea of the size of the United States as she rode sixteen hundred miles, the first part through desert: Phoenix, El Paso, Tucson, and Houston. For three long days and two sleepless nights, Helga watched the landscape slide past through the windows of Greyhound buses barreling eastward toward the Deep South.

At one of the stations, she sat on a bench awaiting the next bus.

"Wrong bench," a voice said.

Helga turned to find an African-American man regarding her with a puzzled expression.

"I'm sorry, I don't understand."

"You're on the bench for the blacks," he said. "Can't you read?"

"Yes, I can read."

"See that sign? It says blacks only."

"What is a black?"

"Negroes, lady." He shook his head. "You ain't from here, are you?"

Her experience with class distinction as a child in Germany and a young woman in Japan had not given witness to the level of disrespect and hatred that existed in some parts of the southern U.S. between Caucasians and African-Americans. In fact, she had almost no exposure to African-Americans. In her short time in California, Helga had seen Mexican and Filipino workers, but on her tour through the American South, it was African-Americans who served food in the dining car and carried luggage. When Helga asked a white woman about the separation between races, the woman had replied, "That's the law. They're separate from us. It's better this way—for both races."

Jesse hadn't told his mother much about the young lady who was coming. Initially, he simply told her he had met a girl. For months, his mother Pearl had assumed that her son was dating a Japanese girl. When the visit was planned, Jesse sent Helga's photograph and asked his mom to make her comfortable and introduce her to family and friends.

He did not mention Helga's stepfather's work in the German embassy, or her father's association with Nazis as their physician, or Helga's past as a Hitler Youth. It simply did not bother him. He figured it was all in the past. But he saw how Helga struggled with her various cultural identities, how she worked internally to deal with anti-German sentiment. He had no doubts that his family would welcome his beautiful fiancée with open arms and crawfish gumbo.

Pearl brought her Cajun mother along to greet Helga at the Eunice bus station: the two women recognized Helga immediately from the photo Jesse had sent. They were smiling and friendly and talkative, but Helga understood only part of what came out of their mouths.

Jesse's mother, Pearl Bellow, had deep French roots. The colorful muumuu dresses and the French-Cajun brand of English spoken by Jesse's relatives were unlike anything Helga had ever encountered. They spoke only Cajun between themselves, which was nearly indecipherable to Helga's ears.

Jesse's family lived in the middle of nowhere in rural Louisiana. The general area of St. Landry Parish was a wide part of the road called Swords. The road in front of the house had no official name; it was described in official books as "starting at Willie Moreau's house and heading north at the Parish Line."

Jesse's father had built the house by hand. It was modern by the standards of the day and place, which meant that it had indoor plumbing. Pearl led Helga to a chair in the living room, then disappeared into the kitchen. Soon she trotted out of the kitchen with a tray of coffee, cream and sugar. Helga found the thick Louisiana coffee with its customary chicory absolutely horrible. She drank it, but the thick concoction made her heart beat so fast that she politely refused all Cajun coffee afterward.

The next day word had already gotten around Eunice that there was a stranger in town. A tribe of relatives and friends soon gathered in the living room. Helga did the best she could to understand, but for the most part, she simply listened. At dinnertime the family specialty was served: homemade gumbo with crawfish caught by hand in nearby streams. Helga did her best to enjoy the meal served, but the spicy heat made her eyes water constantly.

Most people in Eunice had learned English as a second language. Only Cajun French was spoken in the house when Jesse was a boy; when he entered first grade, he learned to speak English out of necessity. Becoming a self-taught bilingual at the age of six may be one of the reasons he later was a whiz at telecommunications. Translating words came naturally.

Jesse had assured Helga that Cajuns spoke English. However, listening to all the family members speaking half English and half Cajun-French around the dinner table, Helga chuckled to herself. *I don't feel like such a foreigner anymore; my English is better than theirs.*

When the locals in Eunice heard Helga speak, they recognized an accent but couldn't place it. "Are you from the north?" they would ask.

Language wasn't the only glaring difference between Helga and the family of her betrothed. She struggled to find cultural equilibrium in the informality of the Cajun household. Jesse's family was very kind to Helga—attentive to her needs—but the lifestyle differences were jarring. In the front yard, chickens clucked and pecked at the ground.

Helga had eaten nearly every meal of her life with sterling silver utensils, china, and a fine linen tablecloth. Her mother and father dressed formally, even in the home. The women in Jesse's family wore tent-like dresses and used plastic dinnerware on a bare table. They ate cabbage but not salads. They served more meat in a day than Helga usually ate in several days, and much of it had been caught wild on the day it was cooked: crawfish, shrimp, mussels, squirrel. For breakfast they served plenty of fried eggs and pork sausage, whereas Helga was accustomed to eating a slice of fresh bread and a small chunk of cheese. It seemed to her that the Americans wasted food.

Helga began to wonder: What is Cajun? Within a day or two, her ears had acclimated to the strange accent, and she was able to decipher some of the Cajun French. Perhaps most clearly of all, Helga began to comprehend the tribal bond between Cajuns: the pride of the pack, the strong family ties, and the shared past of surviving expulsion from France several generations earlier. Helga began to understand the earthy poetry of the language: *Cajun blood runs thick as bayou water.*

Jesse's family home wasn't far from the segregated neighborhood where the African Americans lived. "We don't like them in our neighborhoods, and they don't like us in theirs," a family member explained. "You don't go down there unless you got business there."

Cultural differences aside, Helga and her future in-laws enjoyed each other. "My family liked her right away," Jesse said. To help her feel more comfortable, they took her to meet German-speaking people: members of the growing German community who had moved to Louisiana before the war.

Helga rode the bus through the American countryside and back to Coronado, relatively content that life in America with Jesse would work out. But she did not want to ask him for any money. She would ask him to help her pay off the Watsons only as a last resort. "It would have been much cheaper to have married him in Japan," she decided. "Everything, including my trip to America, would have been paid for. But this way is better for his career, and so this is the way we will do it."

Now with the confirmation that Helga was indeed leaving, Mrs. Watson began training a new maid and sent Helga to live with the colonel's parents for the next week. The elder Watsons offered to pay Helga the same salary she had gotten from the colonel, but she refused.

"I will live with you for a week and I will help you—but I will not take money from you," she told them. Her fiancé was coming to buy her way out of servanthood. She wanted to show her gratitude to the elder Watsons for the days spent in their home, but she also wanted to sleep as late as eight if she chose, not rise at 6:30. She wanted to feel like a free woman.

"We arranged that I would stop in San Diego and we'd get married and travel together from there to Louisiana," Helga remembers. Passenger trains had been a sketchy form of public transportation in the United States since the early 1900s, rising and declining in popularity in relation to the economy and the use and availability of private automobiles. Railway companies included Pennsylvania, Chicago, Denver and Rio Grande Western Railroad, and Western Pacific.

Jesse took a train from northern California to Coronado, booked a hotel room, and then headed to Colonel and Mrs. Watson's house, where Helga had returned. When she first opened the door, Helga didn't recognize him at first glance, in his civilian outfit of a turtleneck sweater and jacket. She introduced him to the Watsons, and the four of them chatted in the living room for a while. Jesse thought to himself, *"These people have a soul. They don't want to hold her back from an opportunity to make a life for herself. They're being pretty nice about this."*

The men went into the den to speak privately. It wasn't long before Jesse came out of the room and joked with Helga, "You come cheap." He had paid two hundred dollars to complete her agreement with the Watsons.

The next day, Jesse and Helga set out to complete the tasks necessary to marry: having blood tests, getting shots—and visiting a Catholic priest.

As a Cajun boy in Louisiana, Jesse had heard the stories hundreds of times: his ancestors, French Acadians, had sought refuge in Louisiana because they refused to pledge unconditional loyalty to England. They refused to forsake the Catholic Church. Jesse was raised Catholic; he had served as an altar boy. He had given serious thought to the reality that his wife would be most responsible for parenting while he worked and traveled for the military. He also believed in religious freedom and would not ask his wife to forsake the church of her childhood, the Lutheran Church.

The priest had a different idea. "The children will need to be raised Catholic."

"But the children should be what my wife is," Jesse answered. "We'll be traveling across the world, and I will be gone a lot. Helga will be their teacher, their number-one parent."

"Also, since you're not Catholic, the wedding can't take place at the main altar; it must be at the side altar."

Jesse would have none of that. He was equally determined that Helga would not arrive in the United States as a war bride. A foreign girl who came into the U.S. as the new wife of an American soldier was not given the same respect as a foreign woman who married an American soldier in the U.S. Besides, he wanted to be married to Helga before launching their future across the South to Louisiana. The wedding, which was simple and frugal, took place on December 22, 1948, in the San Diego Lutheran Church, officiated by the Lutheran pastor and with his wife as the only witness. A three day train ride from San Diego to Louisiana would be their honeymoon.

Life in America—if not as an American—had begun. It was the third country Helga would call home in only two decades. "I was very excited," Helga remembers. "I had found a man I loved and I would have a permanent last name."

Helga entered America armed with an array of cultural survival tactics. From childhood she had been thrown into circumstances that forced her to develop resilience and resourcefulness. She knew how to thrive in unmentionable circumstances. Once again she would adjust quickly: take up a new language, decipher a new monetary system, fit into a new culture. The German child who had survived World War II on two continents entered American society in 1948 as the stunningly beautiful wife of an American patriot. Setting a course for American citizenship, she privately wondered if the paperwork would change her self-image as a German. Time would soon answer Helga's question.

Helga. Coronado. 1948.

Chapter Eleven

Becoming American

THE NEWLYWEDS SPENT THE WEEK FOLLOWING THEIR WEDDING in a most unromantic setting: Jesse's old bedroom in his mothers' house. But after everything they'd been through, perhaps nesting in the family tree for a few days was the perfect move. A few days after New Year's, Jesse's relatives packed up the couple, their belongings, and their wedding presents and drove them to Shreveport.

A stone's throw from Texas and Arkansas, Shreveport was originally Caddo Indian country. Cotton and corn were hauled up and down the Red River that ran through town, making it a natural stop for commerce in the decades to come. The world's largest airfield at the time, Barksdale, had been carved out in the 1930s. During World War II, bomber pilots were trained there. The base also housed a national weather observation center, which brought Jesse Edmonds to Shreveport.

Jesse's work in communications had brought him into what Helga called "the secrecy business." She was not allowed to talk about her husband's work—what little she knew about it.

"If I don't tell you, then you won't have to lie," he explained. When it was time to head out for a new assignment, he would simply say, "I'm on a new project now," and fly off to Africa, or Turkey, or the Marshall Islands. But the simple truth was, he usually didn't know where he was going.

I have no secrets in my life, Helga thought to herself. I have nothing to hide.

They lived in a furnished apartment upstairs from an elderly couple; a convenient location on the bus route so Jesse could get a ride to the base. Although the landlords were pleasant enough, the wife let them know that her beloved brother had been killed in the war, in Germany.

"I'm sorry. . . ." Helga struggled for the right words to fit the moment. How could she give a heartbroken old woman the solace she sought? "I'm so sorry for your loss." She could think of nothing else to say. Of course Hitler was all wrong, but was she, as a German, responsible for the deaths of Americans in World War II?

Jesse took the anti-German bias in stride. "If something was said to me about Nazis, I just grinned and let it go past," he said.

In the coming months and years, Helga would begin to fathom the numbers of Americans and Europeans who harbored a sense of revenge against Germans. Her relatives in Germany regularly detailed the poor living conditions, discrimination, and harassment they received at the hands of Americans and Russians. But it would be decades before the world began to understand that hundreds of thousands of Germans died of starvation and ill treatment in Allied-occupied Germany. "Eisenhower's death camps" became public knowledge too late.

But America in the 1950s, as Helga had hoped, was full of promise. In Shreveport she had the freedom to fashion her own home for the first time. She relished the chance to set up house, to create her nest. It was an exciting time to be a new homemaker in the United States, since postwar consumer industry was exploding with new household appliances and products. Factories that had made weapons, tanks, and planes were easily converted to turn out automobiles and electrical appliances. Electric refrigerators, ovens, washers, and dryers paraded their way across new television sets (showing programs in black and white), Sears catalogs, and newspaper pages. The booming consumer industry birthed thousands of jobs for returning GIs who would now expand their families and were in need of work.

Throughout the 1940s, the War Production Board had lorded over the rationing of basic supplies in the United States, including flour and sugar. A program of resource conservation was promoted across the country. In the 1950s, mass consumerism stepped into the spotlight and never left. Consumption of consumer goods became not only fun and life enhancing, it was seen as a patriotic act. Americans were initially divided: some had lived under restrictions so long that they couldn't wait to begin spending; others had become philosophically if not habitually opposed to wasting resources.

Jesse decided immediately to let Helga rule the house; from her perspective there was no alternative but for him to let her do what she pleased with it. "In our home, she lived the way she used to live in Germany," he said.

Helga created a home that her mother and father would have awarded approval. The table was meticulously set with a complete silver setting, linen tablecloths, and linen napkins and silver napkin rings. Every night that Jesse was in town, the two of them sat together at dinner.

Their apartment was walking distance to the base and to everything a woman of the 1950s could want in a town. Helga had always made friends easily, and she quickly met other German women who were wives of soldiers. They walked everywhere together. Lunch at the cafeteria was sometimes the highlight of the day, choosing happily from a selection of buffet-line hot and cold dishes and enjoying a home-cooked meal at an affordable price. The brightly lit room was made brighter from the spirits of the ladies who were so happy they didn't have to cook lunch or wash dishes.

"A house must have a certain orderliness," Helga told a friend. "I learned orderliness at home. When you use something, you should put it back in its place right away and not leave it sitting around for two or three days, especially if you don't have any house help. My mother always said, 'If you take this out, you put it up; that's not the maid's job.'"

Helga found a good hairdresser who gave her a modern hair-do. Before going out in public she styled her thick, wavy hair, applied lipstick, and dressed in a nice blouse and skirt, nylons, and heels. Like all well-dressed women of the 1950s, she loved to wear gloves and had a dozen pair in different colors. Sometimes she wore a small, stylish hat. She was what one of her German relatives called "the embodiment of an American lady." Jesse, on the other hand, didn't seem like the typical American man to Helga's relatives "because he doesn't drink Coca-Cola, chew gum, or smoke cigarettes."

One of Helga's favorite shops in Shreveport was a small kosher deli owned by a friendly Jewish man who spoke German with her. She delighted in finding dark and light European bread and the kinds of pickles and cabbage she loved so much as a young girl in Germany. Her friendships with German Jews in Shreveport brought her closer to Jewish culture than in her childhood.

The South had its own levels of hierarchy and proximity. Jesse's mother had a black maid who came in and took care of the dreaded hot chore of ironing. When the work was done, Pearl and the maid would sit together at the kitchen table and chat about different people in the community. But everything the maid did took place in the kitchen. She obeyed an unspoken rule not to go into the living space of the house.

Helga thoroughly enjoyed Rubenstein's, a popular department store in Shreveport where she could find the kind of hosiery and finer ladies' accessories she enjoyed. As the weather warmed and the short winter ended, she was able to store her expensive sable coat at Rubenstein's for the summer. One day Mr. Rubenstein approached her and asked if she wanted to work in the hosiery department.

A German woman had just opened a charge account, and Mr. Rubinstein saw Helga's bilingual skills as a great advantage for his store. Helga didn't know what a charge account was but found out soon and also discovered that she was a natural at retail sales in ladies' accessories. Working at Rubenstein's she met other German women and became lifelong friends with several of them.

In early May 1949, Helga found herself sick to her stomach—every morning. She and Jesse were overjoyed to learn that she was pregnant. But it wasn't long before Mr. Rubenstein advised her to stay home, take a break, and come back to work when the morning sickness was gone.

It was a prudish time in America. Even in the media, the sight of a man and a woman in bed was taboo. Married people in movies and in television shows slept in two single beds with a nightstand between them. Famous couples like Ricky and Lucy Ricardo on the *I Love Lucy* show were not seen touching each other or sleeping together. Helga's parents had always slept together in a double bed, so this part of American culture was perplexing to her.

One weekend she and Jesse splurged, rented a car, and hit the road. They drove to Baton Rouge and stopped at a hotel outside of town, where rooms were cheaper. The newlyweds were counting their pennies.

Jesse asked for a room with a double bed.

The hotel manager skeptically regarded the military man and the beautiful blonde by his side.

"Are you married? If you're not married, you can't have a room together. It's the law."

Only after Jesse assured the manager that Helga was indeed his lawfully wedded wife was a room key produced.

Life as the wife of a career military man means one thing: moving, moving, moving. In November they moved to Omaha; Helga, six months pregnant, managed the long train ride without getting sick. Offutt Air Force Base in Omaha housed Strategic Air Command headquarters as well as the U.S. Air Force Weather Agency and strategic bomb and reconnaissance wings.

They were also moving up in the world: Jesse bought their first car, a brand-new Plymouth sedan. A healthy baby girl was born January 25, 1950. They named the baby Leonore Jane—Leonore after Helga's mother, and Jane after the first American baby girl that she ever held in her arms: Cynthia Jane. (When Helga had a second child, she named it Cynthia.) That year was pivotal for Helga: she became a mother and lost her own mother.

Leonore's health, frail most of her life, steadily diminished before she was repatriated from Japan, but conditions in the cold repatriation camp in Germany literally sucked the life from her. There was never enough food. Medical attention was scarce. There were no books, there was no music. There was little to warm the body or spirit. A failing gallbladder sent Leonore into emergency surgery; she died July 7 on the operating table in a Hamburg hospital at the age of 48.

"My mother loved Rilke," Helga said, telling her girlfriend about her loss. "In the evenings, we would read books for hours. We looked forward to our reading time. We'd look at each other and say, 'Let's go finish our chapter!' Sometimes she read; sometimes I read while my mother sewed. She made beautiful embroidery: tablecloths, napkins. She made my doll's clothes. She was constantly working on something."

Missing her mother, missing all things German, Helga took solace in being able to speak her native tongue with a few close friends. "The German language is very important to me," she told her friend. "There are things you can say in your own language that aren't translatable: jokes and stories. Some things just don't translate. Your language is who you are. Your language is where you belong. The language hits your heart."

Helga had been a foreigner in strange lands since leaving Germany as a nine-year-old. Repeatedly she had witnessed the difficulties, sometimes heartache, caused by lack of paperwork. Unable to produce the exact papers of identity and passage required by a government, no one could go where they wanted. Worse, they could be detained indefinitely.

When World War II finally ended, the hated Germans were forced to return to their homeland. Helga had avoided repatriation by signing away two years of her life in servanthood to an American army colonel. She had slipped out of the nanny contract early by marrying Jesse. Now, although she was the wife of an American, legally she was a stateless citizen. When she left Japan, her emigration papers stated her race as "Aryan."

The paperwork wall arose again when Jane was born and Helga inquired about taking her child to Germany. Helga was told that as a German she could not take an American child to Germany, even if it was her own flesh and blood. She would need written permission from the child's American father or American grandparents.

Marrying a member of the U.S. military made Helga eligible for citizenship two years after coming into the country. She had arrived on Valentine's Day 1948 and been granted a green card, which made her a lawful permanent resident without changing her citizenship. Every year she was required to show the green card at the local post office and sign a paper stating her living address and taking an oath that she had not been arrested or in trouble with authorities.

She investigated her options for dual citizenship, but Hitler's ethnocentric laws were still in effect in Germany: any German citizen who married a foreigner lost German citizenship.

As an American, she could file to bring a German relative to the U.S.—and her petition would receive priority over those of non-Americans. If she accompanied Jesse to another country and needed help from her own government while there, a U.S. passport meant the U.S. government would intervene on her behalf. And Jesse's high security status would never be jeopardized because he was married to "a foreigner."

"I think of all these times in the war when people had to show identification to prove who they were," she told a friend. "And Jesse is gone so much. I am a foreigner. I want to have an American passport. I want my child to have an American passport. She will have proof of who she is. My husband is American, my child is American; my life will be American."

In February 1950, Helga initiated the paperwork, sending along two photographs of herself and the application fee. To be eligible for naturalization, she had to demonstrate "good moral character." The paperwork provided a list of actions that might demonstrate a lack of good moral character: crime against a person to do harm, fraud, using illegal drugs, being habitually drunk, being a prostitute, committing terrorist acts, polygamy. No problem there. She needed to be proficient in speaking, reading, and writing basic English: check. In time, she received a letter telling her to go to a certain location to be fingerprinted.

Everything was proceeding perfectly. Next, she would be interviewed and take a test on American civics.

It never occurred to her that in becoming American she would forsake all possibilities of resuming German citizenship in the future.

Jesse was about to leave again and wanted to move their little family to Eunice, closer to his family. Helga agreed. She was reluctant to live alone in a country whose citizens were so fiercely proud of defeating the Germans. She moved back to Eunice, into an apartment within ten minutes' walking distance of his parents' house.

As the months went on, Helga took special classes on American history and government. She must take the Oath of Allegiance.

The Oath of Allegiance

I hereby declare, on oath,

that I absolutely and entirely renounce and abjure all allegiance and fidelity to any foreign prince, potentate, state, or sovereignty, of whom or which I have heretofore been a subject or citizen;

that I will support and defend the Constitution and laws of the United States of America against all enemies, foreign and domestic;

that I will bear true faith and allegiance to the same;

that I will bear arms on behalf of the United States when required by the law;

that I will perform noncombatant service in the Armed Forces of the United States when required by the law;

that I will perform work of national importance under civilian direction when required by the law; and that I take this obligation freely without any mental reservation or purpose of evasion; so help me God.

Home life was calm and stable—until early January 1951, when
Jesse left on another secret mission. One night at midnight, she drove
him and his duffle bag to the train station. She didn't know where he
was going, and he didn't, either. He had instructions to show up on
a certain day and and at a certain place for briefing—then, he was
gone.

A letter arrived from the U.S. government in March. Helga was
instructed to appear at the Omaha courthouse on a certain morning
for her naturalization hearing. She booked a bus for Omaha and left
the baby with her mother-in-law's sister. As the cars rumbled down the
rails, Helga read the U.S. Constitution one last time. The Constitution sets out the branches of government, powers, and restrictions and
includes twenty-one amendments. The 21st Amendment repealed the
18th Amendment, which abolished the manufacture, sale or transport
of alcoholic beverages. Governments of all nations, Helga concluded,
changed their minds and their laws according to who held the balance
of power.

Waiting in the federal courthouse, Helga expected a formal ceremony with hundreds of people and a choir of jubilant children singing,
just like the two naturalization hearings she had attended with other
friends who took U.S. citizenship. But on this day, Helga stood with
just a handful of people. Their voices sounded quietly in the room as
they read the Oath of Allegiance. Then they placed their right hands
over their hearts and recited the Pledge of Allegiance.

In a ceremony that lasted less than twenty minutes, Helga relin-
quished her German nationality. A large American flag watched silently
from a pole in the corner. The stars and stripes seemed to say: *one nation, indivisible, with liberty and justice for all.* An immigration officer
handed each person a piece of paper.

Looking at the certificate, Helga's body flooded with mixed emotions. Something in her heart ached with the realization that she would
never be a German citizen again. In her mind's eye she saw the quiet
streets of Frankfurt am Main, she saw the apartment and the park in
Munich where she had played blissfully as a child. She saw the gentle

faces of her Herzeltäntchen and her Lückchen. Then, waves of relief took over as she realized that she had a new kind of power she did not have before. After long years of being stateless, unable to claim legal citizenship of any country at all, at last she had a homeland. She belonged somewhere. She belonged to America.

Forever after, when Helga was asked, "Where are you from," she would answer: "I was born in Germany, I grew up in Japan, and now . . . *I am an American.*"

Ten Rules to Live By

Asked to give advice garnered from living in dozens of different countries, Helga answers: "I cannot give anybody lessons." But here are some of Helga's thoughts about what matters most to her, gleaned from more than eighty years of living.

1. Be honest.

2. Realize that you have options: you must choose how to live your life. If you have an opportunity, take it; just like I left Germany to come to Japan and then to the United States.

3. Be happy with what you have; make the best of it and try to improve.

4. Education is important: the more you know, the more interesting your conversations and your life will be.

5. Family is important. Try to understand why family members may have done the things they have done. Put yourself in their condition. Don't forget where you came from because that's who you are, that you can't change. Your family forms your beginnings.

6. As a child, my father taught me not to discuss money. He said, "We have money and therefore we don't need to talk about it."

7. Expose yourself to different languages; learning more than one language is important. It helps you to know how to think in other languages. It is especially wonderful to read poetry in its original language.

8. Expose yourself to other cultures and religions: don't just go to work and home and stay in one circle. Respect those who are different from you. You cannot say that one is better than the other. As a child in Germany, I knew Catholics and Lutherans and Jews; in Japan I lived amidst Buddhism and Shintoism. I have known Muslims who are very loving people—men and women who work hard. You owe politeness and respect to all of them. You don't have to live as they do, but respect them. If more people would do that, we wouldn't have these wars.

9. In war, innocent people get killed. The wrong people get killed. Governments should be peaceful and talk with each other and let people live in peace.

10. Everybody cannot be in a democratic society as we are here. You cannot change the world; it is impossible. Be open to other societies; otherwise you make enemies of them.

Helga today.

Epilogue

MOM SLIPPED SEAMLESSLY INTO THE ROLE OF MILITARY WIFE. Although only twenty-three, her tumultuous life had already prepared her for unusual circumstances, strange situations and new adventures. Her new little family relocated often, but she enjoyed a wonderful sense of belonging and familiarity at every new air base. Her new military family provided a welcome sameness no matter where in the world she moved. And move she did – Omaha to Eunice and on to Presque Isle, Maine, then to Ankara, Turkey, in 1952. It was 1953 when Mom finally, and joyfully, reunited with her father, stepmother and three siblings while visiting Germany for the first time in almost twenty years. My sister Cindy was born in Ankara in 1955.

Mom felt at home (and made a home) anywhere Dad was stationed, always creating familiar surroundings for all of us. She was active in the military wives community, with our schools and with a growing circle of friends no matter where in the world we lived. I vividly remember family activities as diverse as poker nights and square dancing, charm school and highland fling lessons, riding camels and visiting World Fairs.

We moved to Pordenone, Italy, in 1956, where Dad's mother came to live with us for a year, and then to Grand Forks, North Dakota, in 1960. Dad received orders to Germany in 1961, but due to international tensions surrounding the building of the Berlin Wall, my mother, sister and I were not allowed to accompany him. How ironic that Mom finally had the opportunity to return to live in her homeland, but was held at a distance once again by political turmoil! We all did eventually join Dad in Wiesbaden in the spring of 1962, where Daddy greeted us holding a furry little wired-haired fox terrier puppy—

replacing the much loved dog that Mom had so sadly lost in 1945. Out last move was to Colorado Springs in 1965, where Mom and Dad bought their first house. Dad retired from the Air Force in 1966 but rejoined Civil Service several months later. As Cindy and I married and started our own lives, our parents once again moved to Germany in 1980 and finally to Pensacola in 1992.

As sometimes happens in otherwise wonderful families, my parents separated and divorced late in life. Mom has created a very comfortable nest for herself, sharing a home with her great friend, companion and care-giver, Brenda. Together they enjoy opera, international ladies clubs, both old and new friends and some travel. Dad married Joan, a wonderful woman who lovingly tolerates his restlessness and his abiding joy in always being on the go. My parents share three incredible grandchildren: my son Steve, a gregarious mechanical engineer who competes in Iron Man Triathlons; my nephew Kurt, a contemplative and studious difference maker who is completing his Ph.D. in economics; my niece Jessica, a social and outgoing whirlwind who is on her own fast track to success in management.

What have I learned from my mother? Without a doubt or pause, the most important lesson has been about family and friends: keep those who are important to you close to you. Be in contact with them. Share their lives, even, and especially, if you don't happen to live next door to them. Because of Mom, my sister and I remain full of interaction and in communication with our extended German family. My grandfather Kurt and Edith both died in Heidelberg, Germany, in 1988 and 1992, respectively. Although my mother's brothers, Hans and Fritz, and Fritz's wife, Edda, have all passed away, as well, we remain incredibly close to Hans's widow, Dorothee and to all our German cousins and their children. Mom's sister Röschen emigrated to Australia, but she and mom speak on the phone regularly, always including Röschen's children and grandchildren in the conversation. Mom also enjoys keeping in touch with her own cousin, Peter, who was born while Mom lived with his parents, her aunt (Herzeltäntchen) and uncle (Uncle Lückchen), in Munich in the early 1930s.

I also grew up knowing and enjoying the company of two very special friends my mother met during her early years in Japan – Anneliese Beyer and Thea Lohmeyer. These two ladies have shared all the ups and downs of my mother's life – her difficult life in Tokyo, her marriage, my birth, my grandmother's death, my sister's birth, our weddings, our children. These three friends remain true and loyal and entwined after seventy-five years—unimaginable if I didn't know them myself. (And because of that, I find it hardly surprising that my sister and Thea, worlds apart in both age and geography, share the same china pattern and that Anneliese and I can still share personal inside jokes!) It just doesn't get any better than that!

Together, Mom and I have worked to tie up loose ends in her life, as well. We've retraced her steps on Schradolfstrasse in Munich; we've visited the very home in the Bavarian Alps where she summered with her mother; she reconnected with the young Watson boys, learned what became of the Valentine officer, and now even knows what became of Cynthia Jane Schwenk. We've had great fun answering all the "I wonder what ever happened to?..." questions.

I continue to be amazed at Mom's life - first as the child of an affluent and intellectual family, then as a German in Japan during the war, then working as a nanny, then living, yet again as a foreigner, in a very conservative small bayou town in Louisiana on her own with an infant. As an adult, she moved and lived around the world, always creating a home no matter where she landed, her family always at the forefront of her thoughts. I grew up hearing many of the stories recounted in this book, always surprised at the resilience, poise, and lady-like demeanor she retained throughout her life, no matter what circumstances arose.

She was born into a life of privilege. She continued her privileged existence even during the horrific times in war torn Japan, and she finally found a warm and welcome continuity within her new military family. For her, it always comes back to family. Hers has indeed been a story of privilege, war and family!

Leonore Jane Lang, January 2013

Family Archives Photos

Else Gleim Zopke
(Omi). Engagement oil
portrait. 1898.

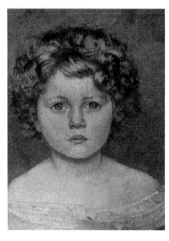

Leonore, three years old.
Oil portrait. 1905.

Hans Zopke. Berlin. 1904. This portrait
now hangs at the Technical Institute of
Berlin. In 1907, Hans Zopke founded the
Higher Technical State Institute of Berlin,
which later merged with two other institutes
of higher learning to become the
Technical Institute of Berlin.

Leonore and Ottony (Herzeltäntchen). Berlin. 1914.

Hans and Else (Omi) Zopke, on tour in Berchtesgaden, Germany. 1908. Else was horrified that she had a visible run in her stocking!

Friedrich Karl Robert Hofmeier. 1914.

Ottony (Herzeltäntchen) Zopke. Germany. 1920.

Leonore and Kurt (Vati) Hofmeier.
Engagement photo. 1922.

Leonore Zopke's engage-
ment photo. 1922.

Helga.Germany. 1927.

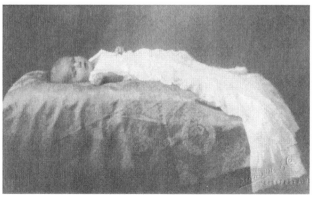

Helga. Christen-
ing photo. Frank-
furt, Germany.
1925.

Leonore, Helga, Else (Omi), and Ottony (Herzeltäntchen). Munich. 1929.

Leonore Zopke Hofmeier. Pencil drawing by Hans Fluggen. 1931.

Helga. Oil portrait by Joseph Uhl. Bergen, Germany. 1931.

Helga wearing a kimono Fritz Kiderlen (Vatl) sent from Japan to her in Munich. 1933.

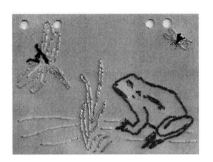

Helga made these bookmarks and sent them to her mother in late 1934, when Helga was nine years old.

Helga. 1935.

Leonore, wearing her Burberry coat and carrying her ever-present cat. Japan. 1935.

Helga and her classmates planting a vegetable garden at their school. Omori, Japan. 1936.

Helga on the kitchen steps of the house in Uehara. 1944, just six months before the house was destroyed in the firebombing the night of 10 March 1945.

The Japanese Education Minister Kunihiko Hashida (center, in the Japanese National uniform waving a small crossed flag) spoke to German, Italian, and Japanese children about the Tripartite Alliance. Next to Hashida (without glasses) is the mayor of Tokyo, Tomejiro Okubo. Helga stands next to Mayor Okubo. December 17, 1940.

Helga. Tokyo. 1946.

Helga. Hakone. 1947. In war-ravaged Japan, she is having tea with a full set of fine china and a hand-embroidered linen tablecloth.

Jesse Edmonds in uniform.
Tokyo. 1947.

Helga and Fusako, the maid. According to Helga, Fusako was "the most
kind, correct, disciplined, honest and
true person I have known." Hakone.
1947.

Jesse in front of the Hakone house.
1947.

Leonore. Tokyo.
1948.

Kurt Hofmeier (Vati).
Germany. 1948.

Helga in Coronado in 1948, holding the Watsons' god-daughter, Cynthia Jane Schwenk. With them are Col. and Mrs. Schwenk. On the back of the photo, Helga wrote, "What do you think of my daughter Cynthia Jane Schwenk?" Helga named her own daughters Jane and Cynthia after this baby,, the first American infant she met.

Helga. Coronado. 1948.

Helga and Jesse. Omaha. 1950.

Helga and Jane. 1951.

Fritz Kiderlen (Vatl). Germany. 1962.

Helga. Japan. 1947.

Letters and Documents

March 10, 1932
Dresden

My dear little Helgchen,

I sent you loving greetings for your birthday and I hope you are all feeling better; why don't you write to me and let me know what the little angel *[Helga: they came for birthdays and brought gifts]* brought you this time. But you have to do it tomorrow so I can have the letter here in time because we are going on a trip on Tuesday. Your mother is still sick and in bed but I think I am getting better and are going to get up tomorrow. In your honor I will drink a glass of wine at the noon meal to toast you in hopes you have a good birthday. Just think about my dear if our thoughts cross, that is a very dear feeling in my heart and yours and let me know how you feel about that. I send loving regards to Uncle Lückchen and Herzeltantchen from Dresden. *[H -I had gone there to visit but I don't remember who these relatives were.]*

This is my first outing since I had not been feeling too well so I think tomorrow I will stay again in bed. I am expecting Tante Gerda to visit. Think about it and maybe you can remember her sweet talk and how she looks and how much we always laughed with her. The stories we shared are still in our minds and I think this is good not to forget.

Your loving Mutti
[Helga turned 7 the next day]

March 25, 1932
Dresden

My dear Helgchen –

Pretty soon there is Easter and see what the Easter bunny is going to bring. Children have to be good so they get many sweet eggs. How is Almut, I hope she is not sick.

[H - Almut was my favorite doll. My dolls also got sick, I took their pulse, put a cloth on their heads, took their temperatures]

I hope she can share your birthday cake with you. Now take care and have a wonderful time and think of your mother who loves you very much.

March 25, 1932 continued on the same day – I haven't received a letter from you in several days. Maybe you wrote to Hamburg and maybe I find a letter from you there.

[H – my mother and Fritz went to Hamburg to visit his mother before they went to Japan]

Since you asked to have a picture of me I am sending you one. I'm wearing the new hat that I bought and that you liked so much.

[H - that must be the passport photo I liked so much...she is wearing the hat. She was not yet in Japan. All I remember is that I went to bed one night at my aunt and uncle's house and the next morning I woke up and she wasn't there and she didn't say goodbye. I have forgotten a lot of that part of my life - I shut it out or I don't know. I was just told she had gone to Japan]

Uncle Rolf, whom I like him very much visited.

[H – Uncle Rolf was my stepfather's younger brother]

He is sending you a birthday present. He also came to see me in Dresden and we all decided to tell the Easter bunny to take the eggs to Munich.

[H -because that is where I was living with my aunt and uncle at the time].

As we were talking he pulled a big picture book out of his suitcase and thought that would be good for you. The book is about how life is in the forest with the little animals.

[H - I loved that book. It was the rabbit school and a family of rabbits. The rabbit children have to go to school. They have tables and chairs and live just like we live, even the teacher is a rabbit.]

I thought that was a great idea and I know you will enjoy that because I know how much you like your books. Remember when you were in Munich one day we went to an exhibit of picture books and your enjoyed these so very much. Just imagine that same books we saw then were painted by this man who did this book! Ha!! I know how you liked when we walked thru the woods. You liked to sit and listen to little animals and I think we always had a good time then. I think on Easter Sunday you will find many big marzipan eggs.

[H – The eggs were filled with almond paste, had a chocolate coating, and the whole egg was wrapped in shiny paper foil].

Now we have to close, und hope to hear from you. If you can write everything you want to tell me, please ask Omi and she will probably help you and you will finish.

Goodbye from your Loving Mother and Uncle Fische.

[Helga is 7 years old]

Helga's drawing of Easter and Spring. Sent to her mother in Japan. 1937.

April 5 1932

Hamburg

My dear Helgchen –

When I woke up this morning I found this beautiful little book with a note in it at my bedside and it said "For Mutti's birthday" It is so nice of the little angel to think of us wherever we are.

[H – My mother's birthday was the 6th of April. I had a birthday angel, I still have it. A famous German company puts out wooden angels with white clothing and green wings with white dots in it and they all play a musical instrument. I have the whole orchestra. I had my birthday angel who was my own personal angel; when I was good, it made sure I was given what I asked for. He had a horn and he blew in the horn to announce my birthday. He was always on the table, next to a wooden thing with the candles, depending on how old I was. On my 10th birthday, it had 10 candles, and my angel stood on the side of that. Usually it was brought in for breakfast on your birthday with a gift. There are so many of these wooden things in Germany; handmade things made in the mountains by the people who cannot work outside because it is too cold in winter so they made Christmas angels and nativity scenes, a whole industry, including the nutcrackers, and so on.]

Remember the book which Omi gave you, how it looks like in the flower heaven.

[H – as a child, I had a book about flowers on the meadow and how they have to die, When we children asked what happens to flowers when die, the answer in the book was that the flowers go to flower heaven]

All the flowers now are going to come out soon, it is a lovely time of year because flowers wake up to their winter sleep. Next time you go to the Englisher Garten be sure to look at how many flowers and crocuses and so forth. They all have come out and are looking for the sun. How are you these days? When does school start? I hope you continue to enjoy your school like you always did. I hope you still have time to write me so I can know about these things with you and know what your thoughts are. Uncle Fische is also sick; he has a throat infection. I have visited the family of Uncle Fische in Hamburg, also his mother. They all send their greetings to you, I think you would like to visit them as well because they are all very nice and have such nice stories to tell. Until next time when we hear from each other, give my love to everybody, until we write again.

Much love and thinking of you, your loving mother.

[Helga was 7]

June 1932
Hamburg

My dearest Helgchen –

What a joy to get the nice letter from you with all the pictures and I am very grateful for that. I am amazed at what a grown-up girl you have become. I almost did not recognize you. And how well you can write and how well you seem to do in school; pretty soon you will be able to write on your own without any help.

[H - sometimes I asked my grandmother now to spell, I would sit in her room at her desk, an old- fashioned desk you could open and close.]

When I come back to see you, you have to show me all your things and I can also see the new apartment on Prinzregentenstrasse and meet some of your friends. Neto called me today and asked me if I wanted to go rowing with him.

[H - I learned to row a boat from my mother]

Maybe one day we can go rowing again together. He sends greetings to you

Let me know whether you can read this letter by yourself. Let's try that.

With a big hug and a kiss, loving mother
[Helga was 7]

Helga's drawing of the ground-breaking ceremony at the House der Kunst Museum. From her apartment window, Helga was able to watch the museum being built across the street. Munich. 1932.

July 30, 1932
Genova, Italy

My dear Helgchen –

To say goodbye I send you a beautiful golden charm bracelet. I know you wanted one for a long time. Uncle Lückchen is going to tell you all about our trip to Japan.

[H - my aunt's husband, Uncle Albert Witzel, I called Uncle Lückchen. It sounds like lucky, and it was his nickname. This must have been was when I was first told about my mother moving to Japan to marry Fritz Kiderlen.]

Your loving Mutti
[Helga was 7]

August 15 1932
Colombo

My dearest Helgchen –

We are now on an island in the Indian Ocean.

[H - On my trip to Japan we could not go ashore in Colombo because they had fighting with natives who were uprising from British regime – it was a rich island. The ship did not allow passengers from ships to go ashore. They have elephants there and I really wanted to see elephants.]

From Colombo with many kisses, I'm sending you two elephants which you can hang on your bracelet - the little gold chain that you already have - for when you play to be a princess. A black Indian sold them to me. Here they have many palm trees, but I haven't seen any monkeys

[H - they were little elephants made out of ivory that would hang on the bracelet. She sent me two. I was sad she hadn't seen any monkeys. I was always interested in monkeys]

I love you - Mutti
[Helga was 7]

21 October 1932
Tokyo, Japan

My dear Helgchen –

I am writing you today all for yourself; I was so very happy to receive your letter. How wonderful you can write now all by yourself, I am very proud you are doing so well in school; after a while it becomes easier to write. Omi tells me many things about how you are doing in her letters to me. I have also heard that you now can play "Zoom, Zoom, Zoom" on the piano. I think that is fabulous all the things you are learning, until the time that we see each other again, would you play for me?

[H - my grandmother had sent me to piano lessons in Munich. I never got to play piano in Japan because our house so small. Most Japanese houses have one room with wooden floor covered with rice mats].

Here it is raining all the time and is not as nice as in Munich. That is a good reason to let you stay in Munich with your friends and that you remain friends with them. The Japanese boys here are very "ungezogen" - without manners and very unpleasant. and I know you wouldn't like that. The little girls are all very well behaved.

[H - in Japan little boys are never punished and they can get away with anything. A little girl has to help with family chores, but the boys are like little gods. A girl ten years old will have her baby brother strapped to her back and the parents will say "Go play." The girls have to take care of the boys and the boys were never corrected.]

Just think - I am seeing here so many children your age who have to carry their little sibling on the back; tied to their back, and that's the way they play by the hour with them. If they are carrying little babies, their little head hangs crooked and bobble back and forth. They do not have buggies for their children here; everything happens on the back of mother or someone else and they go everywhere, even to the movies and the theatre. Sometimes they scream but the Japanese don't care; in Germany this would hardly be possible. Uncle Fische works now at Mercedes Benz with his uncle who is the boss there. Now that Uncle Fische is back in Japan, he has to make up for the time he was with me visiting all the relatives in Germany. He sends his love too. He has now gone to work and has to work hard. He starts at half past nine until one; then two to six in the evening, isn't that a long time. Give my greetings to Hertzeltantchen and Lückchen from me and Uncle Fische and also greetings to Omi. I hope you can read everything I wrote by yourself; let me know my dear child and tell me what you are doing.

From your mother - hugs and kisses

[Helga was 7]

24 November 1932

Tokyo

My dear Helgchen –

Today your mother has for the first time sent you a letter for Christmas and she puts you in her arms and gives you many kisses. She wishes from all her heart that you have a wonderful Christmas and that you stay healthy and happy and lots of attention from Uncle and Auntie. I am sure that Christkindl is good to you and leaves many things under the candlelit Christmas tree and also did not forget to bring the little package from Japan. The little tray with the tea things is for your Japanese children (dolls). They don't like milk or sugar in the tea. The shawl is for your new blue coat, and with the stationery you can write to your family. The calendar you will need again for your room. Also I included a Japanese story book written in English that I hope you will enjoy. I hope all your dolls are getting along.

[H - I played with dolls until I was 14. I enjoyed playing with dolls. In fact behind you is a little tansu, a Japanese chest of drawers. That is where I put my doll clothing at that age when I was in Japan and I brought it to the States with me. It's made of special wood called Kiri wood, a soft wood with leaves very large and look like fingers. When the tree blooms, it looks like a little candle. The white flowers are the crest of the Japanese queen. The chrysanthemum with 16 leaves is the Kings 'crest. The Kiri is almost a sacred tree for the Japanese.]

I can hardly wait for your next letter to tell me all about what you are doing and how everybody is. And also ask Omi to write about the Christmas Eve and all the gifts everybody received. Here in Japan they don't have Christmas trees. If you want one you have to ask the angels to bring one from the forests from Germany.

I am very anxious to hear all that and I will tell you next time what we did. My thoughts are always with you.

Many hugs and kisses, Mutti
[Helga was 7]

22 December 1932

My dear Helgchen –

Your Christmas letter came so punctual which was a great joy to us so I am answering you right away, especially since Omi told me you are able to read my letters easily alone without help. So now in the future we can correspond with each other as we like. Remember when we used to sit in our couch?

[H - we had a little corner couch, at a right angle. I loved to sit together in our little sofa corner and read and chat.]

If you read this letter, your mother is with you in her thoughts and is really so proud that her little girl can already read so well. Please continue to work hard in school because more you learn more can understand things in the world and that is much fun in everyone's life. You probably noticed that already. And now you've already started to do ice skating; when I was small we did the same and I enjoyed it. In Hamburg there was not much opportunity to do that because Uncle Fischi and I as children skated together in the one skating ring we had. Omi probably told you how she danced the Ice Waltz with Uncle Otto, her brother. It's a little bit hard but if you practice you can learn it.

I have a question. Did you really embroider the beautiful little placemat yourself? I think I can hardly believe that - so let me know how you learn that. It is a lovely little thing and we have used it already and are happy to have it. Uncle Fische and I thank you very much for all the things we received and are using everything. Uncle Fische was downtown yesterday, he saw the little gift for you - Yukisan, the doll, which we enclose here, in one of the little books, and handkerchiefs (as Japanese always carry with them), and also jewelry for special occasion and a barrette for your hair. It's the pin with flowers and a hangy thing and is to put in your hair for special occasions..

[H – Japanese ladies have a brocade, like a coin purse, with folded paper napkins in there. They constantly have runny noses, terrible problems with noses; all the little children constantly have runny noses, their noses are flat to the face and they seem to have lots of breathing problems.]

In two days it will be Christmas and I'm really waiting to hear from you and am curious if the little angel with the Japanese gifts can fly quickly enough to get the mail to the mailman so you get all our things. We're still looking for a little Christmas tree and maybe we will find one. We have found some Christmas music for our gramophone Maybe you can play some of these Christmas songs already on the piano and that you have learned a poem this year.

[H - every Christmas I had to learn a poem and recite it before the gifts were opened. In that way, the children participate in the evening. Sing a song and tell poem then we all kiss each other, say Merry Christmas and went to look for their gifts under the tree. It was a quiet evening, nothing wrapped, everything visible, look at it and share it around. (Helga smiles remembering).]

I have to close now so this letter will reach you in time. Many greetings to all and many kisses to you my dear little one.

Your loving Mutti
[Helga was 7]

]

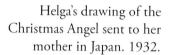
Helga's drawing of the Christmas Angel sent to her mother in Japan. 1932.

December 1933 Tokyo

My dear Helgchen –

This is Christmastime and I still have to write a letter to you and send you in my thoughts many kisses. We will think of you on Christmas Eve and hope that you have a happy get-together. I wonder what little Dieter, the baby, thinks and how wide he will open his eyes when he sees the lights on the tree. I hope I get photos again from you at that time again. We send with the Christkindl a little toilette table (a vanity/dressing table), and a nail file and a nail polisher for you so you always have clean fingernails. I hope you enjoy it and see how beautiful it works.

Have you been able to play some Christmas music on the piano? You don't write much about your piano playing lately, so now I am anxious to see all the good things you received at Christmas and how your poem was appreciated, and especially if the Christ child hears that you love your gifts. He is always in a hurry and has to go quickly to someone else's house. I am going to go to bed now because it is late.

With hugs and kisses, your loving Mutti

[H - we always celebrated in the evening on Christmas eve and Christmas day is just a family day, people come visit and have Christmas dinner. Christmas Eve my grandmother made a fish salad and we had that, made

with sour herring. It was very good, she spent a lot of time the night before, cutting up the fish, and then it sits overnight. We cracked nuts and played a game. We had one game played with the dice, you go around a board and different things happen to you, an old, old game that was played in German families for years - my grandmother had played it as a child. It's the Hammer and the Bell game - "Glaucher und Hammer". We only played it once a year, at Christmastime.]

[Helga was 8]

Nov 26, 1934
Tokyo

My dearest Helgchen –

Today is a very wet and foggy November day it is a time to be inside in a warm room. Our kitty is sitting by the stove and purring, she is almost snoring because she has a cold and I think she has a sore throat because when she purrs or she says meow, she is hoarse. She also doesn't want to eat, poor little thing. I bake Christmas cookies all day and I really missed your help but maybe we can do it together next year. I know it is early but here it is time to start with these things. We are excited already for the holiday. It takes a long time to mail things; I think a package could take almost a month, maybe six weeks. I even was thinking of not sending anything since you're going to be here soon. But I thought you may enjoy it and should have something there with you, and for the long trip to Japan. You can also use maybe some of the things I am sending for the trip.

[H - she is talking about my trip so they probably have decided a date for me to go over. They wanted me to have the first three years of school in Germany because the school in Japan was not very efficient in the first three years. Whether It was the ,teachers I don't know. I went immediately in Japan to fifth grade and started with English and Latin with a German teacher. We had two men teachers and two new women teachers and I came that year. I suppose my mother left years before me because she wanted to see how Japan was, and maybe she would come back, that is what she told me

later on, but she didn't want to make it difficult for Uncle Fische, either. He liked his job in Japan so she thought she would give it a try. I never thought about it as a kid because we did what we were told.]

I have everything, including all your silver, under the Christmas tree. I think you are much too small for things like that but later on you will be thankful that you have it, and it could be a lot of work, too, to have beautiful things, because they have to be cared for. I think you will enjoy it if you have pretty things to put out here and there. I wonder how many pieces you already have. Let me know sometime before you leave, and we know when we are going back to Germany then you can find some more pieces. We eat with our silver every day and really I like your pattern better than mine. Have you used any of it yet? Don't bring your silver here, though, I have enough silver for us; let's keep it over there for when you are grown. I even have cake forks exactly like your pattern.

[H - at that time I already received, many German families for Christmas and birthdays receive them, silver spoons and forks and things, usually given by godparents - they are the ones who initiated that. I had all kinds of silver spoons and forks and little spoons and soup spoon and teaspoon. I had my own silver place setting for the table already in the pattern I would have, but rest was for when I was grown.]

I have many things from Schradolfstrasse here and I know you will enjoy seeing many old things again. Did you get pictures from our house that I sent? I am so glad to be able to see you again; even Almud [H- my doll which had been her doll). When you pack your suitcase, see if you can pack your dolls very carefully between your clothing because it would be terrible if they were broken.

[H – my dolls were porcelain with real hair that was made in France, but they were German dolls].

I imagine you are busy now packing, etc. I hear it's going to be very cold in Germany this winter; maybe you have a chance to go ice skating before you leave. Your new skating boots seem to be very nice. Didn't you say they were the ones with the skate blades attached? I guess Omi has paid for the new lessons.

*[H – My mother was an enthusiastic ice skater all of her life and want-
ed to get me on the ice first thing. Before she left Germany, she bought me
the skates for the second winter, the boots with the attached skates. Before
that, I had only ones where you have to screw the blades on, but it was all
much easier with the attached blades.]*

I have to go around and look at the skating facilities; I have heard
they have some that are good, small and very crowded. In time they
will enlarge so to be more like Europe. But other things here you may
enjoy. Please tell Uncle Lückchen to take a picture of you skating and
also of you and your girlfriends, and a family picture with everybody
in it who are in Munich. Only a few days and Christmas comes around
and you don't have to go to school anymore. Be sure and keep involved
with your school work. Also work a little bit on the ship with the
Bunten girls so you don't get behind when you get here. How old are
the two girls that you travel with? I have forgotten. And what grade are
they? I hope you get along well with the children on this trip. It may
be difficult to be with strange children; don't be more friendly with
one than the other because may get jealous and that won't be good. So
it will be best for all four of you to play together and get along. Also
the parents that you get along well with them, and the mother of the
children, so you have to be on your best behavior, it will be easier that
way and it is only for a short time.

The other day we both went to look at the German school, and I
can tell you it was a beautiful school, everything was new. The school
looks rather small, has three classrooms. One for kindergarten, a teeter-
totter, a room for painting or drawing with a huge blackboard to draw
on, that is also used as for chemistry, physics and geography. It has a
gym, shower room, toilets for boys and girls, a reading room, an entry
with little places where you hang your clothing and gym clothes. There
is a big area at the back, everything elevated like a little mountain. We
were driving and from here at home to the school is an hour and a half,
and too bad it is so far from where we live.

I still have to send packages for Christmas, only a shawl for

Herzeltantchen and a pillow I'm sending to your sister in Berlin in your name.

Goodbye for now and *[writing is sideways]* for today and much love. Mutti [Helga was 9]

Jan 1935
Tokyo

My dearest Helgchen –

If this letter reaches you, almost half of your cruise is behind you and you will be in the land of the monkeys that play on the beach. I saw them in the region close to Singapore where it is so warm, these animals come out to the beach and go in the water, and also if you possible visit the botanical garden in Singapore can tease them with bananas and they come to you and look at you very curiously. I imagine you will go there and also to Colombo.

[H - The botanical part and the animals are different in these areas. Colombo has a lot of elephants and it's a large island compared to others. Different birds, etc. Singapore has a lot of monkeys. I remember them well, - they climb a tree and hang and look down, and they swoop and take your banana.]

I have also sent you a short greeting card; I hope you received it. How do you like your ocean cruise? Was it very shaky? I hope you didn't get seasick. I am sure you had a good time with a lot of laughter in your cabin. Please give regards to the Bunten family. I am looking forward to meeting them as well.

Four days ago we received Christmas letters we had really waited a long time for; packages came on time on the 23rd and the joy was great. We can use everything well as you will see yourself soon. We were so happy to read your beautiful school grades. I hope in this school here you can achieve the same. How do you get along with the children? I hope well and you have a chance to read to them and talk to them about school. I am glad you are remembering to send postcards to Munich from your different ports; we are all anxious to see that you are enjoying this cruise and that you are well. Everybody wants news: write, write, write.

Your loving Mutti
[Helga was 9]

Jan 30 1935
Tokyo

My dearest Helgchen –

We can hardly believe that you are coming closer and closer; if you receive this greeting you have been already in Manila. Uncle Fische will have had his birthday before you get here. We had to celebrate again without you. I had the news from Munich that you had a nice Christmas this year and we enjoyed the picture. Dieter is precious dressed as a little angel and you also make a good angel. Your pictures have also the one skating on the ice. We enjoyed them very much; you look well and like you can handle the ice. I hope you can skate here as well; we have to try it as soon as possible. Do the Bunten's children also skate? I am sure you enjoyed all the new things you saw on this long rip. In Manila I liked especially the beautiful dresses of the young women with the beautiful puffed sleeves.

[H –The Filipino women wore formal long dresses, gathering near waist, with huge puffs at shoulders. Years later, I was invited to a Filipino coming-out party at the naval air base here in Pensacola and the women have not these huge sleeves anymore but smaller white sleeves. While in Manila on my trip to Japan, we went to the cigar factory. Women were all sitting on the floor in rows, hand rolling cigars with stuff in center. The smell of tobacco, has to be wet so sleeves stay together, was overwhelming. The women wore the puffed sleeves dresses doing this nasty work on the floor.]

I hear you are going to change ships in Shanghai because the ship you are on will sail to other ports first and will not be here in Tokyo until March 6. I don't want to have to wait for you that long. Please ask Mr. Bunten, if he is kind enough, to send us a telegram from Shanghai so we know exactly when you arrive. We certainly don't want that you standing alone on the pier at Yokohama — that would be a terrible thing. I hope you are well and not seasick. I think the other children have done this trip several time already and are used to it and have told you some things about Japan already. Our little cat is also waiting for you, too. I have to bathe her so you can see her from her most beautiful side. I carry the little cat everywhere and she travels with me always. Over new years she was with us we spent four days camping from the car, with a special place for cat. Even though it was very cold we slept in there with the leather seats folded down. It's an old English car with a trunk high in the rear that looks like a suitcase, that we could put suitcases inside. Rudolf Ratjen always had a hissy cause we don't drive a Mercedes. The Fuji mountain you can see is beautiful when you approach land. You see we have a lot to talk about. I hope everything goes well with the last stretch, for you to have a good time and that you are soon released from the Buntens.

Many greetings and kisses. [sideways writing] love,
your mother

[H - I took the train to school every day and had to change twice. There were Japanese kids and adults and everybody going to work. People were so protected. We were not so protected. I was told to take care of myself and not to talk to people I didn't know, and so that's what I did. And nothing ever happened to me. Even in Germany I walked alone 20 minutes to the city to school. I remember in the beginning in Japan someone went with me to school, and after that I had it written it down, where to get off, where I had to change tracks, the two times I had to go up the stairs and go down the other side to another station. It worked and everybody did it. I never thought it was a big deal to do this at alone at age 10.]

[Helga was 9]

Zehlendorf, 8 December 1935

My dear Helga!

I'm writing you a letter for Christmas. How are you doing in Japan? Do you also celebrate a real Christmas there and do you have a Christmas tree? Or is it as warm there as in the summer? Does it snow where you are? Are you happy it's almost Christmas? What are you hoping to get? A pair of snowflakes just fell from the sky. They are the first. I'll explain what I'm hoping to get for Christmas. I'd like a clothes chest for my doll clothes and a coat for my new doll, Elisabeth. She's really big, can close her eyes, has braids and says Mama. I can even weave her braids. Lotte sewed a little dress with white and red squares for Elisabeth. I also want a parachute (Fallschirm) and a tricycle and a Berchtesgadener jacket. Der Dicke is hoping for a train set and a telephone and lots of soldiers and horsemen. He wants one more thing but I forget what it is right now. He just drove away with Vati. Every morning we go to the garage with him and often ride with him for a time. Der Dicke is already getting big, almost as big as me. He already goes shopping at Doells alone. He cries a lot when things don't go his way – he really screams! He can be pretty bad. But he can play very nicely and can also build really good. Twice a week I go to kindergarten. I made an Advents card for Mutti, using linseed oil to make it transparent and did lots of gluing and coloring. I can also cut really well now. I'll cut something out for you. Have you seen lots of Japanese people? Have you seen any Chinese men with a long braid? What kind of school do you go to? Do you speak Japanese there? I really like school. Do you know what the Zinnowaldschule is? I'll be going there after Easter. Rudi will go, too. Do you know who Purzel is? That's Uncle Koziol's dog. She had seven puppies, but five died. One puppy is named Blanca and is gray/brown and the other one is called Fockerle. He looks just like Purzel. They can already bark a little. I've told you a lot and I'll stop now. I send you hugs and kisses. Der Dicke does, too.

Kisses, Röschen

[Helga was 10]

26 July 1938
Karuizawa

My dear little Mother –

Your lovely letter just arrived so I want to answer right away.

You don't need to worry about the cooking at all. Both mornings and evenings I eat just as if I were at home and Fusako always cooks something yummy for lunch. I'm certainly not starving. Anyway, Fusako keeps everything in order. She does it all on her own and everything is clean. Our neighbor, Frau Buhre, is astounded! It was really dirty here, especially tracking the dirt in. But it will eventually all be pretty. A new stove for heating has arrived, since we have no chimney. I can still use a small area rag-rug.

I don't like your plan very much either. If you don't want to come up here, then I'll just have to do it all ourselves. I would, of course, much rather have had you up her and I think you'd begin to feel better here. Frau Oetmann just drove back to Tokyo and that trip will probably be too much for her, too. On the first night here, I had a terrible headache and a 101 temperature. I was shivering in spite of the warm cotton batted kimono.

It's pouring right now and it's so foggy that I can't even see 10 meters away. Yesterday, Ingrid Buhre and I went to the swimming pool. The water was pretty cold and we laid in the warm sun for a while. I bought a season ticket that cost me three yen. You can swim and lay around in the sun whenever you want. Otherwise you have to pay 50 sen every time you go in. You can take great walks here. I recently walked to the mossy spring with Ingrid – the little river eventually runs into the sea. It's so cool and gorgeous there – pine trees, birches, chestnut trees – just like in Germany!

Vatl has probably already told you that one of the duvets for the down quilts did not arrive. There is a striped duvet, but it's the one used for the mattress futon. I did find one duvet for Vatl, but just can't find the other one.

Right now, I'm in the process of lining all the cabinets with white paper. We only have one small mirror, from the bathroom, for the whole house. And I've only found one egg cup and no tea cups. I'm drinking out of the pickle jar.

The Buhres are no problem at all. Ingrid and I play together every day, she here or me at her house. Sometimes we ride our bicycles. It's not hard, usually straight or up little hills. If we see a big hill coming, we pedal fast downhill so it's not so hard to go back up the next one. I'm always careful when I see a car, and usually just get off my bike as one passes.

Goodbye for now, it's already quarter past nine. I've chatted long enough – just like you and I always do, Mother.

Think about your plan very carefully again. You know that I'm much happier when you are here – but if it's just too much for you, then we'll just do it your way.

[Helga was 13]

1 August 1938
Karuizawa

Dear little Mother –

Frau Schmidt got here in good shape yesterday, as did the trunk and another stove. Many thanks for your letter and the 50 yen. I am happy to get the money, I was broke. I bought dishes and asked around about petroleum fuel for the stove. It's still available and costs 4 yen a can, but it's not standard oil. Should I buy two cans anyway?

Frau Schmidt brought me a book and some playing cards. I'm always playing Solitaire because Bezique is much harder. Mrs Schmidt and I went down to the little town this morning. She thinks its heavenly. I've been invited to Inge Lietzmann's birthday party Thursday. I have to get her a gift. There's a lot to choose from up here. Yesterday I went to church with Inge – the pastor got mad because not many people were there, so we both walked out early.

The white blouse fits good, but the white bra is too big in the back. Please bring the hammock with you when you come. Frau Schmidt thinks the down quilt is too warm, so she is using a blanket she brought.

She only uses one pillow. There were already two good mattresses in the house when I got here. I took one and the other is on the chaise lounge. I bought a new, all white, futon for 8.30 yen. It fits my mattress just fine. I haven't bought tablecloths yet. I want to wait until you get here. It's fine without one for the time being. Bring little placemats with you – we can always use those.

There isn't a coffee pot, so I make coffee by putting coffee grounds in a piece of netting and pour the hot water over the top. It works fine. There are no enamel cans here. I don't need the white shorts anymore. I have plenty others here. I saw Hella Janson the other day and asked if her sister Erika was coming up. Hella said that because her Dad was here, Erika couldn't come until next week. The blue curtains are really sweet – Frau Schmidt is altering them to fit our windows.

How is my little Wutsche? Bring all the cats with you when you come! It will all work. Please come soon, with the old grouch and all the cats! I have my fingers crossed.

Your babydoll

Please write soon. Many fat kisses to you – and to the old grouch (Vatl), as well. Tell him he needs to change is attitude a bit. He was wonderful when he was here. Tell him hello and don't yell at him too much!

Your little babydoll
[Helga was 13]

5 August 1938
Karuizawa

My dear little Mother –

Thanks for your letter. All the delicious goodies also all arrived. It has been pouring every day since last Sunday. Today is the first clear day and so the metal worker came today. They don't have the white rocks to build a chimney with here, so I ordered sheet metal. The workman is going to repair the stove and that, along with the sheet metal and the connecting pipe, will cost us 4.50 yen. I don't think that's too expensive. I pay 6 sen for icebox ice, 750 grams of eggs are 70 sen, milk is 10 sen, and all the vegetables fluctuate in price. I write everything down and still have about 40 yen and that will suffice until Vatl arrives.

We always eat well. Every morning I have milk and puffed rice, an egg, bread with jam and cheese and a tomato. Frau Schmidt doesn't like jam. She eats only tomatoes and bread, butter and egg – that's her passion! Sometimes I buy breakfast rolls at Fujiya and toast them over charcoal. At noon we eat vegetables with onions (I know you hate them!), potatoes and either meat or fish. We have tea and cake every afternoon. Fusako buys her own cake because she doesn't like ours. At night we sometimes eat noon leftovers, but we usually just have cold sandwiches. We can get liverwurst up here – it's good, but not as good as Lohmeyers! So you see, you don't have to worry about me eating enough!

Please bring the iron up, as I sometimes have to iron a bit. And don't forget the hammocks. The sun umbrella would be great, but we don't really need it. The sun isn't that strong and we usually sit on the veranda anyway.

We don't need the petroleum heating stove yet, but if we come here in January, we'll need it for sure. I'm buying just one can of petrol. I also need coat hangers.

I got your letter this morning, along with the pajamas and the dress. Thanks so much. The pajamas fit good, the pants are a little long, but who cares? I can use the dress. I wore the red dirndl to Inga Lietzmann's party – most girls all wear them. Eight of us were at the party and had a great time. I'll tell you all about it when you get here.

I can't get it into my head that you don't want to come up here. I haven't told anyone, not even Frau Schmidt, because I think that you'll eventually come. I could do it alone, but you know that it's so much better when you are here! Think about it again.

I took the money from Fusako right away. Now she has no money, but it's a good lesson. Now she's constantly cleaning all day. I borrowed a Latin book from Ingrid and we're doing our vocabulary words now.

We don't even think about swimming these days. It has rained constantly and everything is swimming. The tunnel is repaired, but the road is still a work in progress. Hella just came by and asked if I wanted to go to Kutsukake with her, but Frau Schmidt said you didn't want me to go out traveling alone and that I needed to wait until you got here. I invited Erika over for next week.

So I close – but you think about coming here!

Love and kisses from your babydoll.

Oh – I'm invited over to the Buntens tomorrow.

[Helga was 13]

Ferch uber Potsdam
Burgstrasse 2
2 August 1939

My dear child!

It's been just too long since I have written you a real letter. We won't discuss how that came about, there are many reasons. I had always hoped that we would see each other again this year and we all would have been thrilled. But nothing came of it, so I wanted to send you a good long letter.

I'll get back to the most recent letter you've sent me, for which I lovingly thank you, by the way, but first I'd like to tell you what has happened to us over the past few years. We'll start with our extended family – to our great joy, the dear grandparents are by and large doing quite well. Grandfather is almost 81 years old, yet in admirable health and always full of great plans and ideas. At his last birthday celebration, one that was very nice and festive, he gave a speech that he's now decided to stay around to celebrate his golden anniversary with Grandmother. That would be in 1941. We all hope that happens – they both remain as active as they are now, although Grandmother always has something going on with her legs and sometimes her mobility is a bit measured. She continues to use her immeasurable energy to overcome all obstacles. Both grandparents just spent a few weeks on holiday and came home feeling great.

Aunt Irmi is doing great, too. She still has lots to do, but she says she manages just fine. She just added another house to her hospital compound, and is using that as an additional laundry facility and nurse living quarters. She has rented out a large part of her house. She continues to be active, sometimes too much so.

As I think you already know, the Hupertzes were relocated to Nordhausen about 8 months ago. They found a lovely little home there, and have finally, after many long years of sorrow and worry, created a really comfortable home. Uncle Gerhart has gone completely gray, you wouldn't know him. He likes Nordhausen a lot, really doesn't have that much he has to do and enjoys his independence and freedom. For several years now, Helmut has been attending a boarding school in Schulpforte and has become a staunch Hitler Youth. He took part in a rather large military camp last summer and right now is on vacation with his parents. Little Fritz, now 3 years old, is a real square shooter and happy boy. Very blond and independent, and in many respects resembles his recently deceased baby sister.

So now we get to us. Tante Edith is doing fine. She's really busy now that we have the new house I'll tell you about in just a minute. I think she'll probably add a few lines to this letter. Röschen, who talks about you all the time, even though she probably has no idea what you even look like anymore. The dear little lass goes gladly to school every day, to the Queen Elisabeth Academy in Dahlem. She jumped a grade and has already begun to learn English – "school is over, oh what fun, lessons finished, play begun" was her first poem in English. You probably know it, too. She's always fresh as a daisy. She hasn't grown very much, but that will come in time. She has her own bedroom now and has become a little lady. Her brothers worry that she's growing up too fast. Hans Melchoir, now in his second year at school, seems to have made something of himself, even though he remains very sensitive. He's gotten a sassy Berliner mouth, but because of school, that's inevitable. The little Fritz is completely different from both of his older siblings, and usually has both of them in the palm of his hand. He is lively and always incredible active.

Now I'll tell you a bit about me. I've just completed a very full year of work that I'm happy to say was full of much success. You know that I was given the Children's Hospital in Berlin in the fall of 1934. I took on a huge task, but after four years now, it has become a well respected institution. Then, in an incredibly extraordinary last year, I qualified as a professor with a book that I had written during 1937 and I also qualified as a lecturer at the University of Berlin last September. You can't imagine what all that means for me, but I can tell you, it was very hard for me because I was deemed unqualified so many years ago and had to overcome much resistance to succeed this time. It all required a lot of energy and discipline as I to worry about my own hospital and my rather large private practice at the same time. On the first of October last year, I was named Chief Administrator of the Children's Hospital Kaiserin Auguste Victoria Haus, an institution that is known around the world. So my work has not been reduced, but has grown immeasurably. There hasn't been a permanent administrator of this hospital for several years, merely an acting administrator. My predecessor only had to worry about the hospital on a part time basis. It is, however, a fabulous hospital, and, if all goes the way I envision, I'll be happy. I hope you'll be able to see it next year. Just so you have an idea of what kind of a place it is, I'll send you a copy of a keynote speech that I gave to celebrate the 30-year anniversary of the hospital.

So there has been outward success, but the workload has also increased. My day includes 12 to 14 hours of work, with no break and I don't even have time to go home for lunch. So I don't see the family very much and there isn't very much time to socialize either. We don't have much opportunity to maintain friendships and have very seldom even been to the theater. It's all very sad but can't be helped right now. Over the next few years, as I create change here and have the right team around me, things are sure to get better.

We have taken some nice vacations over the past few years, though. In the Fall of 1937, we were in Rome for the International Pediatrician convention. I was actually part of the official German delegation.

It was, naturally, very interesting. Lots of military exercises followed, as big changes are a concern for everyone. Last year was also entirely full of hushed political tensions that left no one untouched. In spite of this, we've been able to record successes that we certainly hadn't thought possible before. All are working with a passion that few people outside of Germany could even begin to understand. There is never enough manpower, all plans are being accelerated and everything is taking place at an unheard of pace. It's not always about the timeframe, but right now, if we want to take a lead and keep it, we have no other choice. It can't continue this way with Poland. While I managed the German portion of the battle for the eradication of rickets, I was in the Sudetenland and in Prague. It was so interesting for me and I understand the country and the people like few others.

So now you know what it looks like with us. You all are all living through a lot of unrest because of the war with China. It can't be easy for you there. I recently had a visit from an older female Japanese doctor from Tokyo. Unfortunately I've forgotten her name and I don't have my calendar handy. We drank tea together. The conversation was incredibly slow, since she didn't speak a work of either English or German, only Japanese. Her son acted as interpreter, but he spoke only English. I had called in my assistant who had spent two years in Japan and we all toiled valiantly for over two hours. She was surprised with all she saw here. From what I understood, the Japanese medical system is pretty pathetic. They are unbelievably diligent, but still seem to be a very strange and foreign people. No one would understand that better than you.

So, my dear child – you've probably grown into a real Backfisch [moody teenager] by now and I have to stop and remember what a grown daughter I have. To my distress I've heard that you haven't been well for a while and have even had a fever. Since I don't have all the details, I can't offer any advice. One thing I do think, however, is that you need to get out of that very unhealthy climate for a long while – and come back to Germany. I've heard from many others, including Uncle Ernst Ramm, how bad the climate there is for sensitive and nervous people, and that certainly includes you. I really think you'd feel completely different in the German climate, so you have to just see how you can get back here. I hope that won't take too long. How are your studies going? I don't have a very good opinion of school there. I think that you need to have several more years of study in Germany, as it is, of course, completely different here than in a foreign school. In a few years time you'll also have to deal with the career question. So it's time for you to come back so we can discuss it all. I'm certain that your mother has made some plans, but I want to have a say in them, as well.

I know the new Ambassador Ott in Tokyo fairly well. He lived here in Zehlendorf as a Major and later Lt Colonel for several years. Did he bring his wife and children with him? Your Uncle Ernst Ramm is now the Consulate General in Wellington, New Zealand. He likes it there. His wife has been there a while with him and they now have two children.

I thank you very much for your latest letter and photographs. I don't have any photos to send you right now, but will do so soon. We haven't taken a lot of pictures lately. As you see from my return address, we are in Ferch am Schwielowsee near Potsdam. We bought a little house there last spring and spend our holiday vacations there. It's really lovely and comfortable and rural here, and that's exactly why I love it here. The children will learn to love it as a piece of home and Tante Edith and I love it as an escape. I'm never really at home in Zehlendorf because of the infernal telephone! We had to do quite a few renovations to the house and are now, except for a bit on the inside, almost finished. The bedrooms are all done, but we want to address everything we need to do to be able to spend a few days here in the winter, as well. I don't know if we'll be able to complete all that this year. Everything is normally expensive now, but the distance from Berlin makes this doubly difficult. We soon have a great Autobahn and when it's complete, as it should be later this year, it will only take about half an hour to get here, and that's nothing.

So, dear little Helga, I'm going to close now. I will tell you that I'll be lecturing Finland in September – you'll get a kick out of hearing that, I'm sure. Let me hear from you soon, preferably all good news. I'd especially like to hear about your plans for the next year so that I can arrange everything.

My best wishes to your mother and to Mr. Kiderlen, as well. If you don't hear from me often, don't think that I've forgotten about you, because I remain always your very loving Vati.

[Helga was 14]

Helga's 3rd-place award in skiing, from the Hitler Youth Winter Camp. 1940.

Zehlendorf, 20 June 1940

My dear Helga,

I got your latest letter just as I returned from a trip and I thank you very much for it. I had so much to do around the house when I got home, that I'm just now getting around to writing you back. Your dear father just left for his holiday and there was much I had to do to prepare for his departure, as well. It's probably just like that at your

house, too, when your Vatl leaves for holiday – always a lot of things
to do!

I was finally able to connect with the director of Röschen's school
– everything is so difficult now with the war. Thank goodness that
there are now uniform regulations in place for all schools and they look
like this: From first to fifth grade, the children have English, from
sixth to eighth grade French is compulsory and Latin is an elective. To
graduate school in Germany now, you must have French. Your mother
is exactly correct when she says that French is a basic building block to
all education. When I was in Rome for an International Pediatrician
convention, I thanked my lucky stars that I knew a bit of French. I was
able to understand a bit of both Italian and Spanish through my French.
One of the directors of the convention was so nice to me. She didn't
know a word of German and I don't know Italian, so we just conversed
in French. We were also able to speak French with another delightful
couple we met who were from Portugal. I'm really mad at myself for
not knowing more about speaking foreign languages – they get you farther in life, they are much easier to learn when you are young, and you
never know who you're going to marry. Often it's absolutely necessary
for a wife to master a foreign language- just think about Emma Ramm.
I have to master different languages now that your dear father travels
internationally so much. He prefers to travel with his wife, so I have to
learn to converse so I don't disgrace him when we travel. I do love to
travel and I'd love to have the time to spend learning more languages,
but now, with the children there is always so much to do, and now,
here in Berlin, just doing the food shopping takes forever. Since I can't
handle too much as I tire easily, the language instruction just has to
suffer. You, however, are young, healthy and fresh and can learn properly, so put your big girl panties on (as we say here in Germany) and
get to learning your English and French! You'll never regret it. I can
tell you from personal experience how horrible it is to be with lovely
people in a foreign country and to be unable to say a nice sweet word
of appreciation when the need arises. It's a tough time here with books
right now. All the French language school books are impounded, most

schools can't even get them. Even if I had one and went to the post office today, because of a recent ban, I wouldn't be able to mail a French book to you now. A new regulation called "Education and Teaching in High School" was recently passed by the National Ministry for Science and Education that has the entire lesson plan that each teacher abides by. It also requires that books can only be sent from bookstore to bookstore, so check with your local bookstore to see if they have a French language book. If they don't, you can order one from Webersche Bookstore, Berlin Zehlendorf, Ladenstrasse, and you can get it right away. Even though students here cannot find French language books, you should be able to find them in Japan, and if your teacher requires you to have one, you shouldn't have any problem anyway. I can get good French/German dictionaries here, so if you can't find one of those, let me know and I'll have one sent to you. I wish I had better news to share with you. I only hope that the war ends soon. Then everything would be different and I'd be able to send you any book you ever might ask me for.

I spent last winter in Poland and it wasn't easy. I had my own work and otherwise helped out however I could. I taught Dickus (Hans) and did all the children's laundry myself because I certainly didn't want to add to Aunt Irmgard's work load. I came home in April, and did all the deep spring cleaning myself. It was a lot of work and I certainly could have used your help. When I finished all the cleaning, I picked up the boys, got Röschen from her boarding school and then Vati from the hospital. We were all so happy to be together again, especially Röschen since she hadn't been feeling well at all. I found another Polish housemaid back with me – we just cant find anyone here, they are all working in the factories. This one is not as clean and tidy as Ida was, but at least she is quiet and friendly and cooks very well. I just had to let Ida go. She was so ill-natured and back-talked me all the time that it just didn't work anymore. I'd get so angry with her that I wasn't sleeping well. Now all is quiet and wonderful, I just have to work more with this one, but that's fine with me. I also visited our wonderful Lottchen on my last trip. She asked about you right away and sends her best regards.

She is now in a hospital in Halle where she tends to the wounded.

I also have a young Romanian nanny who's very sweet and just on vacation right now. Fritzchen has become a real cheeky little lad who looks complete different from the others – looks a bit like Ludendorff. He is so full of energy that I believe your mother is right - it won't be too long until he starts in on Dickus. He's always happy, in a good mood and is loved by everyone here. Dickus remains quiet and moody, and it's not always easy with him. He screams when something doesn't go his way, but he'll grow out of that. And even though he's lazy and never does any more than he absolutely has to, he's doing well in school. Röschen would be a wonderful little sister to you, it's so sad that you don't live closer to us. She doesn't have many little friends other than Dorle, I think she has written you about her, but she lives pretty far away and that's sad. Sorry that I don't have any pictures of the children, but I promise I'll take some and send them to you. I thank you for the photos you've sent us, the larger one is especially nice. You and Röschen share a similarly shaped larger nose, but that makes no difference. What's important is that you are both so good hearted.

So, little Helga, I have to close now to get the evening meal ready for the children. I hope things continue to go well for let you and that you rejoice with us in our glorious victories. It's a shame that you cannot experience this time with us here. Everything is incredible. We are all so proud of our soldiers and our Fuhrer. There will never ever be another time like this on earth. I'm sure you all see it exactly the same way and you are all proud to be German, too. Do you get to buy German magazines or get to see the weekly German newsreels? I allowed the two older children to watch one of the recent newsreels with me and they were astounded, especially Dickus. He knows all the different airplanes better than I do.

I really must close now. Best wishes to your dear mother and be a good girl.

Loving kisses from your dear
Tante Edith
[Helga was 15]

Berlin – Zehlendorf
Reimeisterstr.39A
Tel: 84 42 00
15 February 1941

My dear Helga!

I'd like to add a few lines to Vati's letter, he's right next to me writing a letter to you, so I sat myself down at my writing desk. It is nice that the letter finally gets to you via the mail now, so we can actually write about everything.

First off, all our love and best wishes on your Confirmation! That must have been a memorable day for you, but sad, too, to have to say goodbye to the pastor who, I'm told, had done so much for you. As I was in Pabianice, Aunt Gertrude was just telling me that Helmut is just not succeeding with his instruction and that he probably won't be confirmed. I don't know, we'll just have to wait and see. In any case, I hope you have a grand celebration, one that you can remember for the rest of your life. We certainly are thinking about you at this time. Sadly this letter will get to you late, as we initially thought that you were to be confirmed in April. I hope you like the ring. We looked for it with much love and think the stone is especially nice. I wonder what kind of dress you'll be wearing – white or black. Please take lots of pictures and send us some.

I'm so thankful for the letter you recently wrote for Vati's birthday. I still enjoy rereading it. In the meantime, you should have received a school textbook. The bookstores had not been allowed to ship books for such a long time, so I now hope that you can get back to your French lessons. Do you think it's hard? I thought it was easier than learning English and Latin. I had to learn Latin, too, but I have forgotten all of it already! Röschen has absolutely no talent for languages, English isn't any fun for her, She likes history, geography and math much better. It's sad, because we need to know those other languages as we get older.

You certainly seem to be joining in everything there. I'm sure everything is beautiful and interesting for you, But don't you think you might want to come back to Germany for a few years?

I was just in Halberstadt, in the Harz mountains, with Vati, as he visited with one of his very ill little patients. I was waiting in our hotel, when I saw an Illustrierte Beobachter Zeitung with a photo of you with one of your little girlfriends in Japan. You'd already sent the photo to Röschen, but I loved seeing the photo in the paper so much, that when I got back to Zehlendorf, I bought three more copies of it. I'm going to send them to Röschen and to your grandparents – they'll all love to see it. You look so nice in the photo, as does your friend, Ursula Ott.

Vati had surely written you that our family has been scattered to the winds. It's so sad that it has to be this way, but the bombing here in Zehlendorf was just too difficult for the children. We all hope that the war ends this year, at least in Europe, then I can gather my children back up again. Aunt Gertrude was so sweet to take on both the boys, Röschen is also doing fine, although I have to get mad at her for still not writing you. As far as I know, she thanked you for the chocolate; I know I did so on behalf of the boys. Funny enough, two jars came on exactly the same day, but the third arrived much later. It was a heavenly confection. Know it will all be honestly divided and shared. I thank you again for sending it.

The children are doing fine. Since we just returned from Ferch in November, I'm not going to go back for a while. You were right – it has its advantages and disadvantages, I still have the Polish woman working for me. She cooks really well, but I have noticed that she's not exactly honest and that's simply terrible. So now I have to lock everything up. I'd much rather be with Vati alone and do everything myself, but then I'd run the risk of not being able to find someone to help out later. It's here just like it is for you there – everyone wants to work in the factory, but they work hard for just a few hours a day, and the girls want to be free every evening. Here in Dahlem, and in all the best neighbor-hoods in Berlin, the ladies sit in their huge villas without live-in maids, and can hardly even find hourly help. It's absolutely terrible. I'm eas-ily reminded of your dear mother who was so angry some evenings that things weren't properly completed that she couldn't sleep. I'm the same way – and then I also begin to feel physically miserable, as well.

Hopefully the end of the war will come soon, you'll all be able to come back here and your mother will really be able to convalesce properly.

Starting next week, for four weeks, I'm going on holiday to freshen up before things get busy for me again. But if those English return with their horrible bombs, I will leave again, although I am reluctant to leave Vati in the air raid shelter alone even though I have fixed it up quite nicely with bedding and all kinds of things. The children always slept well there at night, waking only when the bombs feel especially close to us. Dickus thinks everything is absolutely terrific – for him it's all about the airplanes and woe is me when I can't immediately identify a plane he sees in the air! That frustrates him immensely and very indignantly he tells me "You have to know these things!" He cries a lot less now. He was really miserable in Ferch, so I decided to have his tonsils out last December. He handled the operation very nicely and is now feeling much better. He remains the most fragile of all the children. You know, dear Helga, the little Spatz (Fritz) has much more going on between his ears; Dickus seems to take everything so seriously and only acts happy for show. Right now I don't have any new photos of the two boys, only of the two Fritzes – but those will make you laugh anyway. I only have a picture of Röschen at the piano with her little friend Dorle. You see, how my sloppy daughter runs around, caring less whether her collar is straight or if her braids are half undone! But it's a cute picture anyway, so I'm sending it along to you. The photo isn't mine, so I need it back. Please, when you have time, do return it.

So, my dear Helga, I have to close now. You wanted to know when my birthday was. Well it's exactly 14 days after Vati's and exactly when Autumn begins, so I'll let you figure that out.

I send you lots of heartfelt thoughts for your birthday and wish you all the best. Hopefully, this letter gets to you before your birthday, Hopefully you can really enjoy your day and that your mother feels better, I know that's always your utmost wish.

Loving thought and once again,
all our love for your Confirmation and Birthday –
Your Tante Edith

My apologies that I wrote you on a typewriter. I've had a splinter under my left middle fingernail since Christmas, it got infected, and I still can't write properly, especially a long letter.

[Helga was 15]

Helga and Ulla Ott, daughter of the German ambassador to Japan (photo in lower right). Taken as a propaganda piece at a German/Japanese sport day in Tokyo, the photo appeared on 6 February 1941 in the German newspaper *Illustrierte Beobachter*. Edith talks about this photo in her 15 February 1941 letter from Germany to Helga in Japan.

Riehen
25 February 1943

Dear Helga!

So I thought I'd write you again. I have been sick and I am now recovering in the Berner Oberland. We live in Strassburg in the Alsace. Vati is a professor at the Childrens Clinic there. We are all doing well. Fritzchen is already going to school. We all like it there. We have a big house with a big garden with a river, the Aar, in front.

How are you doing? Has your mother recovered from her illness? We had a good time at the grandparents' golden anniversary. You got a nice silver plate that Mutti will keep for you. The grandparents are doing well. Uncle Paul, I don't know if you know him, died shortly after the anniversary. Uncle Hanschen in Charlottenburg has also been really sick. Uncle Hans Gunther was wounded, but he's doing better now. I'm doing well in school. Vati has a lot to do. Mutti has to do everything by herself now, as we don't have a helper. But thank goodness all is going well for us now. Uncle Gerhard is in Italy and Aunt Putzer lives in Wartheland. Is Ursul Ott now in Berlin?

Many heartfelt wishes to you from all of us and our best wishes to your parents, too.

From your sister
Röschen
[Helga was 17]

29 September 1943
Karuizawa

My dear Mother –

I was running around all day today trying to find information about a stove. I'm writing because a telegram would be too long. There are no stoves to be found up here anywhere, but Burikia-san (the Tin Man) can build one for us. He has to come here, take measurements, and write down what he needs—probably three or four pieces of tin. The paper goes to the German Embassy for approval and they send it to the Gaimusho (Ministry of Foreign Affairs) for their approval. If all agree, Burikia-san can buy the tin he needs for our job. The tin will cost about 60 yen. It might be more because of the long exhaust pipe needed to reach from the stove to the outside. I discovered that Frau Tiedeman has never bought a metal stove. She had a tile oven built because she had special metal flooring in her house. Mr. Altendorf is the man who handles this at the Embassy, so Vatl can speak with him about it. I spoke to Frau Schultze and Frau Deppe and Eisendorf—they have all spoken to Mr. Altendorf about stoves, but no one has heard back from him yet.

Burikia-san had a stove in for repair when I was at his shop today. I think ours will look like the one I saw—it's on metal legs and stands about 80 centimeters tall. He says it should give great heat to a 10 to 12 tatami sized room. So the only question left is where we put this stove. I think it should go where the floor lamp currently is—that way it can heat both the living and dining rooms at the same time. We can send the smoke pipe up through the bedroom on the second floor and then straight up through the roof. The pipe will also heat the bedroom nicely. It looks like a stove has been in that same place before, anyway—there are already holes in the living room ceiling and in the upstairs bedroom ceiling that have just been covered up with piece of tin. Let me know if you have any questions—I want to let the Tin Man know when he can come get his measurements.

I got a really great pottery teakettle today. It's not very big, but it'll work for tea. Do you want me to bring it down to you?

I hope you are feeling well—the weather here is great. On Sunday I should be able to get a big basket of apples and some blueberries, as well. I hope Vatl picks me up at the station. Please answer right away

Your Helga
[Helga was 18]

24 November 1943
Yokohama

My dear Mother –

Many thanks for your letter and the delicious cake. I still have some of the cookies left. I couldn't write yesterday, as the Bergholtz's came to visit me, as I'm sure Vatl told you. They thank you for the cheese.

My stomach is getting better all the time. I stood up for the first time last Friday, but I felt really shaky. The doctor thinks that I can come home next Monday or Tuesday. Nothing hurts anymore, not even when I laugh or cough, but the incision still feels really tight. It's a lot longer than an appendix cut.

Sleeping is still the same. I had to take a sleeping pill last night. Maybe it will all get better as I am more physically active.

Helmut Jannsen was here yesterday and brought me a bouquet of roses. Otherwise, he was as usual, a bit boring. Dr Schroeder is always very nice to me, but is always incredibly busy. Inge Teutner was here Sunday. She stayed quite a while and we had a real nice time together. She is feeling better and her attitude is better, too.

It's gotten quite a bit cooler lately. I don't mind it a bit. I even lie in bed in short sleeves when the window is open, much to the dismay of all the nurses. They are all nice to me, even the Mother Superior. I had quite a nice chat in English with the Mother Superior – they don't speak German at all.

How are you – I hope well. We'll see each other again soon.

My love to everyone and a kiss from your Helga.

[Helga was 18]

28 December, 1946

Dear Helga,

It's still hard to write you now because I don't know if it will even get to you or if writing you even matters. That simply paralyzes me. Please be absolutely assured, even when it didn't seem to be so, that we've thought and talked about all of you often. Our long separation has pained me deeply…we could never have imagined what we have all had to experience and suffer through.

Your grandparents and both aunts were in Eisenach when the Americans came through. Uncles Gerhard and Helmut were away. Fritz Hupertz had escaped to Mecklenburg with them and will be going to the Ramms in Charlottenburg to recover. The Russians were the next to come through Eisenach. Grandfather got really sick just before Christmas 1945 and after spending over 14 days in the hospital, he finally went to his eternal rest on 5 January 1946. We lost so much with him but we can envy that he no longer has to deal with this entire tragedy and that he can now rest. You cannot imagine how difficult it was for me that I couldn't go there to comfort your old grandmother.

They have all had to give up their homes; Aunt Irmi had to give up her clinic. They all now live at Schillerstrasse 15 in a tiny room in the attic. After being captured, escaping, and then very ill, Uncle Gerhard died in March of this year in Oberkaufung near Kassel. He was just able to see Aunt Tutzer and Fritz before he died. Helmut lost his left foot in Normandy, recuperated in Strasburg, and was then captured. He was held prisoner of war for about six weeks. I was able to eventually see them both in Frankfurt and found them both in fairly good shape. They are all back in Eisenach now and we stay in constant touch.

Life is so difficult for everyone, they barely have even the most basic necessities of life. But your grandmother has incredible courage and is an example to us all. I hope I'll be able to get to them early next year. I have such a longing to see them all. The last time we were all together was Christmas 1944.

I'll only briefly mention the beautiful, unforgettable and successful times in Strasburg. Those days were the high point of my life. The Americans came through on 23 November 1944. Even though I was the one and only clinician, I was able to get all my staff out early that morning before they would have had to endure a certainly painful and degrading capture. We—me, my wife and Fritz—(the older children had long been in Eisenach)—got in the car and drove toward Eisenach and then Berlin. We found accommodation for Fritz with friends who had rented our home in Ferch. I then returned to Tübingen to join the pediatricians there. There wasn't an express need for me there, so I returned to the field [he rejoined the Medical Corps where he had been a reservist] and stayed out in the field for over a year.

Months after I left, under incredibly dangerous conditions (there are absolutely no safe connections anywhere) Tante Edith was finally successful in gathering all the children together and back to Tübingen where we had safely stored some of our meager possessions, everything else was lost. We didn't even have a bed anymore! On my return here to Tübingen, I had to go through the French lines. I was detained for a short time, but then released and was very lucky not to have been taken prisoner. Since then, we're here—accidently able to find this little attic home, but it's ours alone and we are all healthy. I initially took a job as a General Practitioner, but since April this year I have not had a real job.

All of our assets were lost in Eisenach, as the Russians took over all the banks. I'm naturally continuing to look for work, but there is a huge number of unemployed here—I'm sure you've heard about it. In the bigger picture, we need to be thankful that we are still making it. The horrible fates of countless relatives, close friends, and acquaintances that we heard about during this last year, reflect to a terrible extent the full misery of what has befallen our homeland. So now when you think about us, you'll know where and how we all are.

I often worry about what you and your dear mother have had to endure. Vatl Kiderlen is probably still interned, but I hope you are all still in communication and that his situation is tolerable. Is there any news about when you will all be returning to Germany? We're hearing about repatriations from China and the British Indies. But what will you find here in your once beautiful homeland? You can't even describe it and I won't even try.

Life goes on and we continue to try to remain brave and not let things get us down. One day I'll get another job and once that happens, everything will be easier. The children are all getting older and we have worried about them a lot. In four weeks, Röschen will be 17, Hans Melchior, certainly the most difficult, is usually in an international school in the Black Forest, but he's home on holiday now. Fritz is entering high school soon. I hope I can prepare them all for a good future, because after school they are on their own. I can't do any more for them.

We send you all loving thoughts and above all, a happy new year. Maybe we'll be able to see each other soon—I long for that time. Please write me as soon as possible—from now on I'll write you every month. My dearest thoughts and wishes from your very loving Vati.

[Helga was 21]

Kurt Hofmeier's letter of 28 December, 1946 (above) expresses clearly the misery of the German citizenry in the aftermath of the war. A quarter century later, he looked back in an autobiography. Here are excerpts:

A partial autobiography published in limited edition for family members. Ein Bild Meiner Zeit. Erinnerungen von Kurt Hofmeier. Geb am 9 September 1896 in Konigsberg i. Pr. Gewidmet seinen Kindern und Enkeln. Published in limited edition by Kurt Hofmeier, September 1971.

The half century my life has spanned is less noteworthy because of the tired wanderer I have become, but because during that time things have transpired that can only be deemed unspeakable. Fate has set me in the midst of these events, even though I can't say that I have had the least influence on them, but they had a deciding impact on my life.

The following notes should first of all be a description of my life and of specific people I have met. I believe the younger generation, and especially my children, cannot imagine the times of my youth anymore. However, what I write here is neither to justify myself or practical wisdom. Should my children read this, they will get a picture of what shaped the man their father has become, who especially in the last years has been so hard for them to understand. That was bound to happen and probably will remain so.

I start these notes on the 5th of August 1948 in Stuttgart in the Robert Bach Hospital. Impoverished to the ultimate degree, with few marks in my pocket, and with deep concern as to support my family in the next months, until the income from my office, which I opened 10 days ago, can become our livelihood.

[The book gives an account of his father's career in the Prussian Army. His father's promotions through the ranks bring with them many moves, so until high school, Kurt has no chance to make lasting friendships. The military with its parades for the Kaiser of Germany and the King of Prussia has a big influence on the boy. His parents have social obligations because of their position. He warms to the detailed story of his early childhood. Loved by parents and a large extended family, he is close to his mother, but nannies take care of the everyday work of child-drearing. From an early age the children are sent to spend summers at the grandmother's estate (his mother's mother). Even on the train, they travelled in the company of servants. He receives a classical education; at the end of high school (Abitur) he is deemed too frail to continue his education, was to spend six months to a year at his uncle's estate and maybe study agriculture. August 1914, WW I breaks out; his father gets special dispensation from the Kaiser to become Fahnenjunker (an officer cadet). He comes out of the war a lieutenant. His memoir alludes to things in the future, he meant to come back to them, but then instead of continuing with his life story, he talks at length about his parents. The 17-year-old student Kurt reaches home after a lengthy ski trek totally exhausted. At night he has strange symptoms. He experiences: racing of the heart, arrhythmia, panic, which was probably due to the instability.]

Even though, at my physical before going into the army, there were no objections to letting me don the many-colored coat. I don't know any particulars, only that through the years of war I bore all hardships and not the lesser emotional stress without damage.

The Prussian Army:

The German army was a federal militia, made up of separate detachments, from each state. In war time, the Kaiser was commander in chief. The armament, training, and general staff were uniform.

I will take it upon myself to make a few explanations about this unique aspect in the history of our homeland. These facts are historically interesting, and also I want to clear up some of the misconceptions that you hear and read about again today; they are born of ignorance and pejorative propaganda. And besides, I have been part of the bitter war years and have been able to form my own opinion about a few questions. I draw from my own experience. About a general view I rely on diligent studies undertaken by me after the war, and from accounts of my father's.

The Prussian Army was often considered "the school of the nation."

That was without doubt true of the more distant past and also of the time frame I am talking about. Nothing has elevated and strengthened the national sentiment more than the compulsory military service. For many young men their enlistment period was the only time, at least until the end of the last century, that they had the chance to poke their nose out of their very restricted existence.

To wear the king's coat was to most everyone an honor, to 'serve' in the same unit with his father the greatest wish. Most regiments drew almost exclusively from volunteers, as their number was sufficient every year. A man who had served was to be trusted, and was proud to enjoy that trust. That may seem to be exaggerated today but it is a fact.

The bond to the king was strong in the general population. For the soldier it was without question. They had sworn their allegiance to him.

Without the noncommissioned officer corps the high degree of training that the army reached in 1914 would not have been possible. I myself have encountered excellent and conscientious men during the war and as a young officer have learned much from them.

Officers were never allowed out of uniform in public except when on vacation or at sporting events. Many wore their uniform at home, but my father changed into civvies.

At the start of World War I, the Prussian army had surpassed its zenith as unique and culturally important for future time.

The Question of the Jewry:

In view of later occurrences, it seems important to me to at least touch on how the question of the Jewry confronted me, and what attitude towards Jews was instilled in us.

The first contact with Jews was at the estate of our grandmother. I already talked about the highly-regarded Jewish doctor, Dr. Simon, and the merchants Pelz in Wirsitz. In the province of Posen lived many Jews, and they dealt primarily in the buying and selling of livestock and grains. In school there were a few Jewish students. I never had any quarrels with any of them. They differed from us only because of their religion, they were never looked upon as a different race. They were Prussian citizens and they enjoyed the same rights as everyone else. But somehow, I must say they were looked down upon. They could not become officers but had to serve in the army as everyone else did.

The family had no contact with Jews, even those in the higher echelons of society in Berlin.

There was never any derogatory talk at home about Jews, and in Lissa, an area with many of them, unleavened bread was served at Easter time.

Without a doubt, there were circles in society where a rift existed between Jews and them. I only became aware much later of a rabid anti-Semitism. My parents had nothing in common with those circles.

Early on we heard about heavy persecutions in Russia and especially in Russ.-Poland and in the Ukraine.

(As a student in Freiburg, Kurt was befriended by a Jewish boy named Levi and invited to his house. The boy's father showed Kurt his wonderful stamp collection, and the visit went well, and Kurt talked happily about it at home. When his parents said, You know they are Jewish?, the boy answered: Absolutely not; his mother is Dutch. But Kurt's parents would never have forbidden him to visit the Levis.)

With these few observations I want to end this discussion about the "Jewish Problem" of that era. You may say the Jews were not loved, that one did not seek contact with them, but that there was no talk in my youth of hatred of Jews or of racism.

Helga's Japanese identity card. 1947.

AFFIDAVIT OF SUPPORT

United States of America)
State of Illinois   )
County of Jefferson   ) SS
City of Mount Vernon   )

I, Albert Watson, II, being duly sworn, depose and say:

1. That I am a native of the United States of America and 38 years of age, and have been a legal resident of the United States for the past 38 years. My present residence address is: 402 N. Tenth St., Mt. Vernon, Ill.

2. That I am an American citizen by birth, and have always maintained my citizenship.

3. That I am married and that my wife has read and concurs in this affidavit of support, as evidenced by her signature hereinafter subscribed.

4. That the following are the only persons dependent upon me for support:

Anne Bucher Watson		Wife	Wholly dependent
Albert Watson, III	7	Son	Wholly dependent
John Bucher Watson	4	Son	Wholly dependent

5. Colonel, United States Army; annual pay and allowances $7884.00.

6. Assets:

| Cash: | National City Bank, Tokyo Branch | $465.06 |
| | Union National Bank, Lewisburg, Pa. | 287.00 |

Real Estate: None

Personal Property: 1942 Packard Sedan
                    ¼ Ton (Jeep)
                    2 horses
                    1947 Packard Sedan

Investments: Stocks $2,717.00
              Bonds $34,500.00

Life Insurance: Straight Life $16,000.00

7. That I am a friend of Helga Hofmeier, who now resides at Yoyogi Honcho, Shibuya Ku, Tokyo, Japan and desires to enter the United States for permanent residence.

8. That I hereby solemnly swear that I will receive and care for her and that I will at no time allow her to become a charge of the United States, or of any State, territory or subdivision thereof.

9. That I freely incur this obligation because of friendship and a desire to assist the applicant in becoming an American citizen.

10. That I make this affidavit for the purpose of inducing the United States Consular authorities to grant a visa to the above-named person.

11. That I have never given similar affidavits of support.

ALBERT WATSON, II
Colonel, U.S.A.

ANNE B. WATSON

The Watsons' declaration of assets, in support of their application to sponsor Helga's residency in the United States.

Part of Col. Watson's required documentation in support of his sponsorship of Helga's residency in the U.S.

Helga's Affidavit of Identity, issued by the American Consular Service in Yokohama, 1947. This affidavit served in lieu of a passport for her journey to the U.S. as a quota immigrant.

Confirmation of Colonel Watson's commission in the U.S. Army, as part of the documentation in support of Helga's residency in the U.S.

Document listing names for repatriation back to Germany. This page shows Fritz and Leonore Kiderlen and Helga Hofmeier. Instead, Helga went to the United States.

Helga's visa for the U.S.

Helga listed on the ship's manifest of the USS *President McKinley*. It lists her national-ity as "German" and her race as "Aryan."

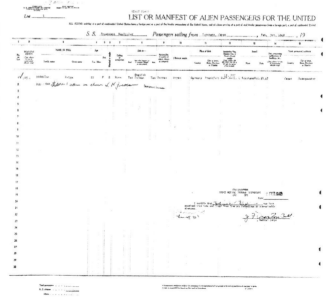

23 February 1948
Coronado

My dear Mother –

I've been here in Coronado for five days now. I left Yokohama the morning of the 4th of February and arrived in San Francisco on the 14th. I couldn't get any space on a ship any earlier—I'm glad that my sailing on the 18th of January didn't work out because this ship was much nicer. I sailed first class. The *President McKinley* is about the same size as the *Quito*, a freighter that took a few passengers. There were 8 of us, all Americans except for me. I had a nice cabin that I shared with two other ladies. We had our own bath with a WC. It was a very nice cruise. All were very nice to me and very worried about me because I was so all alone. The food was wonderful and the service was exceptionally attentive—almost all Negroes. Sadly, we didn't cruise via Hawaii, but rather cruised the northern route by the Aleutians. It was very stormy and cold, but I never got seasick. The departure from Japan was very hard for me. Japan had become a real part of me.

I sold our kura, pool, and what was left of the house and property to the Oinuma's for 70,000 yen [$886 in 1948 exchange rate]. I couldn't buy dollars as it was just too risky. For 65,000 yen [$823], I bought a stunning dark brown sable fur coat. I got it for about half price at my friend's shop in the Imperial Hotel. I thought this was the best way to handle the cash. Chingai finished my teeth just in time. My braces were taken off two days before I left, but I still wear a night guard. That all cost 12,000 yen [$152]. I received all my crates. The total freight was $18 with an additional $7 customs that I paid in San Francisco. My crates were all inspected both in Yokohama and in San Francisco. I had declared absolutely everything I was bringing, so there were no surprises. The officials saw I was honest and were very friendly.

Col. Watson's parents, who were in San Francisco, met my ship. He is a retired Colonel, about 70 years old. She is a bit younger. Both are very nice and are, for their age, very active. The picked me up in their new car, a black Lincoln. They drove me through San Francisco all afternoon and showed me all the sights. It's a beautiful city—

everything is so gorgeous. It was a beautiful sight to sail under the Golden Gate Bridge the morning we arrived—I'll send you some photos. We spent two nights at the Canterbury Hotel. I had a room on my own with my own bath. That first evening we had dinner in the restaurant and then went to the movies. I happened to meet a young Lieutenant that I had met at a party in Tokyo about a year ago. We were both so surprised to see each other and we spent all day Sunday together. He showed me the "intimate" side of the city—he took me to some little cabaret bars and then to a bowling alley—I'd never seen anything like it. It was jam packed. People carrying their kit and caboodle, men in shirt sleeves, children sucking on lollypops and women in the most unusual attire I've ever seen. Jazz music played and everyone drank Coca Cola and ate popcorn. We ate lunch at the Fairmont Hotel, which is the largest in town. The whole building is like a little city with lots of restaurants, shops, entertainment places, and bars. Across from it, was the Mark Hotel—the tallest building in town. At the very top is a bar with a beautiful view of town. I had trouble everywhere with what to drink. They only serve alcohol and only those over 21 are served. No children are allowed in the bars. I look so young that when I said I was 22, no one ever believed me until I showed them my identity papers. At night we went to the Fairmont to dance. The people were all very elegant.

Monday morning we drove on in the Lincoln. I had the choice to go on the train or to drive with the elder Watsons, and I chose the car drive. It was a beautiful drive all along the coast. We spent the first night at an idyllic small hotel in Santa Maria. Flowers are everywhere. It is such a pleasure to drive here as opposed to driving in Japan. The roads are so nice that we drove at 50 miles per hour. Col Watson did most of the driving; his wife spelled him every now and then. We spent Tuesday night in the Ambassador Hotel in Santa Monica, a suburb of Los Angeles. We got there in the afternoon, so took a drive into Los Angeles, all the way to Hollywood. There were flowers and palm trees everywhere—just like in the movies.

We arrived in Coronado on Wednesday afternoon about 3 pm.

There were many greetings, as Mr. and Mrs. Bucher, Mrs. Watsons parents, are also here, so altogether nine people said their hellos. The younger Watsons have purchased this lovely house, right across the street from a golf course. There are two bedrooms and one bath upstairs and another two bedrooms and bath downstairs. There is a large living room and dining room and a large and practical kitchen. There is a separate room for the clothes washer and dryer, with a door leading to the outside. My room is next to that and I have a view of the back yard. My room is about eight tatami. I have a lovely bed, a chair, a vanity and a chest of drawers. I have my own bathroom with a shower and toilet. I have my own key to the back door so I can come and go when I want. I'll take some photos and send them to you. My work here isn't very difficult. There are so many electric appliances and everything is so practical. Mrs. Watson doesn't expect too much and she lets me clean and take care of everything as I please. The big thing is that the meal is punctual. Even the meals aren't a problem for me. All together they eat only as much as Vatl ate all by himself. You can get almost everything pre-made at the grocery store. Even the bread is already sliced!

All the laundry, except the bed linens, is washed at home. That means, I dump everything into the tub of the washer, let it run half an hour, then I dump it all into another tub and it rinses all by itself. I don't have to wring it dry, I only have to hang it all up. I do the laundry twice a week. The ladies do their own bedding, I just dust their rooms. The big cleaning is done every Thursday by a Negro woman and she also does all the ironing. I get all of Thursday off. I get $55 a month and I can eat all I want. I get up at 6:30 am every day except Sunday, the younger Watsons and their two boys come for breakfast at 7:30 am. The parents and in-laws come for breakfast as they get up. Lunch is at 12:30 and is usually cold, salads, bread, cold cuts. I'm finished in the kitchen around 2 pm and usually don't have anything to do until about 530 pm. Dinner is served at 6:30 pm. Mrs. Watson usually helps and both her mother and mother-in-law usually add their opinions, as well. I haven't seen anyone do any darning or sewing. Mrs. Watson's parents are very nice. Her father is already 80 and a bit doddering. He is usually underfoot in the kitchen because he likes to chit-chat with me, but he stutters a bit.

Sometimes we sit together in the Bucher's room and chat. This is usually the younger Col Watson's office. It has a Murphy bed and is used as a guest room when the Buchers visit. The younger Col. Watson calls it the "gossip room" when we are all in there talking. I usually go to bed at 10 p.m. at the latest. I'm dead tired by then. The climate here is heavenly. It doesn't get very cold; I just turn on the little heater in my room. The mornings are glorious and there is always sunshine. Coronado is a small island. There is a ferry to San Diego every five minutes—night and day. It's about a 20 minute walk from here to the ferry. I've added a few postcards to your package. This package is going out today. I can send one 22 pound package to you every week. I bought you an iron, but cannot get the voltage changed to what you need. Hopefully you can take care of that over there. I'm sending Crisco and sugar in the next package. It would have been too heavy for this one. The chocolate is for your common birthdays— Herzeltäntchen, you, and Vatl all get a sweet! I got the pralines as a gift, but I'm sending them to you because I don't like them. I couldn't find any other kind of darning thread, but I'm going to San Diego on Thursday and I'll see if I can find any there. I can't find any silk sewing thread anywhere at all. These nail scissors are the best I could find. I'm including the only hair curlers I could find. I know you are used to the canned bacon we used to get during the war, but they don't have that here. The jam only comes in jars and I can't send glass. I hope this is the right kind of ink pen for Vatl's birthday. I've been thinking about him a lot—please give him a kiss for me. I write down everything you need, and I look for it and buy it when I find it. I cannot send you cigarettes or cosmetics at all.

I'm concerned that I haven't heard from any of you. I hope you've received all my letters. I already have six letters from Herbert. Vati and Röschen wrote me in January. I'm sending you some photos I took a week before I left Hakone. The pictures of Jesse are not very good. He looks better in person. We have planned to marry next summer. (I already wrote Herbert about that.) Jess has to stay in Tokyo until March

1949. He wanted to marry me right away, but we decided that I should go first with the Watsons. If I had stayed and we had married, we would not have been able to get dependent housing for nine months. I met him the first part of October, but I think I mentioned that already. He wants to stay in the military and hopes that he will eventually be assigned to Germany, That would really be wonderful, but that will all be decided after he gets back from Japan. He is from Louisiana, and like me, has two fathers. His mother is divorced and lives with his step-father. He has a younger brother and married sister. We get along so well, the good-bye was very difficult but had to be. If he doesn't get assigned to Europe, he wants to live in St Louis.

I hope you enjoy the pictures of Fusako. She is now working for the American Captain who is renting our house in Hakone. She has all her things in Hakone now and apparently is thinking of getting married. She has been flirting with a man there. She helped me until the very end and I really needed her. She washed all my laundry. I did everything else myself. I gave her a few of my things and paid 3000 yen for her teeth. She was delighted with the gifts, but was so sad when I left. I'm happy to hear that Frau Schmidt found a home. Please give her my love and greetings—I'm so glad she left with you. Do you want to stay in Hamburg? I hope that Vatl finds work soon—things have got to pick up for him.

Since you don't have a permanent address yet, I'll send your packages to the Kienlin's in Hamburg. Let me know when to do something differently. I'm also going to send you most of my winter clothes. I don't need them here—and when I marry, I'll certainly be able to buy new clothes. You can sell my clothes or give them to the relatives. There are no galoshes here that I can send you because it never rains here. I do need Vatl's footprint so I can figure out his size. Shoes are very expensive here and I'd need his exact size.

So my dear ones, don't worry about me here. I have more than I need. I worry about all of you and will help you all out as much as I possibly can. My best wishes to everyone, in Oberammergau as well, and to Uncle Otto, too. Send photos when you can. Do you need film?

I took all my photos with the little box camera.

Good-bye for now, I'm exhausted. I have lots of letters to answer. A thousand kisses to all of you–

Helga

How is the new little kitten, Chibi?

[Helga was 22]

3 March 1948

Dear Mutti and Vatl,

I have sent another package; you cannot insure packages to Germany but I hope it arrives. I walked around to find butter and lard in cans, so I could mail them to you, but you can't find that. Since the war is over, nothing is made in cans anymore. People tell me repeatedly that only the military can get food in cans. Also egg powder I couldn't find. Artificial powder we used to get. Also noodle soup, but I keep looking as I go along. The next thing I am going to send you is clarified butter. I'll just keep sending you care packages.

I am also sending a package to Herzeltäntchen. But my finances are not very good and I cannot spend too much. I have not really any savings and I haven't been to the movies. But that is not so important. It is difficult to sell things, not as easy as in Japan. I sold a few things of mine in an antique shop, and the lacquered trays, but there were lots on the market so they didn't bring much.

Maybe I could sell jewelry, but I hate to sell my pearl ring and my broach that I was given by a young man. So I am sending only when I can afford it. I also don't have much time to go to town, only once a week. I am worrying about you because things are so bad over there. I hope you have a room for yourselves by now.

The Watsons don't know of anyone who is going to Germany. Cigarettes are not allowed to mail. Are your packages opened before you get them? I don't want to smuggle anything because that makes only difficulty. I can't send you any jam because it is only in glass containers, and you cannot send milk either. Also the regulations of what to send to Germany are rather strict and rather ridiculous I think. I was trying to find some sewing silk thread and also a thicker yarn to sew on buttons. I hope you like the white wool jacket that I found for you, Mutti. I am going to try to find some warm winter things for you soon. Here you don't need warm underwear due to the climate, you don't get that cold.

I'm doing quite well here I'm always very tired. I have to be up at six thirty every morning and on my feet until about eight thirty at night, therefore I also have to do my laundry and iron and do the sewing repairs. I am missing my sleep in the mornings . . . for some reason I need that very much, my morning sleep. I could lie down in the afternoon but I don't have much time. Thursday is my free day; after breakfast I wash the dishes, then it is 9 then I wash my hair and clean my room and after lunch I go to San Diego to look around for shopping. Before it gets dark I want to be back again because the sailors are swarming then. If you cross the street in front of them, there is whistling, whistling, and they ask, Where are you going, beautiful?

I am also trying to eat at home to save money. I am lonesome and don't have many friends here. I hope the year is over soon and Jesse is arriving and I think things will be easier for me. I still care for Herbert very much but I am waiting for Jesse.

Just imagine, next Thursday I will be 23; it is hard to believe and it is time that I get married, don't you think? I have to stop now and go to the post office; all the other questions I will answer next time.

Greetings and kisses. I think of you all the time.

Helga

[Helga was 22]

671 Alameda Blvd.
Coronado, Calif.
April 2, 1948

Dear Mr. Kiderlen,

I received your letter of March 6th yesterday. We are all quite concerned that you haven't heard from Helga, as she has been writing to you ever since she arrived in the States the 14th of Feb. But we hope by this time the letters have started to come through to you.

She arrived in San Francisco the 14th of Feb. Col. Watson's family met her at the boat and drove her down in their car to Coronado. I was so glad that the plans worked out that way as she got such a good view of the West Coast of our country on the trip.

She is just fine and a joy to have in the house. She is of invaluable help to me and is so willing and pleasant to have around. We are having an awfully good time together and I feel sure that she feels the same way. She hasn't seemed to be the least bit home sick since she has been here.

On her birthday we had a birthday cake for her and I think she really was surprised.

She asked me to tell you that she has sent you four food packages and one CARE package. The first food package she sent after the 20th of Feb and she has sent one each week. We hope that they will soon be reaching you. She has been having a lot of fun going to the food stores and selecting things to send you.

Yesterday when she went into San Diego shopping she came home with a darling dark blue straw spring hat. I want to take a picture of her in it and send to you. This is the second article of clothing she has bought for herself since she has arrived. The other was a very pretty green flannel sport jacket. She can't get over the stores here and has more fun just looking at all the things.

We have bought a very attractive house here in Coronado. We like it here so much. The climate is wonderful, warm and sunny all winter. Helga has her own room and bath and I think she is very comfortable.

We have had quite a houseful with us. Both Col. Watson's parents and mine have been with us. Next week my family is going back to Pennsylvania but the Watsons have bought a house here, too. So they will be living very near us. We are so glad.

We do hope that soon you will be getting Helga's letters. Please don't worry about her as she is very happy here. Remember us to Mrs. Kiderlen,

Sincerely yours,
Anne B. Watson
[Helga was 22]

22 May 1948
Coronado

My dear Mother –

You are probably angry because I haven't written, but I just haven't had the time. I need some peace to write to you, but now I'll tell you what's been going on.

First, my heartfelt thanks for your lovely letters. I got yours from the 8 of April last Monday and Vatl's from the 14th of April. They always take such a long time—I hope you can start to send via Air Mail soon. In the meantime, I've sent you all several new packages. On the 18th of May—magazines, stationary, 5 dozen envelopes and two cans of shoe polish, two packages of noodle soup, bottles of vanilla, lemon, orange and almond flavoring, caraway seeds, one pound of margarine, two packs of cigarettes, 10 yards of elastic, eye liner, and two pairs of nylons. The darker colors are all in style now.

On the 19th of May, I sent a package to Uncle Otto via your address. Maybe he can pick his up when Vatl picks up your package. His package contains soap powder, sugar, raisins, plums, two cans of sardines, sandwich bags, honey, yeast, one piece of cheese, chocolate syrup, strawberry jam, two cans of deviled ham, one package of Jell-O.

Next Monday I'm sending you a package with Crisco, chocolate syrup, Lux laundry soap, lotion for your hands, dry milk, one pound of margarine, four bars of soap, brushes to wash the dishes with, eye shadow, powdered eggs, flour, two packs of cigarettes, and some children's clothing. The clothes are from our boys and Mrs. Watson was going to give them away. Maybe you can use them for Rolf's little boy. I haven't had very much luck finding used clothing for adults. They have a collection place for needy people called Goodwill. People donate their clothes there, but they are all in very bad condition. The ones that would be suitable for you are very expensive. Everything is very expensive here, especially cotton and wool. Most all the summery clothing and underwear are made from cheap fabric that doesn't last very long. I've been looking for lining fabric for you but haven't been very successful yet. The colors you prefer just aren't available—I think I can get brown [but] I didn't like any of the ties that I saw, so I didn't get one for Vatl. There are many that are burgundy colored, but they have horrible patterns and designs on them and cost up to $15!

I have ordered rubber rain shoes and should get them next week. Nobody here wears the full body aprons like they do there when cooking or cleaning. The ladies here just wear little dainty ornate aprons. I'll buy you one or two washable day dresses that don't need dry cleaning. You can wear those. The summer season is beginning now and I'll see how expensive they might be. There are sales at the end of the month—I'll look around then. I seem to be spending all my money on you. I think of you all so often and try to send everything I possibly can. I haven't bought myself much at all, but that's not a problem! I don't know how I will possibly pay off the Watsons—I still owe $380. Maybe Jesse will help. I am very unhappy to have to ask him, and will only do it as a last resort. It would have been much cheaper to have married him in Japan—everything, including my trip home would have been paid for—but I didn't want to do that. Mrs. Watson says there is no hurry to pay them, but I'm not happy to have to depend on their kindness and patience. It will all work itself out.

Please continue to let me know what you all need. I will try my best to get you what you need, even though it might take a while to gather everything up.

I don't think there will be another war any time soon, the Russians will wait and one day their alliance will all fall apart. Do you have any thoughts about the Marshall Plan? One always tries to console oneself thinking that it's getting better in Germany, but I don't believe it. Anneliese writes me that the inflation is getting worse and worse in Japan. I hear from her every now and then. I'm forwarding you two letters from our friends the Ketels, so that you can keep in touch with what's happening with the Germans still in Japan.

I wrote Herzeltäntchen on the 11th. I hope that Omi and Peti are feeling better. Two days ago, I got a package from her—a lovely dark blue blouse with white polka dots. She shouldn't send me so much—she can sell these things. I enjoyed the blouse so much and was very moved that she wanted to send it to me. Have you all been to Oberammergau? Herzeltäntchen wrote that she was expecting you the beginning of May. I got a letter from Vati on the 21st and another letter from Röschen and one from Fritz. I haven't answered anyone yet—I haven't felt good for the last ten days. I'm trying to get off my headache medications. But they have helped me—my headaches are slowly going away. I'm still taking pills to go to sleep and pills to get me up for the day. Taking pills all the time is crazy. It's a lesson in patience. As long as I'm busy, I'm fine, but as soon as I sit down, I want to fall asleep. Hopefully this will all get better—I'm getting up earlier and that's working out. I take afternoon naps every once in a while, but I lose a lot of time that way. I can't read at all—I fall right asleep. Writing and sewing or mending is also tiring—seems everything that uses my eyes is exhausting. I even went to the optometrist, but he said all was fine.

A young Australian girl that the Watsons had met in Tokyo was just here visiting them for two weeks. She was my age. She's been in the U.S. since March and is waiting for her fiancé. He's coming here for a year to study medicine. She's a very nice girl and we understood each other perfectly. I wish she could have stayed longer, but she had to return to Canada to renew her visa. We had so much in common, she even knew Jesse from working for the Air Force in his same building. We took a lot of color photos; it will take at least a month to get them developed. We went horseback riding along the beach in glorious weather. She invited me, as I couldn't afford it on my own. I love to ride—we have stables across from us here at the Country Club. The old Watsons came to visit last week. They are beginning to move into their new house. It's very nice and has a new refrigerator, and a new cook stove that is automatic. They also have a dishwasher and a washing machine. Our washing machine is worthless—it's broken again. I've had to wash all the clothes by hand. Mrs. Watson wants to buy a new one like her in-laws—everything is automatic. You dump the clothes in a tub and add water and soap. Then you push the button. When the machine stops, the laundry is clean, rinsed and wrung out. Your hands don't even get wet! But the beast costs over $300!! Mrs. Watson has offered me a $10 raise for next month. I had recently told her that other housemaids around here get $65.

I'm learning to drive a car now. I started with the Jeep but am now driving the car. It's a lot of fun. Mrs. Watson says that I can use either the Jeep or the car anytime she doesn't need them once I get my license. I have to do a lot of practice—I still haven't driven in heavy traffic. It's real slow and quiet here in Coronado.

Jesse wants to buy a new car when he gets here. He says I should think about what model I like best. I think a Buick or a Cadillac convertible—but they are all so expensive! But that's far away. Anyway, I'm sending you a picture of him with this letter, but I think his smile looks forced. He wrote me that he has nothing to be happy about since I left Japan, but he wanted to look friendly. I've tried to get a photo of him for the last six months, but like me, he hates to have his picture taken. He hopes you like the picture. I sent one to Herzeltäntchen, too. His hair is wavy like Vatl's and Jesse combs his straight back just like Vatl does. These men are all the same. He's tried to call me via short wave, saying that we could talk for over an hour that way. So far that hasn't worked out. There is always so much interference.

Your request for information about his family is ridiculous. Jesse would never allow that and I would never ask him. I would rather meet the family myself and make my own judgments. You have really funny ideas sometimes. I'm also not going to send you one of his letters, either. His letters are to me, and not for the critique of others! If you want to see his handwriting, I'll send you the envelope from one of his letters to me. He hasn't ever questioned me about my family, even though the military is very strict about foreign relatives. He just wrote that the CIC still watches him. It started the day we first went on a public date. He works Top Secret items and has a special pass for that called a Cryptographic Clearance. Those are only for people with clear backgrounds and without connections to foreign countries. I hope he doesn't lose it when we marry, but he says it doesn't matter. We'll just see how it works out. I have asked for a border permit for Mexico, but I haven't received an answer yet.

Otherwise there is no other news. As usual, the boys are sassy and once in a while I put them over my knee. We seem to get along just fine. They listen to me more than they do their own mother, but that's her own fault.

It's slowly becoming summer here—I've been swimming once. I'm tired, please excuse all the mistakes I've made. I'll write again soon— please write right back. I hope you are feeling better soon—greetings to the whole family!

Hugs and kisses – Helga
[Helga was 22]

Telegram to Germany. 1948.

Eulogy for Leonore Zopke Hofmeier Kiderlen:

It was the wish of our dear deceased, that only a small circle of friends be present as her loved ones gather at her coffin. She wished for only the smallest of memorials. She was averse to an abundance of words and asked that we indulge her in that request. During her years of suffering, she often thought that she might suddenly be taken from us, so she already shared her thoughts with us.

Today, in this place, let us seek how to express our grief and sorrow, while we say our goodbyes yet honor our loved one's request of brevity and moderation.

We will, however, try, in just a few sentences, to remember the entirety of the dear one we all knew – the wise, lovely woman, always the face of life, brave despite pain and physical weakness, equipped to handle the difficult times, but at the same time always ready to help those she actively loved and cared for. She always had, for example, through her courage, her clear thinking, her warm heart, and her joy in working, our best interests at heart.

In these dark days, one singular bit of luck puts a small piece of paper in our hand – one on which Leonore wrote down verses and lines that she must have loved because they mirrored her own thoughts. We wish to, in front of her now, remember the loveliest of these. It is almost as if she walks with us again through these words:

Never say "This I cannot do."
You can accomplish much when duty calls.
You can achieve great things as a result of love.
Therefore, be seasoned by the greatest difficulties.
Great things are required by love and duty
Thus, never say "This I cannot do."

Love and duty, duty and love. Yes, Leonore, you epitomized both to us. We will all try to follow your example. Maybe then will we find some consolation in our sorrow and grief that you were taken from us.

Before we all leave here today, let us also remember those who must be absent from us today – your old mother in Munich, your only daughter and your granddaughter in Omaha. The birth of her little granddaughter was Leonore's last great joy during her illness and suffering.

12 July 1950
Otto E. Ratjen
[Helga was 25]

"This evening at 9 p.m. after gall bladder surgery, your mother peacefully passed away. With love, Vatl."
July, 1950.

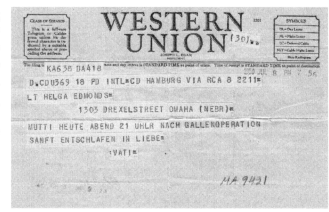

14 December 1950
Eunice

My dear Aunt Edith and my dear Vati –

It's about time I write a Christmas greeting. When you get this letter, you're sure to be in your own home. How nice that you can all live together again and that the long separation is finally at an end. A long separation has just begun for me as Jesse left on the 2nd of December. I miss him terribly. He is still in San Francisco, but awaits his departure on a daily basis. He is homesick and especially misses Jane. I'm so happy that I have this little person. She is full of life and a real wild child. She has been walking since she was 10 months old and already has six teeth with which she thoughtfully chews. She has a great appetite and eats everything that is put in front of her. She tolerated her chicken pox vaccination and her erupting teeth. She is real healthy and I hope it stays that way.

Otherwise, I feel right at home here in my little house. I have two rooms and a kitchen, bath and garage. My landlord is a very nice woman who has a 22 year old daughter who teaches here at the elementary school. They come over every now and then in the evening to chit-chat and I have to always show them my pictures of Germany and Japan. Everyone always says I should write a book about all the adventures in my life, but unfortunately I don't have that talent. I see Jesse's relatives regularly. His mother lives close by. All are very kind and worry about me – the only problem is that a small town like this can get pretty boring. Except for the movie theater, there is really nothing to do. We have to go all the way to New Orleans to see theater or a concert and that is just too expensive. I'm going to try to see the opera Carmen there this winter. Herzeltantchen wrote that the silver spoon and sliver bowl were sent to me right after Christmas and I'm already thankful for them.

The news from Eisenach continues to make me sad. It is really horrible that people are made to live like that! And now the question of war is ripe again – you don't want to think of what might happen. How nice that Grandmother was able to get away.

How are you both doing health-wise? By the way, I have pictures from Grandfather's 80th birthday – thank you for those. You need to write me more about your home – will Hans move to live with you, too? I hope that your practice begins to pick up. Are you still specializing in Pediatrics, dear Vati, or are you also seeing adults? And what's happening with Hans Melchior's England plans?

I have to end for today. The letter has to leave right away. I wish you the best for the New Year. Hopefully the New Year will bring us all peace.

Your loving Helga and Jane

(Jesse sends his best, too)

[Helga was 25]

15 December 1950
Eunice

My dear Grouch (Vatl) –

You need to finally have a real letter from me! Jesse loved the lines you sent him and wanted me to thank you, since he didn't have a chance to do so himself. He will write you as soon as he gets to his station – he left here at 5 am from Lake Charles. His mother and I had driven him there. The goodbyes were very difficult and I miss him terribly. He also seems to have homesickness, too. At the moment, he is in San Francisco and thinks that he will soon ship out. He still doesn't know how long he will be gone, thinks that it won't be longer than 6-8 months. I think that's long enough!

I have settled in quite nicely. I have a living room, kitchen, bath and garage. It's all very clean, has recently been wallpapered. My landlady is a very nice lady who lives next door. Her daughter is my age and is an elementary school teacher. We all get along very well. My mother in law doesn't live far away. The location of the house is very convenient.

Jane is doing well; she gets bigger all the time. She's been walking since she was 10 months old and already has 6 teeth. Thank goodness she didn't have a rough time with them. She's a real wild child and is on the go all day. She talks all the time, even knows a few words – Mommy, with the accent on the last syllable when she's mad. Otherwise, I'm Mama. She says baby to her little doll and to the little kitten who runs around in our back yard. She often tries to repeat what she hears, but just hasn't gotten the hang of it all yet. She has a wonderful appetite and eats everything I put in front of her. I just hope it stays that way.

Just imagine, a portion of our household baggage is still not here from Omaha! We have checked on it several times, but still have no idea when it will arrive. Its really a scandal – all kitchen items and lots of other small stuff, the Christmas tree decorations, dishes and a package with food items that I was going to send you and Herzeltantchen is all still missing. I'm so sad that you will not have anything for Christmas – we just didn't have enough money to fill another box for you. Jesse hasn't been paid since October and he says he probably won't get paid until he reaches is final duty station. Thank goodness I got my monthly check from the War Department a few days ago. I receive $127.50 a month. Jesse gets $100 and $20 of that goes to his mother. He pays $55 every month for the car from his money and I pay the rent of $60. Once we have everything together, I'm sure everything will go better. We still need a few things we have to buy – we really need some glasses and things like that, but its all so expensive. I'm going to send you my mothers painting that Fluggen did. Herzeltantchen thought that you'd like it. I'm hoping you'll send my the lovely picture you have from Fuji. I don't have any Japanese pictures. Do you think you can release it? You both took so many with you. If you come across any pictures that I might like, please think of sending them.. I have only one picture and that's The Politiker. With great joy, I received the copies of the Sunday newspaper inserts – thank you. I haven't read them all yet, but I will get to it right after Christmas. So far I've written 44 Christmas cards and letters. My arm is limp!

I've met many very nice people through the Church here – several with German backgrounds whose parents immigrated here. People here seem to be well off as there are many oil fields. But it's very boring – there is nothing going on. You can go to the movies, but that's about it. It's a shame that New Orleans is so far away – there are theaters and concerts and opera there.

[Helga was 25]

Eunice Rotarians Hear Ex-Resident Of Japan and Germany

EUNICE, La., Feb. 24. (Spl)— Mrs. Jesse Edmonds, wife of Staff Sgt. Jesse Edmonds, stationed in the Marshall Islands, spoke at the Rotary luncheon this week.

Mrs. Edmonds is a native of Germany and was in Japan with her parents at the time of the outbreak of World war II. Her father was engaged in the export trade.

Having spent most of her life in Japan, Mrs. Edmonds answered many questions about the Japanese. She believes the Japanese attitude is to get what they can out of the white civilization and then turn the white man out.

Mrs. Edmonds met Sergeant Edmonds while he was with the army of occupation in Japan. She came to the United States in February, 1948 and was married in December, 1948. She lives in Eunice.

Native of Germany To Become U. S. Citizen

A young Eunice matron, a native of Germany who lived for many years in Japan, is soon to become an American citizen.

Helga Hofmeier Edmunds is to leave Friday by bus for Omaha, Nebraska, where she will receive her citizenship papers.

Mrs. Edmunds has been living in Eunice for the past several months, while her husband, Staff Sergeant Jesse Edmunds, is with the United States Air Force in the Marshall Islands.

Mrs. Edmunds and their one-year-old daughter, Jane, live at Mrs. V. M. Fontenot's apartment on South Fourth street. They moved to Eunice from Omaha, where Jane was born.

Eunice and Louisiana are not entirely new to Mrs. Edmunds, who came to this country as an emigrant in 1948. She and Sergeant Edmunds spent a month here following their marriage, and also lived for ten months at Barksdale Field, Shreveport.

The attractive blonde matron was born at Frankfurt, now headquarters for American Occupation forces.

"We moved around the country quite a bit," she said. "Most of the time we lived in Germany we were at Munich, later to become the birthplace of Nazism."

When she was ten years old Helga's mother and step-father went to Japan to live, and she joined them there This was in 1932, when the rest of the world was becoming acutely aware of the existence of a terrible little man with a square mustache.

"In Tokyo we lived in a German community", Mrs. Edmunds said. "We had the German embassy there, and our own school and church."

It was here that the teen-age girl became a member of the Hitler Youth movement.

"All the boys and girls in our

(Continued on last page)

Native of Germany

(Continued From Page 1)

school belonged to the Youth movement. It was part of our school work. We were taught the ideology of Nazism, but our activities were mostly sports and physical education. We held meetings once a week, attended camp twice a year, and wore the official uniform. German boys and girls from ten to 18 all over Japan belonged to the Hitler Youth."

Asked her personal opinion of Der Fuhrer, Mrs. Edmunds said:

"When Hitler first became powerful my mother had a great faith in him. But we were away from Germany, and we knew little of what was actually happening.

"However, before 1939 we had lost confidence in Hitler as a German leader."

After the war her mother and step-father became repatriated.

"I did not want to return to Germany," she said. "So I asked to come to America as an emigrant." Before her papers were approved she met Sergeant Edmunds, who was with the occupation forces in Tokyo, and fell in love with him.

She sailed for the United States the summer of 1948. Sergeant Edmunds joined her in December of that year and they were married in San Diego, California.

Mrs. Edmunds speaks fluent English, with just a hint of an intriguing accent. She also speaks Japanese, and of course her native German.

Her stepfather, now in Hamburg, sends her German newspapers. All the books in her bookshelves are in German. She has practically all the German classics, including the works of Goethe and Schiller, the German Shakespeares.

Mrs. Edmunds has been guest speaker at meetings of the Business and Professional Women's club and Rotary club, telling of life in Japan during World War II and the American occupation.

She is very beautiful, and her personality and poise denote a background of education and culture. When interviewed by a New Era reporter on Monday, she was making plans to attend the Jane Hobson concert in Crowley that evening, and voiced her pleasure that the concert program included numbers by Shubert, Brahms, and other noted German composers.

She also expressed a wish to meet Grandma Klein, who came to this country from Germany as an emigrant girl of 16.

"When I return from Nebraska, I hope I will have the pleasure of visiting Grandma Klein. I have heard so much about her!"

Partial List of Sources

Germans, discrimination against after WW II
    Taken August 23, 2012, from www.whale.to/b/starvation_of_germans.html
    Koenigsberg: http://canitz.org/index.php/history-of-konigsberg
    Germany
    Eisenach http://translate.google.com/translate?hl=en&sl=de&u=h
ttp://www.wartburgstadt-eisenach.de/05-Seite-Die%2520Stadt-1933-
1945-1.htm&prev=/search%3Fq%3Deisenach%2B1945%26hl%3D
en%26biw%3D815%26bih%3D517%26prmd%3Dimvns&sa=X&e
i=VthAUOLJLpPW8gSmlIDABw&ved=0CC8Q7gEwAw

Kormoran
    http://en.wikipedia.org/wiki/German_auxiliary_cruiser_Kormoran

Hitler in Frankfurt am Main
    Anne Frank website timeline of her life with photos and cutlines:
    http://www.annefrank.org/en/Subsites/Timeline/In-
ter-war-period-1918-1939/Anne-Franks-birth/1931/
A-rush-by-depositors-in-front-of-the-Darmstadt-and-
National-Bank-after-its-collapse-13-July-1931/#!/en/Subsites/Time-
line/Inter-war-period-1918-1939/Anne-Franks-birth/1932/Nazi-par-
ty-election-rally-in-Frankfurt-am-Main-1932-/

Kulmerland Ship

http://translate.google.com/translate?hl=en&sl=fr&u=http://
fr.wikipedia.org/wiki/Kulmerland_%28p%25C3%25A9trolier-
ravitailleur%29&ei=rm5qT7bGBIrXsgL_lrnqBQ&sa=X&oi=t
ranslate&ct=result&resnum=5&ved=0CEIQ7gEwBA&prev=/
search%3Fq%3Dhamburg-amerika%2Bfreighter%2Bkulmerland%
26hl%3Den%26client%3Dfirefox-a%26hs%3DJSr%26rls%3Dorg.
mozilla:en-US:official%26prmd%3Dimvns

http://forum.axishistory.com/search.php: 5.51 Other submissions
point to the presence of Japanese milk bottles in the possession of the
Germans as somehow proving that a Japanese submarine was involved
in the action. However, *Kormoran* was resupplied by *Kulmerland*, which
in turn obtained supplies from Japan. It is therefore not surprising that
some of the items would have Japanese markings on them.

Omori, Japan

http://www.japan-guide.com/e/e5853.html
http://www.japan-in-motion.com/jim/item/mov_282/
http://www.warsailors.com/POWs/imprisonment.html#omori

Silkworm Industry in Japan

1 Bird, Isabella L. (1911). Unbeaten Tracks in Japan: An Account
of Travels in the Interior, Including Visits to the Aborigines of Yezo and
the Shrine of Nikko. John Murray: 25.

2 Watkins, Thayer; San José State University Department of Economics, "Meiji Restoration/Revolution." Retrieved on 2009-05-08.

Wartime Japan

Shapiro, Isaac. Edokko: Growing Up a Foreigner in Wartime Japan. 2009.

The United States Strategic Bombing Survey Strategic Report, issued
July 1, 1946, WAR DEPARTMENT, HEADQUARTERS OF THE
ARMY AIR FORCES, WASHINGTON

The B-29 Strategic Air Campaign Against Japan by Henry C. Huglin Commander, 9th Bombardment Group (VH), 313th Wing, 20th Air Force, Tinian Island, Marianas, March-Sept. Source: http://www.9thbombgrouphistory.org/B29air_campaign.pdf

Guillain, Robert, *I Saw Tokyo Burning* (1981); Werrell, Kenneth, *Blankets of Fire: US. Bombers over Japan During World War II* (1996).

The Incendiary Bombing Raids on Tokyo, 1945, EyeWitness to History, www.eyewitnesstohistory.com (2004). Visited site in May 2012.

Lt. Robert Copeland's diary. Source: http://flgrube1.tripodcom/id13.html. Visited site in May 2012.

Tokyo's History, Geography, and Population, http://www.metro.tokyo.jp/ENGLISH/PROFILE/overview01.htm Visited site in May, 2012.

"1945 Tokyo Firebombing Left Legacy of Terror, Pain." Associated Press, March 10, 2005.

A Guide to the Microfilm Edition of A UPA Collection, from Confidential U.S. Diplomatic Post Records. Office of the Political Advisor for Japan, Tokyo, Japan, 1945–1952. Part 2: 1949–1952.

"How MacArthur Shaped PostWar Japan." Taken from: http://www.historynet.com/american-proconsul-how-douglas-macarthur-shaped-postwar-japan.htm.

Ratjen, Rudolf: *In Der Welt Zu Hause (At Home in the World)*, by Helga's grand-nephew. [no date available]

United States Strategic Bombing Survey (Pacific) Interrogation of Japanese Officials [OPNAV-P-03-100], courtesy of ibilio Hyperwar Project. Added By: C. Peter Chen

U.S. Immigration Oath of Allegiance: http://www.uscis.gov/files/article/M-476.pdf